Tom Swift® & Company
"Boys' Books" by Stratemeyer and Others

by
John T. Dizer, Jr., Ph.D.

McFarland
Jefferson & London

Tom Swift is a trademark of Stratemeyer Syndicate,
registered in the United States Patent and Trademark Office

Library of Congress Cataloging in Publication Data

Dizer, John T., 1921-
Tom Swift & Company.

Bibliography: p.
Includes index.
1. Stratemeyer, Edward, 1862-1930 — Criticism and interpretation.
2. Boys — Books and reading.
3. Children's stories, American — History and criticism.
4. Boys in literature.
I. Title. PS3537.T817Z62   813'.52   81-1559
AACR2

ISBN 0-89950-024-2

Manufactured in the United States of America

Published by McFarland & Company, Inc.,
Box 611, Jefferson, North Carolina 28640

To my most tolerant

and patient wife:

Marie Leerkamp Dizer

ACKNOWLEDGMENTS

In my years of research into the subculture of series books, I have called on innumerable friends for help. They have responded willingly and I regret that space permits the listing of only a few to whom special acknowledgments should be paid. They include:

Dr. E.S. Lauterbach of Purdue University, who has been a continual source of strength for many years and an early believer in the value of this research and writing;

Professor J. Randolph Cox of St. Olaf College, noted authority on Nick Carter, who introduced me to both the Dime Novel Round-Up and the Harry K. Hudson bibliography of boys' books and who materially assisted in the editing of the manuscript;

Librarians Alice Griffith, Audrey Sotendahl and Marjorie Thorpe of Mohawk Valley Community College and Carolyn Ann Davis of the George Arents Research library of Syracuse University, who tirelessly retrieved much valuable information from many obscure sources;

E.T. LeBlanc, editor and publisher of Dime Novel Round -Up, which has been for fifty years the leading periodical in its field;

Captain Chester G. Mayo, USN retired, a distinguished writer and true gentleman who loaned me without question his collection of Bright Days, Good News and other rare story papers; and

The following fellow researchers and writers, all of whom have freely shared their knowledge and their books: J.R. Chenu, Owen R. Cobb, William Gowen, George Holmes, Harry K. Hudson, D.K. Kanarr, the late Edward Leithead, Charles L. Messecar and Leo F. Moore, Professor David Mitchell of SUNY Albany, Maurice Owen, Stanley A. Pachon, Denis R. Rogers, Ernest P. Sanford, Jack S. Schorr and John Sullivan, to mention only a few.

A special note of thanks goes to Harriet S. Adams, Nancy Axelrad and the late Andrew E. Svenson, partners in the Stratemeyer Syndicate, who have always been most courteous, friendly and cooperative and have taken valuable time to read my writings and answer my questions.

CONTENTS

INTRODUCTION

The world of letters is filled with the names of writers who have been over-shadowed by their creations. The names of Sherlock Holmes and Tarzan are recognized by many who have never read a line by Sir Arthur Conan Doyle or Edgar Rice Burroughs.

There is a select number of literary creations whose literary fathers, buried beneath a layer of pseudonyms, are known only to specialists in popular culture. "Frank Merriwell" is synonymous with American sportsmanship, but few could call to mind the pen name or real name of the writer who brought him to life. Does the name of an author--even a pen name--come to mind when you hear names like Jack Harkaway, Deadwood Dick, Nick Carter, Doc Savage, or Buck Rogers? These are symbols of certain kinds of stories of adventure, of a unique kind of manufactured folklore, in which the names have passed into the language.

Try some other names, heroes of youth. The Rover Boys, Nancy Drew, Frank and Joe Hardy, the Bobbsey Twins, Tom Swift. Does no author come to mind? These were all the creation of one man, Edward Stratemeyer, perhaps the influential figure of modern children's fiction.

His name does not appear in the histories of literature, yet his books and those of his followers in the Stratemeyer Syndicate, have been read by millions. His significance lies not in any literary merit, but in the vitality with which certain aspects of the American Dream took shape in his stories. The leading authority on the work of Stratemeyer, John T. Dizer, Jr., Ph.D., sums it up best when he says, "he probably knew the juvenile mind, its interests, aspirations and dreams, better than any writer of his time."

Studies of popular literature tend to fall into two groups: the recreation of a long-past era in an attempt to understand its reading tastes, or a journalistic trip into nostalgia. The first uses primary source material, is certainly valuable, but too often dull; the second, based on secondary source material, is too often superficial, lively reading, but repeating wornout assumptions. Human frailty may impart a certain amount of error to both.

Edward Stratemeyer

<u>Tom Swift & Company</u> attempts to blend the best parts of both groups, with none of the worst effects. Dr. Dizer has chosen to examine with enthusiasm, but accuracy, an era within the memory of many readers. The tools of the scholar and the judgment of the critic are at all times weighed against the heart of the enthusiast. This mixture makes the work informative as well as entertaining.

Based on original research conducted over a period of many years, Dr. Dizer's work suggests some of the reasons for the great popularity and influence of the Stratemeyer creations. Before memories could fade, he interviewed writers and publishers, collectors and bibliographers. He built a research collection of Stratemeyer's books in which he has read deeply.

Dizer places Stratemeyer in perspective in the whole field of series books, a genre of popular fiction that too often is not taken seriously. Here is the first attempt at a comprehensive bibliography on Stratemeyer, series by series. Dizer the critic examines the influence that one mass market magazine article has had on the history of series book criticism--a strange example of the misuse of misinformation which should be required reading by all writers of nonfiction.

In a work primarily about Stratemeyer, it may appear strange to find some chapters devoted to other than Stratemeyer books and writers. Not all series books were the product of Stratemeyer and his syndicate and a brief look at some of his contemporaries can be instructive. Dizer sheds some light on the backgrounds of writers for boys like W.O. Stoddard's upstate New York, or the choice of New England as the locale of so many heroic tales. He also takes a light-hearted look at a little known aspect of U.S. military history in the chapter, "The Boy Allies; or, Who Won World War I?"

But central to Dizer's interest is the title character, Tom Swift, perhaps the greatest of all series book heroes.

Of all the characters created by Stratemeyer, probably none arouses more affection than Tom Swift. His adventures serve as a symbol of American ingenuity and technological progress, one part of that American Dream. If is of no small significance that Dizer, a professional engineer himself, is unusually qualified to interpret the wonders predicted by Tom Swift, another professional engineer. Beyond this, the stories may reflect those flights of imagination that can show us the way in a troubled time. The influence may be subtle. How many scientists, or writers of science fiction, may have decided on their professions by reading Tom Swift?

Greatness is not always dependent upon literary quality. A child's favorite story is often simple and direct. It is best remembered that way. None of Stratemeyer's books were literary masterpieces in the usual sense. They weren't intended to be. They were designed to be read with enthusiasm; when one book was finished, the reader still wanted to know what happened next. At the core of their simple stories were myths of heroes and heroines with essential ideas of what was right and wrong. If their ideas did not always work in the real world, they should have.

J. Randoph Cox
Saint Olaf College
Northfield, Minnesota

Part One. The Cultural Issue.

Chapter I

THE MEN WHO WROTE FOR THE BOYS

"We are what we read."   A platitude, certainly, but
with a large measure of truth.   Today, perhaps, it would be
more accurate to say we are what we see, but this is still
not entirely true.   Many young people still read omniv-
orously and others read occasionally, but practically all have
one thing in common: at a formative time in their growing
up they read series books.   Nowadays they read the Hardy
Boys, Nancy Drew, the Bobbsey Twins and Tom Swift, Jr.
In other years they read Frank Merriwell, The Rover Boys,
Tom Swift and Tom Slade.   Still earlier, it may have been
Horatio Alger, Jr., Oliver Optic, Edward Ellis and Harry
Castlemon.

A recent survey will buttress these points.   A group of
librarians listened to the author's lecture on the history of
series books.   At the end of the discussion period, the
chairperson asked each member if he or she had read series
books as a child.   All but one very youthful librarian (and
these are librarians, mind you, guardians of our children's
reading rights) admitted reading series books and enjoying
them--without any noticeable harmful effects.   Some of the
series they mentioned included Ruth Fielding, Betty Gordon,
Tom Swift, Nancy Drew, the Bobbsey Twins and the Hardy
Boys.   Many of the audience were quite unaware that these
were all the product of the Stratemeyer Syndicate.

If the series we read as children had a real effect on
attitudes, values and a belief in what we call the "American
Dream," then these books and their authors are certainly
worthy of research and analysis.   This belief provided the
original impetus, many years ago, for this book.   At that
time the standard texts and guides to "children's literature"
had little mention of series books.   The references in librarians' magazines were inaccurate and unfair.   Neither has
improved much.   There was practically nothing in print
which related to the "subculture" of juvenile series books.
Since then, the climate has changed somewhat.   Baum is
beginning to receive proper recognition.   Several fine books
have been written about Baum and his works.   The same is
true of Alger.   Patten's (author of Frank Merriwell) auto-

biography has been published, as well as My Father Was Uncle Wiggily, a nostalgic story of Howard Garis. Detailed bibliographies of G.A. Henty have also appeared.

This book, as originally projected, was an over-ambitious project. It was intended to include biographies and discussions of all the well known series book writers of the last century. Of particular interest were Arthur M. Winfield (the Rover Boys), Allen Chapman (the Radio Boys and Ralph of the Railroad Series), Edward Stratemeyer (Dave Porter and Old Glory Series), Roy Rockwood (Bomba and the Great Marvel Series), and particularly Victor Appleton. Victor Appleton wrote the Moving Picture Boys and Motion Picture Chums and Don Sturdy, but especially Tom Swift. My training and profession is engineering and I am a lifelong admirer of Tom Swift. Just how much influence Victor Appleton had on stimulating my interest in engineering through his Tom Swift series is difficult to measure, but it was considerable.

It took a great deal of reading and research to find that most of these popular authors were one and the same man, more or less: Edward Stratemeyer. He was such a prolific writer and, through his Literary Syndicate, published so many series that he dominated the field during his lifetime. The book was, therefore, reduced in scope to the offerings of Stratemeyer and the Syndicate with a few additions. Although Stratemeyer had help from such capable writers as St. George Rathborne, W. Bert Foster and the Garises, their names seldom appeared on his books.

Further research showed that Stratemeyer's influence, just on the basis of number of series published and volumes sold, was probably the dominating factor in shaping juvenile attitudes for several generations. It still is, to quite an extent, since his daughter, Harriet S. Adams, continues very successfully to publish the old series and introduce new ones.

To research series books and their influence properly, one must read many of the books, not just a small sample. The first problem is finding them. My collection of something over 6000 represents many years of book searching. The second problem is reading them. Many collectors have magnificent libraries of children's books, none of which they ever read. Possibly because of arrested development as a child, it is not only possible but enjoyable for me to read most of the series.

It is much too easy to draw inaccurate conclusions from isolated examples and it is imperative that a large enough sample be used for accuracy. Some writers with a limited access to the literature and insufficient background have writen extensively on the subject. It is even more important to use the original sources rather than to copy another writer's attitudes.   Several recent articles and books have been guilty of these errors.

As has been noted, much of this book concerns Edward Stratemeyer and his Literary Syndicate.   This is the result both of my interest in his books and a belief in the importance of his contributions to juvenile literature.   Relatively little on the life of Stratemeyer has been included, out of courtesy to his daughter who is preparing the authoritative history of his life.   An important and basic chapter has been included which correlates the early writings of Stratemeyer (as opposed to the Syndicate writings).   It is hoped that this chapter will be of help to future researchers.

Some of the chapters have appeared at various times in other forms as magazine articles, some of which were more thoroughly footnoted than others.   There is a certain amount of Vermont humor in some of the chapters: it seems necessary to mention this as previous readers have taken some of the tongue-in-cheek statements at face value.   The length of the chapters varies considerably.   The article on Stratemeyer's portrayal of blacks is the longest, but it seems important to present a true picture with a maximum of facts and a minimum of opinion.

The chapters on the Boy Allies and W.O. Stoddard were included both because of the popularity of these writers and my personal interest in their books.   Some will ask why such writers as H. Irving Hancock, "Burt L. Standish," "Leo Edwards," Ralph Henry Barbour and Percy Keese Fitzhugh are not included.   There are two answers.   Others know more about these authors and are planning to write about them, and there is just not space.

The many, many writers of series books have formed, reinforced and perpetuated youthful attitudes towards life and our society.   Their impact has been largely ignored. This book is an attempt to provide some additional insight into the great excluded area of what used to be called boys' books.

Chapter II

BOYS' BOOKS AND THE AMERICAN DREAM

What is the American dream? What effect could boys' books have on it? Who was responsible for spreading and perpetuating a belief in the American dream? Is there any virtue in the American dream and do people still believe in it? These are good questions. They cannot be answered completely here, but will be discussed.

In connection with the term "American dream," four assumptions are commonly made: (1) Hard work and diligence will bring just rewards. Hard work itself is a virtue and, being a virtue, will be rewarded. (2) The American society is basically a classless one and any worthy boy by effort, ingenuity, and persistence can succeed to positions of responsibility and financial success. "From Log Cabin to White House" is accepted as a legitimate goal. (3) Opportunities exist in all sorts of enterprises. The Young American may be an Indian fighter, boot black, gold miner or circus performer. (4) The moral virtues, particularly those considered typical of the biblical wisdom literature, are accepted without question. Honesty, cleanliness, thrift, industry, charity and sobriety are accepted as desirable qualities to be cultivated and encouraged. Chances of personal success, presumably, will increase as these qualities are developed.

The characteristics mentioned above are common to many people's concept of the American dream. This dream may be a stereotype, it may be fading, it may never have been true, but it played a large part in the development of America. John Tebbel writes, "In contemporary terms the dream is often regarded as our 'image,' the aspect we present, or believe we present, to other peoples, and endless controversy surrounds it. The fallacy in this concept is that it does not take into account the radically different 'images' held by differing groups of Americans." He adds, "A far more important difference is the popular vision of the nation, nurtured by the stereotypes which pass for American history in our educational system, and the general view held by those who have made a professional study of that history." This seems as important as worrying about whether Shake-

4

speare's Julius Caesar presents Roman history accurately. The point is, there was an American dream, and dream or reality or combination of both, it dominated American life for at least a hundred years.

A strong influence in perpetuating this dream was children's literature, particularly the so-called nickel and dime novels and the boys' and girls' hardcover series books from the Civil War period on. It is possible to examine in some depth the guidelines established by certain publishers for their writers and thus to say the publishers were responsible for the social patterns of their output.

It is possible to prove that many dime novel or series writers wrote from a strong conviction of what should or should not be presented to youthful readers. It seems a bit ironic that writers like Adams, Alger, Patten, Stratemeyer and Garis should be criticized for producing heroes of unbelievable virtue and manliness while at the same time their writings were called sensational, lurid and unfit for youthful consumption. It is also possible to assume that, since the literature was commercially successful, it reflected current social attitudes or possibly common aspirations. It should be stated that books which did in the past and do now influence young Americans are the ones they read or are still reading. This may be a truism, but it is one often missed in the smokescreen of vituperation against series books emanating from self-appointed creators of good taste in juvenile literature. More American boys were influenced by Frank Merriwell's ideas of fair play, manliness and physical fitness, more boys were stimulated by Alger's commands to strive and succeed, and more boys developed a leaning toward invention and engineering from Edward Stratemeyer's Tom Swift books than from all the other, even award-winning, juveniles ever published.

One sometimes wonders whether librarians are truly concerned with the quality of series books or just unhappy with their commercial success. A single book may be a classic, but if the demand for more adventures of the hero produces a series of books with the same characters in new situations, then the author is labeled a hack pandering to popular tastes.

The books under discussion here many self-respecting librarians will barely admit exist--and discourage their appearance on the library shelves. These are books virtually ignored in histories of children's literature, except as horrible examples to avoid.

It is interesting to see the frantic efforts many critics make to push their brand of literary history. (Though occasionally there is mild enough notice taken: in Fifty Years of Children's Books, Dora V. Smith, writing about the "Landmark Story," notes, "children wait for the next Land-

mark book much as an older generation waited for the next
Little Colonel book or the next Tom Swift title.") More
often, however, their vituperation gets away from them, as
when Smith quotes the following from Alice Jordan's book,
From Rollo to Tom Sawyer: "Oliver Optic, a school principal, had written one hundred and sixteen books in cloth
bindings exclusive of those he produced in paper, among
them his young America Abroad series, filled with drunken
youths at sea, gambling, pillaging and stealing."

The first part of the complete reference in Jordan's
book is as follows: "Oliver Optic, who was responsible for
the issue of 116 volumes, in cloth bindings, not published
by Beadle but by more reputable firms, was the pen name of
a Boston teacher and school principal. His books were
circulated freely and long by public libraries. In the 1875
catalogue of the Cambridge Public Library, seven series by
Optic are listed, and other libraries agreed in naming him as
among the most popular fiction authors, whose works were
read by men as well as boys and girls. Some contemporary
reviews called his stories pure and ennobling, 'improving the
taste and elevating the mind, while at the same time they
stirred the blood and warmed the heart.' Yet before his
death, his books were ruled out of most public libraries."
Then Jordan tears into Optic, somewhat as Ms. Smith noted.

The Jordan book itself is certainly not objective to start
with, but the partial quote by Smith is obviously less so.
Let me read you two actual samples from Optic.

From the Yankee Middy written in 1865: "...but with
Kennedy's glazing eyes still before his vision, he felt how
vain was all human glory. He readily obtained permission to
return to the bedside of the dying rebel, and hastened down
into the steerage for the Testament which his mother had
given him, and which had not been an unused companion in
his leisure. He found Kennedy was sinking fast, on his
return, and, with the patient's ready permission he read to
him a chapter from his Testament."

Or from The Boat Club: "Perhaps my young friends
cannot fully appreciate the amount of satisfaction which a
parent derives from the good character of the child. Though
the worthy shipmaster had a beautiful estate and plenty of
money, if his son had been a liar, a thief, a profane swear-
er,--in short, if Frank had been a bad boy,--he could not
have been happy. If a wise and good father could choose
between having his son a hopeless drunkard or villain, and
laying his cold form in the dark grave, never more to see
him on earth, he would no doubt choose the latter."

Now it must be admitted, regardless of the literary
quality of the above, that it doesn't sound too much like the
"drunken youths at sea, gambling, pillaging and stealing"
impression. Whatever one may think of Oliver Optic, these

quotes are a lot more typical than Dora Smith would have you believe.

In a section called "The Immortal Four," Smith discusses with obvious relish the attack by another librarian on Finley, Optic, Alger and Castlemon. I have already given her comments on Optic. Let me read from the rest of the section:

"The last quarter of the 19th century saw the tremendous spread of cheap, tawdry fiction, akin to the dime novel, one hundred or more books written according to an established pattern by a single author. Caroline Hewins, from her vantage point as librarian of the Young Men's Institute in Hartford, Connecticut, struck out against 'the immortal four.' They were Martha Finley (pseud. Martha Farquharson), author of the Elsie books; Horatio Alger, Jr.; William Taylor Adams, popularly known as Oliver Optic; and Charles Austin Fosdick who wrote under the name Harry Castlemon. Horatio Alger's errand boys who carved new roads to fortune were bombastic heroes setting forth false values.... Harry Castlemon's Frank on a Gunboat ... and the like harked back to the days when the author had run away from home to join the navy during the Civil War. Miss Hewins worked through letters to the press, talks to parents, and, above all, through vigorous promotion of better books to offset the influence of the series."

Harry Emerson Fosdick, interestingly enough, turned out rather well in spite of the pernicious effect of his uncle, Harry Castlemon.

Having demolished the popular writers of the last century, Smith took care of this century in one paragraph. Here is part of it: "Then came the syndicate for mass production of cheap juveniles. Tom Swift celebrated his fiftieth anniversary in 1960, having apparently thrown the glove to English teachers and librarians as early as 1910. His first inventions were a motor-cycle, an electric runabout, an airship, and a submarine (1910). Today, Tom Swift Junior is busy in the caves of nuclear fire (1956) and with his ultrasonic cycloplane.... In 1908 Edward Stratemeyer had formed his syndicate to turn out boys' books on a mass production basis.... He wrote some one hundred and sixty books under syndicate pseudonyms, fifty or so under his own name, and devised plots for about eight hundred others which were farmed out to hired hacks."

Calling writers like Howard and Lillian Garis, W. Bert Foster and St. George Rathborne "hired hacks" is a little extreme. One is forced to believe that such critics dislike series books so thoroughly that they are incapable of a fair evaluation of them. Incidentally, series writers occasionally get back at librarians and other disdaining critics. In The YMCA Boys of Cliffwood, by Brooks Henderley, a part of the story concerns an unpleasant and narrowminded librarian (male, in this case) who will not permit wholesome, action-filled boys' books of good moral tone in the town library, so the YMCA boys, with adult help, start their own library. Eventually, the librarian sees reason, of a sort.

The point here is, and it is important, that some librarians and English teachers tend to emphasize, or "push," so-called "good" literature for children; the carefully written, well printed, beautifully illustrated, and expensive books that picture life as they want it presented to the children. But children, and even adults, don't like being spoon-fed beautiful literature. They want a story. They want action. They want characters they can identify with. They don't have to have a plausible story to enjoy it. Escape literature is none the worse for its escapism, regardless of whether it is science fiction or Frank Merriwell at Yale. And when children like a story they want another with the same characters in other situations, and so the series are born. Obviously, not all series books can be characterized as the acme of juvenile literature. Many, however, are carefully plotted and well written, and to categorize all series books as trash shows a rigid intolerence more typical of a bible-belt evangelist than an enlightened educator.

There are two significant points in this digression. The first point is that the series books were and are tremendously popular. A second point is that series books are recognized as having a significant impact on the young (harmful, of course, in the eyes of many). Pliable young minds must be molded judiciously. Both points are pertinent to the theme under consideration. To repeat, it is the books children read, not the ones they are supposed to read, which have the impact.

Getting back to the theme. Before mass production as we think of it was known, such publishers as Beadle & Adams and Street & Smith--and many others--were flooding America with the 5¢ and 10¢ action-filled novels. Buffalo Bill and Nick Carter became household words. Many writers wrote both for what we would now call the pulps and for the more respectable hardcover book publishers. The influence of Edward Ellis, Harry Castlemon, or L. Frank Baum, just as examples--all of whom were, or in the case of Baum still are, tremendously popular--should not be minimized.

Just four men will be discussed in this chapter; they perhaps have had the greatest impact on America. They are William T. Adams, who wrote mainly as "Oliver Optic;" Horatio Alger, Jr.; Gilbert Patten, who used "Burt L. Standish" and at least a dozen other names; and Edward Stratemeyer, who used "Arthur M. Winfield," "Roy Rockwood," Allen Chapman," Capt. Ralph Bonehill," "Laura Lee Hope," "Victor Appleton," and many other names. These four writers are all acquainted, all used a similar literary formula and all were tremendously popular and influential. The first was Optic. Two quotes from him have already been given, and the esteem in which he is held by librarians indicated, though as Jordan honestly admits, he used to be perfectly socially acceptable. Optic wrote from 1853 until his death in 1897. He was a Sunday-school teacher for twenty years, principal of Harris School in Boston for about twenty years and editor of various magazines from 1858 to the 1880's. His fame, however, is based on the series of stories he wrote which started with The Boat Club in 1854. The Boat Club, incidentally, went through 60 editions. His first series were so startlingly successful that he followed them with several on the Civil War--the Army and Navy, and the Blue and Grey series being just two. Optic was so popular that about 22 serials which had appeared only in Goldon Argosy and Golden Days magazines were published in book form ca. 1912, 15 years after his 1897 death, and did quite well. The general tone of Optic's books was one of moral uplift, plenty of action, general acceptance of the social customs of the time with rather more preaching than today's youth would buy. Compared to many other juvenile hardcover books of the period, which were designed to educate only, however, Optic reads well. He entertained, at least, and the boys could accept a reasonable amount of moralizing if the entertainment were there.

Oliver Optic published stories by Alger in his Student and Schoolmate when Alger was turning to the writing of juveniles. Both Optic and Alger published about the same number of books, in Optic's case 127 or so juveniles and in Alger's about 123 juvenile and adult books, and both were active during the same period (Alger died in 1899). Their backgrounds were quite different. Alger had studied to become a minister and had published his first book unsuccessfully in 1856. Not until his publication of Ragged Dick in 1867 did he hit his stride. From then until his death and long afterwards Algers poured from the presses.

It is interesting to note in passing that Alger was not a particularly good selling author in his lifetime, with the one exception of Ragged Dick, and that his total sales were not more than 800,000 at the time of his death, according to Frank Luther Mott and John Tebbel. It was when the paperback publishers started reprinting Alger in 10¢ and 25¢ editions that he really sold. Even so, a reasonable sales figure is about 16 or 17 million in all. Jack Bales, editor of the Alger Society Newsboy agrees with this figure. However, book sales do not indicate the number of readers and Alger's influence extended far beyond the 800,000 or so who actually bought his books during his lifetime. Many of Alger's books concerned life in New York City and all were based on the same theme: poor boys who succeed, generally in business, either slum boys of the city or country boys who came to New York. The significance of Alger has been analyzed in countless papers. His stories fitted the times and the changing patterns of postwar America of the 1870's and 80's. He restated Franklin's and Emerson's thoughts on the values of human individualism and the old Puritan values of piety, courage, thrift, alertness, and hard work. His books provided a picture, of sorts, of contemporary economic life. As inperfect as they are, they contain a detailed social documentation which has been compared to Dickens, without, however, the reform element of Dickens' novels.

Alger's books were made real to his readers, as Russel Nye says, "by life itself, for they embodied the great American dream that any right-thinking and right-acting American boy could by Struggling Upward succeed in Finding a Fortune." Two popular misconceptions about Alger's books must be corrected. First, his heroes did not become millionaires, they became moderately wealthy only. Secondly, while it was necessary to work hard and to practice all the virtues, it was a lucky break somewhere along the line that almost always made the difference. Wealthy merchants, saved from harm by Alger's heroes, invariably gave them jobs and the prospect of a partnership and marriage with the merchant's daughter, generally, as well. Alger emphasized that traditional middle class virtues were still important in the competitive urbanized society of the late 1800's, and in addition gave a good deal of practical information on living and getting on in the big city. It is possible to say that his books helped ease the transition from a rural to an urban society.

By the turn of the century, the nature of American life was again changing. Other interests had developed and the day of the rags-to-riches millionaire was becoming a thing of the past. In the 1890's and the early years of the 1900's, baseball and football became important spectator sports. Preparatory schools and academies were fashionable and prep school athletics were widely popular. Gilbert Patten wrote hundreds of stories dealing with sports and prep school activities and in his principal character, Frank Merriwell, created an American folk hero. The 245 Merriwell stories alone sold about 125 million copies. Patten had written for Beadle & Adams and Street & Smith, both dime novel publishers, and in 1894 had written a science fiction serial for Street & Smith. But it was in his Merriwell books and stories written for Street & Smith, that Patten particularly tied together morality and athletics in a popular and profitable manner. Patten preached, by his heroes' examples, the doctrine of a clean mind in a clean body. In writing about his books he said, "I did my best to keep them clean, and

make them beneficial without allowing them to become namby-
pamby or Horatio Algerish." Patten convinced his readers
that morals and manliness went together.

His heroes did not smoke, drink or swear, not because
these things were "wrong," as earlier books had preached,
but because these habits interfered with athletics. There is
less emphasis on material success in Patten and much on
leadership by example, playing the game and doing the right
thing. Frank Merriwell found that "in athletics strength and
skill win, regardless of money or family."

George Jean Nathan paid tribute to Patten in part as
follows: "For one who read Mark Twain's Huckleberry Finn
or Tom Sawyer there were ten thousand who read Standish's
Frank Merriwell's Dilemma. For one who read Thomas Nelson
Page--or Judge Shute--or even for that matter, Horatio
Alger, Oliver Optic or Edward S. Ellis--there were 500 who
weekly followed with avidity the exploits of Standish's magnificent Franz--his influence on American young men was
vastly greater than any of these."

Without question, the most important single influence in
American juvenile literature has been the Stratemeyer Syndicate. Where most writers produce a handful of books in
their entire career, Edward Stratemeyer produced hundreds
before his death in 1930. Since that time his daughters,
together with Andrew E. Svenson, have very successfully
continued the Syndicate and have published an additional
estimated 500 volumes. When today's children read the
Bobbsey Twins, Hardy Boys, Nancy Drew, Honey Bunch and
Norman, Tom Swift, Jr., Happy Hollisters, Bret King, Linda
Craig, and on and on, they are reading offerings from the
Syndicate. The Syndicate has been the subject of several
patronizing, misleading or downright inaccurate papers in
recent years. The comments made here, while frankly
reflecting a strong personal bias, are backed by letters from
the Syndicate and very friendly visits there, as well as
much literary research. Let us first picture Mr. Stratemeyer as seen by Andrew Svenson, late partner in the
Syndicate. "You are right of course, that these books had
an immense and salutory effect upon the American ideals of
good character and fair play, and time will prove that these
stories are American classics.... Edward Stratemeyer was the
founder of the so-called 'Fifty Center' in 1910. As a young
man he had a burning desire to write. This did not please
his father, who wanted him to go into the commercial field.
Edward secretly wrote his first short story on brown wrapping paper and sent it to Golden Days. His success in the
field of children's literature was immediate. He went on to
write over four hundred titles, innumerable short stories,
and to direct the story development of more than one thousand books in all before his death in 1930. Among the best

known written completely by himself are the Rover Boys,
Dave Porter, Colonial Series, Old Glory Series, Frontier
Series, Flag of Freedom Series, Pan-American Series and
Popular Series.... Edward Stratemeyer was a man of simple
tastes, fun loving and imaginative. He hewed straight to
the line of the high moral concepts of integrity and loyalty,
and, through the vast circulation of his books, instilled
these ideas into the minds of millions of young readers."

Stratemeyer wrote for Munsey's Argosy and later joined
Street & Smith as editor of Good News, a boy's weekly. He
published a number of series, in particular the highly successful Old Glory series (it went through over 20 editions)
in the 1890's, and started the Rover Boys series in 1889.
Over 5,000,000 Rover Boys were sold, though this figure is
dwarfed by Tom Swift's apparent 20 million. While editor of
Good News, Stratemeyer worked with Alger, Oliver Optic,
Edward Ellis, Harry Castlemon and Gilbert Patten. He was a
particular friend of Horatio Alger, although Stratemeyer
was 30 years younger, and obviously copied the Alger formula in some of his early books.

In fact, Stratemeyer completed 11 manuscripts that
Alger had left unfinished at his death in 1899. He also
finished Oliver Optic's last book after Adam's death. It is
obvious from a study of Stratemeyer's own writings that he
took very seriously the same moral precepts and ideals of
Alger and Optic. Even his titles published under the house
name of Frank V. Webster show this influence. Only a Farm
Boy, Tom, the Telephone Boy, and Bob Chester's Grit,
published from 1909 to 1911, sound much like Alger. Ralph
the Train Dispatcher, published in 1911, can serve to illus-
trate Stratemeyer's philosophy: "Ralph had his enemies.
From time to time along his brisk railroad career they had
bobbed up at inopportune junctures, but never to his final
disaster for they were in the wrong and right always pre-
vails in the end."

Keeping his pulse on the interests of Young America,
Stratemeyer gradually turned away from the "economic"
approach of Alger to current American interests such as
motor cars and inventions. His Motor Boys series in 1906
was an instant success and his Tom Swift series, starting in
1910, was equally so. There has been much controversy in
recent years over who actually wrote the Motor Boys and
Tom Swift. Howard Garis is often credited with both series,
which is unfair both to him and to Stratemeyer. To explain
more fully, Edward Stratemeyer had such a fertile imagination that he was able to outline and plot books faster than
he could write them. Quite early in his career he copied the
Dumas procedure and became literally a fiction factory. This
is to say he would outline a series with plots and characters.
He would then turn over the plots with rather explicit details

to staff writers who completed the books. Stratemeyer personally read and edited all his books and then issued them under one of his many house names. There is no question that Howard Garis wrote for Stratemeyer; that, because of his ability he had wide latitude in writing, and that he is personally responsible for many of the Tom Swift and Motor Boys books, as well as many others. However, it should be remembered that these books were written under contract to Stratemeyer, based on characters and plots developed by him; the format and even main situations were his.

How good was the Stratemeyer science fiction? Considering the period in which it was printed, it holds up surprisingly well. Looking at our favorite hero, Tom Swift, we note that he invented an electric runabout in 1910, a phototelephone in 1914, synthetic diamonds in 1911, a TV detector in 1933 and an electric rifle and giant searchlight, just as examples, in between. It may sound absurd today for Tom to talk about designing and building an aeroplane in three months, but Tom's achievements at this point followed closely those of Glenn Curtiss who was known in 1910 as "the fastest man on earth." Curtiss established a motorcycle record of 136 mph in 1907 using an engine he designed himself and in 1911 he designed and built his Golden Flyer airplane and won the speed event at Rheims, France, with it all within one month. As Donahey notes, "Stratemeyer certainly built an image of the boy inventor which profoundly influenced generations of young men.... Stratemeyer spoke to his readers at their most impressionable age, and he must have sparked an interest in science in many of the men who are today leading scientists and engineers."

When Lindbergh flew the Atlantic in 1927 Stratemeyer had the first volume of Ted Scott, Over the Ocean to Paris, finished in two weeks and had it in stores in less than four. In Castaways of the Stratosphere, a 1935 Ted Scott adventure with high altitude balloons, we find this statement regarding an atmosphere for the gondola: "You see it's better to purify the earth air which is in the gondola when it is first sealed up, than to use straight oxygen, for in case of a fire nothing could stop a blaze where there was just pure oxygen." It was a prophetic statement and a shame that NASA took so long to find this out.

It may come as a surprise to learn that the Hardy Boys have been around since 1927. Both this series and Ted Scott were issued under the house name of F.W. Dixon. However, the Bobbsey Twins, who are also still having new adventures every year, hold the record, having been active since 1904! They seem to hold their age well. The Syndicate is still very successfully competing in the juvenile field as indicated earlier. Stratemeyer's success was based on a

good product and a fair price. His editing sense was fabulous and his publishing ability and mass-production techniques gave him a dominant position in the juvenile field.

There was a strong similarity in emphasis among the
major authors. Action, there certainly was. A certain
thinness in characterization or similarity in plot there often
were. But dominating the whole field of series books have
been the ideals of success through vigorous effort, of fair
play and honesty, of physical and mental vigor and of adher-
ence to strict moral standards. Perhaps the heroes were
larger than life. Perhaps it was impossible for anyone,
ever, to be the athlete Frank Merriwell was, or the inventor
Tom Swift was, or the detectives the Hardy Boys are, but
young people don't know this or care much anyway. And if
they choose to pattern themselves after their heroes, perhaps a little of the American dream will still rub off on them.
And who are we, anyway, to say that this is bad, either for
the youths or for America?

Chapter III

FORTUNE AND THE SYNDICATE

"Whom the Lord loveth, he chasteneth." And the Lord must dearly love the Stratemeyers and their writers because he certainly has chastened them. It may not be entirely the Lord that chasteneth since some librarians, educators and social reformers seem to feel that the Lord needs their help. This help they give willingly and with enthusiasm. As some churches have insisted on their particular brand of salvation, with damnation to all unbelievers, so have some critics insisted on their brand of literary salvation with damnation to all readers of other kinds of books.

Now this may sound slightly dramatic, but it is no more dramatic than the criticisms of series books that can be found in print. Perhaps only hell hath fury like a scornful librarian's. As the following pages will show, series books have frequently not been considered worthy of serious attention, scholarship or accurate research.

Gentle readers who are outside the librarians vs. series books combat arena may wonder at the persistence and intensity of the critics' attack. Criticism of series books is a matter of more heat than light, and will probably continue to be. Reasoned arguments are wasted unless there is agreement on the nature of the disagreement. The frames of reference of the protagonists are poles apart and it would be easier for Beelzebub and Gabriel to agree than for some librarians and some series-book enthusiasts. Standards may have changed since the days of Peter Parley and Rollo, but attitudes have not changed as much as one might suppose.

A basic premise, therefore, may be stated. Articulate critics--primarily librarians, school teachers and professors who teach librarians and teachers--look disapprovingly upon series books, and the Stratemeyer series books in particular, as unfit fare for the young. Some will say that in this enlightened and permissive age the premise no longer holds (if indeed it ever did) and that I am beating a dead horse. Would that it were true. A cursory examination of library literature, however, shows that the same old prejudices, myths and opinions are being perpetuated and expanded. Even the titles of the articles are provocative. "How Serious

Is the Series Problem," "The Last of Horatio," and "Why Not
the Bobbsey Twins," give something of the message.

Several summers ago a course in library science was
given by Indiana University. At the first meeting, the
students were given a reprint of Janie Smith's "History of
the 'Bobbsey Twins'" (South Carolina Library Bulletin, May
1956, pp. 3-4). The article was not an enthusiastic encom-
ium. In fact, it reads more like a garish expose. This
expose has had excellent mileage, perhaps for that reason,
but more of this later. The students were also given a
handout called "A Replacement List for Series in Juvenile
Fiction" (by Frances Sullivan, Small Libraries Project, American Library Association, Chicago, 1963). The introduction
reads as follows: "What shall I buy to replace Bobsey [sic]
Twins and the Hardy Boys? This question has led to the
preparation of a list of replacements. It includes titles of
more lasting quality and of more literary merit than those
outmoded and poorly written series."

The Bobbsey Twins are to be replaced with the Henry
Huggins series, Ginnie series, Little Eddie Series (all by one
publisher, Morrow) and by others. The Wizard of Oz is to
be replaced by the Miss Pickerell and Pippi Longstocking
series, Mary Poppins series, C.S. Lewis titles and the
Borrowers series. Anne of Green Gables: replace with the
Betsey books; and the Cherry Ames series, replace with
Sue Barton and Penny Marsh series. Five Little Peppers:
replace with Laura Ingalls Wilder and Sydney Taylor titles.
Nancy Drew: replace with Lenora M. Wever, Betty Cavanna,
and many other titles. And so the minds of children are to
be molded into "right" habits. Nancy has survived for 50
years, the Bobbsey Twins for 76 years and Oz for 80 years;
and I know there is a message of some sort there. It is also
interesting that this list includes Five Little Peppers, but
does not mention the Rick Brant or Tom Swift, Jr., series.
One could wonder if the Wichita City Librarian and the
Children's and School Librarians Section for the Kansas
Library Association, who prepared the list, had the slightest
idea of what the kids were reading. Heaven forbid that
they actually have Oz and Nancy on their shelves and are
looking for suitable replacements.

It might be noted that the Small Libraries Project are
recommending replacing series in many cases with other
series. This brings up an interesting point. Apparently,
series books are anathema per se to some librarians while to
others only certain series are proscribed. There is, however, a general resistance on the part of librarians to any
series offered by the Stratemeyer Syndicate and librarians
react automatically to the Bobbsey Twins and Nancy Drew.
Since few critics actually have read series books to any
extent and their resistance is, therefore, apparently not

based on critical analysis but on Pavlovian conditioning, it may be interesting to examine the causes of these reflexes. It is beyond the scope of this chapter to analyze librarian and educator attitudes over the past 100 years or so towards all series books, but it is possible to pinpoint the source of many attitudes towards Stratemeyer. The "History of the 'Bobbsey Twins'," already referred to, was based on the 1934 Fortune article, "For It Was Indeed He," and practically every critic's discussion since of the Bobbsey Twins, Hardy Boys, or Nancy Drew in literary journals harks back to this one article. Since the critics' reviews tend to dwell on what they think is important, we should examine both the reviews and the original article.

Library criticisms of juvenile fiction, or books about juveniles, is not a 20th-century phenomenon nor is it limited to series books. The Boston Transcript, March 17, 1885: "The Concord [Mass.] Public Library committee has decided to exclude Mark Twain's latest book [Huckleberry Finn] from the library. One member of the committee says that, while he does not wish to call it immoral, he thinks it contains but little humor, and that of a very coarse type. He regards it as the veriest trash. The librarian and the other members of the committee entertain similar views, characterizing it as rough, coarse, and inelegant, the whole book being more suited to the slums than to intelligent, respectable people." This passage points out objections often made of series books. They are also called coarse, inelegant, and trashy. Another review of Huckleberry Finn and other Twain books makes this comment: "They are no better in tone than the dime novels which flood the blood-and-thunder reading population.... [T]heir moral level is low, and their perusal cannot be anything less than harmful" (The Springfield Republican, as quoted in The Critic, III n.s., March 28, 1885).

Such comments about Twain are a fair indication of the attitude towards dime novels, and through a little osmosis, the modern series books, in particular Stratemeyer. The Fortune article takes pains to point out the connection between Stratemeyer and dime novels.

"For It Was Indeed He" is a detailed examination of all aspects of series books and their writers, with particular emphasis on Stratmeyer-Garis productions and discussions of the Mathiews-Stratemeyer feud. No author is indicated, no author is ever mentioned in the reviews of the article, and this writer has been unable, in correspondence with Fortune, to determine the author. Only in educational and library circles could an anonymous article published over 45 years ago still be accepted so blindly.

We can forgive the early delighted references to it, but the continued use of the material is inexcusable. Let us

first trace the effect of this article before examining the
article itself. The first reference in print was apparently in
1934. Hope White, who was the children's librarian at the
Moline (Illinois) Public Library, gave a speech on "For It
Was Indeed He (50¢ Thrillers Exposed)" which was duly
reported in Illinois Libraries (October 1934, pp. 113-6).
She starts by saying: "Every now and then we realize that
among the various roles a children's librarian must play is
that of the reformer and that even now after thirty years of
reforming, we are still pioneering in this field. An article
which appeared in the April issue of Fortune for this year
impresses us anew with this fact. It is called "For It was
Indeed He" and tells the inside story of the writing, the
publishing and the distribution of the fifty-cent thrillers, or
what are more often referred to as the cheap series--the
Rover Boys, Tom Swift books, the Bomba series and their
like. It is this article which I shall review for you this
morning." And what a job she did. Continuing, "...we
should also add that one man wrote or conceived for others
to write more than eight hundred of this type of book.
That same gentleman holds the all-time record for quantity
production of one man's work. This arch-fiend was none
other than Edward Stratemeyer ... but more about him
later."

      "There is no need to enumerate to this group the
undesirable features of these series. We have all been
preaching and acting against them as long as we have been
librarians--perhaps longer. Although we may not express
ourselves as forcefully or as colorfully as Anthony Comstock,
we can sympathize with him when he said that 'the love
story and cheap work of fiction ... are devices of Satan to
capture our youth.'

      "The history of the fifty-center is an interesting one.
It is a direct descendant of the dime novel, which was first
issued in 1860.... In 1896, Street and Smith, one of the
busier of the dime novel firms, brought out the dime novel
for boys. It was Frank Merriwell or First Days at Fardale,
written by one William Gilbert Patten.... Frank Merriwell was
the first boy hero, but since the books about him sold for
five cents (most 'dime novels' did) he bore the stigma of the
dime novel heroes and was frowned upon by worthy parents
of the great middle class who, as this article so aptly puts
it, 'appraised literature in terms of what it cost them.' It
remained for Edward Stratemeyer to remove this stigma--not
by writing any different kind of stories, but by putting his
dime-novel in board covers and raising the price.... Edward
Stratemeyer would be a good subject for a Freudian biographer. Very little is known about his life; in fact, it
is guarded as a sacred trade secret by his two daughters
who have been carrying on in his stead since his death in

1930.... Since he alone could not turn out stories enough for his fast-growing public, he organized the Stratemeyer Syndicate which was not really a syndicate at all. It was, instead, a group of some twenty hired hack writers who filled in the stories for the plots outlined by Stratemeyer and signed whatever name the master assigned them...."

White finished her speech with this rousing battle cry: "Is it not evident that we are still pioneering in the field of good books for boys and girls? But let us not be discouraged. Rather, let us pledge ourselves anew to battle the fifty-cent thrillers until they are completely routed."

Note several attitudes here. She can sympathize with Anthony Comstock, the notorious 'reformer.' She feels that librarians should themselves be reformers. Series books are trashy because they are descended from dime novels, which she apparently considers automatically trashy. Edward Stratemeyer was an arch-fiend and a good subject for a Freudian biographer. She admitted that one reason for founding the Syndicate was because of Stratemeyer's fast-growing public, but she has no comment on why his public was so fast-growing. The writers for the Syndicate are a group of "hired hack writers." Just what a hired hack writer is is not explained, but it seems probable that it is any writer who writes books of which White does not approve.

There are probably other references to the Fortune article in the years between 1934 and 1956 of which this writer is not aware. In 1956, however, one Janie Smith immortalized herself by writing the "History of Bobbsey Twins," which first appeared in the Charleston, South Carolina, News and Courier and then in the South Carolina Library Bulletin. She starts her article thusly: "As we have read the articles about the Bobbsey Twins recently published in the News and Courier, we remembered an account that appeared years ago in Fortune, April 1934." She then quoted numerous sections of the article, giving her special interpretation. She writes, "'For It Was Indeed He' begins with a quotation from Anthony Comstock's Traps for the Young: 'The cheap works of fiction pervert taste. They defraud the future man or woman by capturing and enslaving the young imagination. Wild fancies and exaggerations supplant aspirations for that which ennobles and exalts'." Now that is not how the article starts; it is only part of it. It actually goes, "Satan adopts ... devices to capture our youth and secure the ruin of immortal souls.... Of this class the love story and cheap work of fiction captivate fancy and pervert taste."

Pure Comstock is of course a little strong, even for this librarian, and the full quotation does not even refer to series books of the Nancy Drew type in the first place. She writes, "Stratemeyer either wrote himself, or conceived for others to write over 800 books. He employed hack writers ... [who] ... were given from a week to a month to enlarge the outline into a book.... These hirelings were merely cogs in a machine.... These books have few pretensions to literary excellence. They are accounts of the superhuman exploits of adolescent heroes, whose deeds surpass those of the bravest and most sagacious men...."

She writes, "...there should be said something about his [Stratemeyer's] predecessor, Gilbert Patten, probably the first writer to exploit the self-perpetuating series for boys and about boys. In 1896, Patten wrote the first 'Frank Merriwell' that Stratemeyer used as his pattern for the 'Rover Boys.' There was one essential difference, however, the Merriwell books sold for a nickel. Parents who appraised literature in terms of cash, felt that the Merriwells were undesirable. Clever Mr. Stratemeyer, however, who wrote the same things, put his novels in board covers and sold them at prices varying from a dollar to twenty-five cents." Smith continues with a condensed version of the Stratemeyer-Mathiews controversy: "The state of literature in the early 1900's appalled Mr. Mathiews. He took action by going to Grosset & Dunlap, who also published Stratemeyer's books, and induced them to reprint in fifty-cent editions the works of better authors--Altsheler, Barbour, Heyliger...." She then included, in an abbreviated form, a comment by Mathiews: "One of the most valuable assets a boy has is his imagination. Story books of the right sort stimulate and conserve this noble faculty. The cheaper sort by overstimulation debauch and vitiate as brain and body are debauched and vitiated by strong drink." She then quoted the section on the supposed effect of Mathiews' article on Stratemeyer and ended with the Fortune conclusion (which will be quoted later).

In one and one-half columns Janie Smith did a remarkable hatchet job on Patten and Stratemeyer. Her misinformation was equal to that of the earlier reviewer. She also misquotes Comstock in the same manner as Hope White, and apparently throws him in as an acceptable moral guide for librarians. Her selected passages from Fortune served entirely to buttress her own position. She identifies Mr. Stratemeyer as "clever" and notes, "Incidently, he died a millionaire." The point is not clear. His writers were "hacks." She would have you believe that Mathiews attacked this unconscionable Goliath and utterly routed him, when she says "Disgruntled booksellers packed up their Tom Swifts, etc. etc., and shipped them back to the publishers. Stratemeyer was furious. He threatened to sue, but was told by Grosset & Dunlap that if he did, they would be compelled to take sides, and they were not sure which side they would choose...." Virtue is triumphant and the devil is routed. Praise the Lord.

Now you might think that when an article is a condensation of an earlier article, it would be a little suspect as source material. Not for some librarians. The Mississippi Library News (March 1957, pp. 38-39) reprinted the "History of 'Bobbsey Twins'." This article largely duplicates the Smith article except that it gives no credit to Janie Smith. In addition, it leaves out about the last third of the original article, including all the discussion about Stratemeyer and Mathiews.

In December 1961 the Kansas Library Bulletin (pp. 15-17) published their article, "Bobbsey Twins History Told." It begins, "If you have wondered why standard libraries refuse to spend limited book funds for children's serials like the Bobbsey Twins, perhaps the following article written by a Charleston, South Carolina, librarian will explain some of the reasons." It then continues with the entire Janie Smith article of 1956. And then, in the 1970's, as already noted, this same old warhorse was being distributed in at least one library science college course, and the end is not in sight.

Another reason for not having series in libraries was added in the Kansas 1961 reprint. Don't spend limited funds for trash. There would be more virtue in this argument if librarians had to spend limited funds for series books. The usual problem is disposing of series books given to libraries by well-meaning donors. The author once had a very amicable arrangement with a library director to dispose of their unwanted gifts. Numerous Bobbsey Twins and Hardy Boys, to say nothing of Oliver Optic and Alger, found a welcome home and the library was spared the potential embarrassment of being caught with such stuff.

It might be helpful to examine the Fortune article, "For It Was Indeed He," more closely at this point, both to mention a few items the librarian reviewers left out and to clarify some of the concepts. The heading of the article contains these words, "the 50-cent juvenile, which Anthony Comstock included among his 'traps for the young'" and then continues with a quotation from Traps. This quotation itself was a condensation of Comstock, which was further abbreviated by the reviewers as previously noted. We can question if the anonymous writer of this article seriously expected Comstock to carry any weight. It is also difficult to show any connection between the modern fifty-cent juvenile and Comstock's "traps for the young." Comstock was the chief agent of the New York Society for the Suppression of Vice and as Bremner says in the editor's introduction to the 1967 Harvard University Press edition of Traps "No understanding of American reform is complete without an apprehension of

the mentality and temperament depicted in Traps for the
Young" (p. xv). Continuing from Bremner's introduction,
"As far as children were concerned evil reading encompassed
nearly all light fiction and popular journalism. Comstock's
abhorrence of the daydreaming and vain imaginings inspired
by sentimental novels perpetuated the view firmly established
--or at least often expressed in the Connecticut of his
youth--that reading frivolous literature impeded the mental
and moral development of children" (p. xxii). Would this be
why the librarians previously quoted approved of Comstock?
As examples of unexpurgated Comstockiana, let me quote in
its entirety the first two paragraphs from Chapter III,
Traps for the Young (p. 20), first published in 1883: "And
it came to pass that as Satan went to and fro upon the
earth, watching his traps and rejoicing over his numerous
victims, he found room for improvement in some of his
schemes. The daily press did not meet all his requirements.
The weekly illustrated papers of crime would do for young
men and sports, for brothels, gin-mills, and thieves' resorts,
but were found so gross, so libidinous, so monstrous, that
every decent person spurned them. They were excluded
from the home on sight. They were too high-priced for
children, and too cumbersome to be conveniently hid from
the parent's eye or carried in the boy's pocket. So he
resolved to make another trap for boys and girls especially."
    "He also resolved to make the most of these vile illus-
trated weekly papers, by lining the news-stands and shop-
windows along the pathway of the children from home to
school and church, so that they could not have gotten to
and from these places of instruction without giving him
opportunity to defile their pure minds by flaunting these
atrocities before their eyes."
    Why has this old Fortune article had such a long life?
Possibly it is because the writing is "slick" and impressively
detailed. The article has the air of exposing dark secrets,
long suspected by the virtuous but now actually brought to
light. Many statements are made which, taken at face value,
if not entirely accurate, agree with the critics' prejudices.
If they are not true, they ought to be. Examples follow:
"These [Bomba, Nancy Drew, et al.] are the successors to
the former eminence of the much maligned dime novel..., the
pattern from which they were cut." "By definition every
one of these books is pure, wild fancy, exaggerations of the
unreal; in short, what reformers, intent upon ennobling,
dub 'cheap.' And that is no reflection on the price."
"Unobtrusively, like so many Guy Fawkes heaping gunpowder
in the cellars of Parliament, three publishing firms annually
unload well over 5,000,000 explosive fifty-centers on the
American adolescents, the foundation stones of human society." And so on.

The Fortune author writes, "On the surface, none of this is insidious enough to undermine the morals of the nation. Then why the great hue and cry against the fifty-center? It is the embodiment of success-story idealism. If not exactly literary, it makes up by action for what it lacks of art. Certainly it will not fill the adolescent mind with ideas that adults might think too mature for it. The reformer's answer to all of this is that the fifty-center is overexciting. A child intoxicated with Tom Swift would be not only intolerable, but permanently warped by an over-stimulated imagination. At least that was the cry of one Franklin K. Mathiews whose enmity for the fifty-center will be particularized later. Of all the scalps, Mr. Mathiews would have liked to hang on his belt, that of Edward Stratemeyer would have pleased him most...."

Another reason for the longevity of this article is probably the prestige of its being printed in an expensive, classy magazine. A more expensive magazine naturally means a better magazine with better writers and better facts. Still another reason is the singular paucity from the critic's standpoint of critical articles on series books and Stratemeyer in particular, at least in the popular literature. Corey Ford had a friendly article on Stratemeyer called "The Father of Those Famous Rover Boys," which was published in New Age Illustrated in April 1928 (and reprinted in Readers Digest May 1928). Gilbert Patten himself had written "Dime-Novel Days" for the Saturday Evening Post, February 28 and March 7, 1931, and James M. Cain had also written favorably about "The Man Merriwell" for the Post, June 11, 1927. So, if Fortune could come up with an expose of the machinations of the fifty-center publishers, it was just the kind of ammunition the critics had been longing for. If the critics were to be completely honest, they would probably admit that the Fortune one is the only detailed article criticizing Stratemeyer and series books that has appeared in a major magazine of the popular press in the past fifty years, as far as is known by this writer. Small wonder the critics get as much mileage out of it as they can.

To return to the article itself. Much of the material described the publishers, writers and fifty-cent novel itself in flamboyant, if not particularly accurate terms. Here are excerpts: "The nucleus of the fifty-cent theme is the fact that a hero cannot fail. With the definite finality of a chemical formula, The Rover Boys at School is the pattern of elements from which every succeeding fifty-center has been compounded. Holding each volume together are the threads of some hair-raising adventures. Poverty empties the pockets of dastards only. Lack of funds in anyone so middle-class as a Rover Boy would be something of a sin. Virtue and success are synonyms, for virtue is resolved to the business of thwarting the villains in their frantic efforts to appear greater men than the heroes...." "With rare justice, he [Stratemeyer] made the most money.... That was his reward for discovering in the late nineties that, like many another resource of the time, the reading capacity of the American adolescent was limitless. As oil had its Rockefeller, literature had its Stratemeyer." "Today, librarians and champions of 'better books for children' would like to think that the fifty-cent thriller was interred with Mr. Stratemeyer. But that is a reformer's dream. They forget the Writing Garises ... who today thump out fifty-centers faster than ever. They forget the Stratemeyer Syndicate founded by the late great Edward and lustily carried on by his daughters...."

When the Fortune author enters the Mathiews-Stratemeyer controversy he raises some interesting questions. Franklin K. Mathiews was Chief Scout Librarian, Boy Scouts of America, and a Don Quixote par excellence. According to Fortune, "And more than Dan Baxter and all the great gallery of black hearts, he hated the guts of Richard Rover." His first step was to talk Grosset & Dunlap into reprinting acceptable juveniles that could be sold for fifty cents like the thrillers. His second blow was an article for the Outlook, which had a circulation of about 100,000 at the time, entitled, "Blowing Out the Boy's Brains" (November 18, 1914, pp. 652-654).

The Fortune article claimed that "Blowing Out the Boy's Brains" was a tract that swept the country. "Women in Portland, Oregon, stood beside the counters of bookstores discouraging would-be buyers of fifty-centers. Disgusted booksellers packed up their Tom Swifts and shipped them back to the publishers." Actually, this Mathiews article appeared in 1914, only four years after the first Tom Swifts. By far the greater number of the forty Tom Swifts in the canon were written after the Mathiews article. If there was any lasting effect on Tom's sales, it is hard to find it. Not only that, in the actual article Mathiews doesn't even mention Tom Swift or Stratemeyer by name. He does mention Frank Merriwell and ridicules the Submarine boys, missing the science fiction overtones of the Submarine Boys entirely. Fortune admits that in the 1926 Winnetka Survey of 36,750 pupils, 98 percent read fifty-centers, and most of them added that they liked Tom Swift best. "By 1913 Tom Swift had passed The Rover Boys as best seller.... Today [1934] the sale of Tom Swift is the record of all time: 6,500,000 copies of thirty-six volumes...."

Referring again to "Blowing Out the Boy's Brains": Mr. Mathiews' main argument seems to be that reading series books overstimulates a child's imagination. He writes: "One of the most valuable assets a boy has is his imagination. In proportion as this is nurtured, a boy develops initiative and resourcefulness. The greatest possible service that education can render is to train the boy to grasp and master new situations as they constantly present themselves to him; and what helps more to make such adjustment than a lively imagination? Story books of the right sort stimulate and conserve this noble faculty, while those of the viler and cheaper sort, by over-stimulation, debauch and vitiate, as brain and body are debauched and destroyed by strong drink."

In these days of television, comics and modern movies, if a boy has any imagination left to overstimulate it's a wonder. Notice the use of "viler and cheaper" together. Mathiews was shrewd enough to recognize that the boy craves excitement, has a passion for action, and that "something much be doing" all the time. He attempts to make a distinction between Treasure Island and a modern "thriller." "A Stevenson works with combustibles, but, as in the case of using the gasoline, he confines them, directs them with care and caution, always thinking of how he may use them in a way that will be of advantage to the boy. In the case of the modern 'thriller,' the author works with the same materials, but with no moral purpose, with no real intelligence. No effort is made to confine or direct or control these highly explosive elements. The result is that, as some boys read such books, their imaginations are literally 'blown out,' and they go into life as terribly crippled as though by some material explosion they had lost a hand or foot."

If indeed this passage makes sense, which is not certain, it is hard to apply to the Stratemeyer books. No one seriously questions their moral tone. If a boy's imagination is blown out from reading Tom Swift, it must have been in pretty sad shape to start with. And what is "vile" about any book ever offered by Stratemeyer to his reading public? I seriously challenge any critic to show a book by Stratemeyer or his writers or by Gilbert Patten for that matter, that is offensive or "vile." And as far as moral purpose is concerned, a modern criticism is that there is entirely too much moralizing in the older series books. Mathiews brings in several other arguments. "In making a survey of children's reading in a certain Southern city recently, in the very best book-store I found the famous Frank Merriwell nickel novel series bound in cloth and selling for fifty cents. And I happen to know that the author of this series, under another name, is writing other books for the same publishing house."

Inference one is that the nickel novels are "cheap" and "trashy." Inference two is that a trick is being perpetrated on the unsupecting public by binding nickel novels and displaying them in the very best book-store. Inference

three is that any author who writes books under several
noms de plume must be producing inferior work. It is not
necessary to get into a discussion of the quality of nickel
novels except to note that the quality of the writing varied
widely and that some excellent writers wrote extensively for
this market. Good critical studies exist, both of dime novels
and of attitudes towards them. Inference two is at variance
with other criticisms of dime novels, namely, that the printing, binding, and appearance is "cheap." These critics
would supposedly welcome the McKay editions of Frank
Merriwell since these objections are apparently overcome.
Critics have never quite decided whether it is the appearance, printing, illustrations or quality of writing that make a
"good" book. Inference three really bothers Mr. Mathiews.
This is his real hang-up on Stratemeyer: "The public will,
I am sure, be interested in knowing just how most of the
books that sell from twenty-five to fifty cents are, not
written, but manufactured. There is usually one man who is
as resourceful as a Balzac so far as ideas and plots for
stories are concerned. He cannot, though, develop them all,
so he employs a number of men who write for him.... In
almost all of this 'mile-a-minute fiction' some inflammable tale
of improbable adventure is told.... Insuperable difficulties
and crushing circumstances are as easily overcome and
conquered as in fairy tales...."

After reading this 1914 article, it is a little startling to
read the introduction by James E. West, Chief Scout Execu-
tive, to the 1934 Boy Scouts Year Book, edited by Mathiews
himself (New York: D. Appleton-Century Co., 1934). Mr.
West writes, "Primarily, for this purpose, a good book to a
boy abounds in tight situations with hair-breadth escapes.
Take, by way of illustration, the airplane story. What is it
that holds spellbound readers of this latest popular tale?
The same old thing, of course--action, suspense, jeopardy;
life is threatened. That is the 'big moment' for a boy. For
above all, his hero must be brave and courage supreme is to
dare death deliberately.

"Such is the fact, but only half the truth, for while
the boy is interested in 'the dangerous doing of me,' as he
puts it, we know equally well that if a boy can be in the
action, and the hero, so much the better. The fact is the
boy has a master passion for himself. He does not want to
be a man so much as to be a boy and act like a man. That
chance comes to him vicariously in books that tell of his
daring exploits, and while the boy is in the 'wishing stage'
of his development, his exaggerated ego, aching for expression in some big way, finds immense relief in stories that
feature boy heroes." Apparently, it all depends on where
the action is.

According to Fortune, Mathiews next "persuaded Percy

Keese Fitzhugh, who was working on historical encyclopedias for Harper's, to write the Tom Slade scout series. It was the fifty-cent material, but presumably put together more adroitly than a Syndicate yarn. Over 3,000,000 copies of that work have been sold to give Fitzhugh claim to fame as the man whose books have been more popular than all but three Olympians of the Syndicate...." The writer concludes his comments on Stratemeyer on this note: "And the great juvenile he was always going to write was forever lost in the deluge of his 20,000,000 potboilers that bestow upon him the fame of a colossus he never wanted to be." The article itself ends thus: "Tripe they were in the beginning, tripe they are now, and tripe they always will be. But a wise publisher knows to his profit that they are pap to the maturing mind, and from the customer's point of view, most delectable pap to boot." Regardless of one's opinion of the statements in the article, it must be admitted that it is not entirely objective.

Since most of this chapter deals with the Fortune article and its ramifications, and thus presents a highly distorted picture of both Stratemeyer and the Syndicate, it might be fair to present a few other witnesses. The best witnesses are the books themselves. Stratemeyer was a good businessman with a good product and a fine sense of timing. There are few authors whose books are being collected and read 85 years after their printing. His early books, written entirely by himself and published by Lee & Shepard and many other publishers, were favorably reviewed by many respectable publications regardless of Stratemeyer's former connection with dime novels. When he found it impossible to do all of his own writing, he made a point of hiring competent and qualified writers. It was good business to do so. It is quite true that these authors followed a plot laid out by Stratemeyer, using his characters and timetable, but so what? W. Bert Foster wrote many of the Syndicate books, particularly titles in the Ruth Fielding, Betty Gordon and, I suspect, some of the Ralph of the Roundhouse series. Howard Garis's Tom Swifts are minor classics and if you have tried to buy any of the old Tom Swifts lately, you know they are being ardently collected. Certainly, many older series contain stereotypes that are offensive to our modern tastes, as well as characterizations that are less than well-rounded. But again, so what? (Incidently, as background for a larger article on juvenile criticism, I re-read The Water Babies, Hans Brinker, the Princess and the Goblin and a number of other "classics." Edward Stratemeyer, my hat is off to you!)

It was only after he had established the Syndicate and become financially successful that Stratemeyer became the target for the reformers. Here was an obvious target. Of

the hundreds of series published, Stratemeyer's were generally better written, better produced and better promoted and
the sales show this.   A subject for an interesting essay
would be a comparison of series books treatment of World
War I as shown in Fitzhugh's Tom Slade series, Stratemeyer's
Dave Porter series and Clair Hayes' Boy Allies series, for
examples.   It does not appear that Stratemeyer is a bit
bloodier than Fitzhugh and his style is equal to Fitzhugh,
Mathiews notwithstanding.   But it was Stratemeyer who was
successful, who was innovative in his techniques and who
provided an obvious target.   Gilbert Patten and Clair Hayes
were thus not perceived as quite the threat that Stratemeyer
was.   The more the kids read Tom Swift, Ted Scott, Nancy
Drew, the Hardy Boys and the Bobbsey Twins, the more the
reformers focused on Stratemeyer.
     Criticism has moderated to some extent recently, and
occasionally favorable comments appear.   There is for example a "Viewpoint," published in Library Journal (April 15,
1970, p. 1455), by Ervin J. Gaines, director of the Minneapolis Public Library.   Among several searching remarks,
Gaines made two that I quote here: "The unwillingness of
children's librarians to relent from their firm position that
Nancy Drew and The Hardy Boys are some kind of trash is a
sign of brittle rigidity that is ultimately harmful to the
promotion of reading.   Carl Sandburg once admitted to
reading Horatio Alger and Oliver Optic, two authors whose
fame has survived the disapproval of librarians.   Many
important men and women who have taken the trouble to
recall their childhood reading habits have testified to a
juvenile taste for what adults forbade."   The second one is
somewhat tangential to this discussion but poses interesting
questions.   "I have raised the suggestion that there is a
cosy closed circuit arrangement between children's librarians
and publishers, which tends to limit the range of children's
literature.   Publishers only want to finance books that they
know librarians will buy--and so long as librarians have
their feet anchored in the concrete of the past, they are, in
effect, controlling the library output of children's literature
--since about three-fourths of the juvenile sales are to
libraries.   Thus, inadvertantly, we may have created an
elitist monopoly, and the only way it can be broken is for
the kids to boycott the library, which is what they seem to
be doing."
     The Saturday Review also put the seal of approval on
Stratemeyer, in Arthur Prager's "The Secret of Nancy Drew
--Pushing Forty and Going Strong" (January 25, 1969).
Try to relate these quotes from Prager to those from the
children's librarians quoted earlier: "Nancy is written in
East Orange, New Jersey, by 'Carolyn Keene,' who is really
a grandmotherly lady named Harriet S. Adams, abetted by

her partner Andrew Svenson and four anonymous ghost writers. This group also writes the 'Tom Swift, Jr.,' series, the 'Hardy Boys,' the 'Bobbsey Twins,' and a number of others." "Mothers who have never read the series examine it and find it harmless, if not downright wholesome. Parents who don't care one way or another tolerate Nancy because she keeps the children quiet and arouses in them an interest in books and reading." "The books have an old, timeless quality. I looked for anachronisms in our 1930 first edition of "The Secret of the Old Clock." Except for Nancy's roadster, with its running boards and rumble seat, there were none." "When I asked my daughter why she had loved Nancy, she thought for a moment, and then said simply, 'You can identify with her'." "The surest clue to an evil-doer in the series is grammar. A Nancy Drew felon reveals himself at once by his garbled syntax." "A day will come when each of them (another generation of first-graders) will discover, either on her own or through the instrument of some fond relative who remembers her own girlish past, the irresistable girl detective and The Secret of the Old Clock, and will turn to chapter one, page one, and read...."

There have been many other favorable articles on the Stratemeyer Syndicate in the recent past. Few people seem concerned to find that Mrs. Adams uses the "Carolyn Keene" pen name and "Laura Lee Hope" as well, or that Mr. Svenson is Jerry West of Happy Hollister fame. There seems to be a recognition that there is something enduring about these series books and that, while they may not all be Treasure Islands or Huckleberry Finns, they are certainly not "devices to capture our youth and secure the ruin of immortal souls."

Let me close with a quotation from the article "For Children: Reform the Reformers," by Carolyn Heilbrun, which appeared in the New York Times in the fall of 1967: "... The writers of children's books have been working too hard to reform the world. I suspect they've been listening to the wrong people: children's books, these days, wouldn't be so dull if the writers would stop trying, on bad advice, to accomplish something besides being readable and making some money."

Part Two.   Tom Himself.

Chapter IV

TOM SWIFT, AERONAUTICAL ENGINEER

Flying played a large part in the inventions of Tom Swift. Many do not realize that he did not invent his first airship but built it to another's plans. Most do not realize the usual nature of his early planes, which combined features of the airplane and the dirigible. Tom had a notable career in aircraft development and, in fact, is still active in the field. His career and inventions now span about seventy years.

It took sixty years for aircraft development to catch up with Tom Swift. A Popular Mechanics magazine has this description of a newly patented combination airplane-dirigible: "Half airplane, half dirigible, this monster hybrid is designed to combine the advantages of both. The rigid, wing-shaped fuselage has the speed of an airplane, but gets added lift from a gas-filled chamber...." Shades of the Red Cloud! Tom not only perfected the same invention about 1910 but used it successfully for many trips until it was wrecked in the Caves of Ice. The Red Cloud, in case you've forgotten, was the first of a long series of airplanes, gliders and dirigibles built by Tom and his associates. It, too, was a combination airplane-dirigible and could take off vertically using just the gas or horizontally as a conventional airplane. It is doubtful if the modern imitation will perform any better than the old Red Cloud. So successful was this design, in fact, that after the Red Cloud was destroyed Tom built another combination airplane-dirigible named the Black Hawk which followed the same design but was smaller, lighter and faster.

To be completely accurate we must admit that the Red Cloud was not Tom's invention but that of Mr. Sharp, the balloonist who was rescued by Tom from a burning balloon over Lake Carlopa. "Mr. Sharp was more than an aeronaut --he was the inventor of an airship--that is he had plans drawn for the more important parts, but he had struck a 'snag of clouds,' as he expressed it and could not make the machine work." Tom and his father, however, not only solved the technical problems but actually built the machine.

How did Tom get his start? In 1910 he was already labeled a young inventor, having patented several machines.

He lived with his father, Barton Swift, on the outskirts of
the small town of Shopton, in New York State. Mr. Swift
had become wealthy by accumulating a considerable fortune
from several of his patents, as he was also an inventor.
Tom started off in a small way. Like many boys he was
tired of riding a bicycle so he purchased a damaged motor-
cycle from Mr. Wakefield Damon, the elderly eccentric who
had attempted to climb a tree with it. This he rebuilt with
help from his father, making some minor improvements in the
machine in the process. He used it for a hair-raising trip
to Albany during whch his father's patent model was stolen
and Tom was mugged. Next he bought a motor boat at
auction which he renamed the Arrow. This, too, he over-
hauled rather than redesigned although he added a new
system of lubrication under forced feed and a better water
pump. He put it in such good shape that it beat the boat of
Andy Foger, the bully, even though his was a racing boat
with three cylinders compared to Tom's two. It was in the
Arrow that Tom rescued John Sharp, the aeronaut, from a
watery grave and it was John Sharp who interested Tom and
his dad in aircraft design.
  "Ever invent an airship?" asked the rescued Mr. Sharp
of Tom as the Arrow carried him towards Shopton.
  "No," replied the lad, somewhat surprised. "I never
did."
  "I have," went on the balloonist. "That is, I've invented part of it. I'm stuck over some details. Maybe you
and I'll finish it some day. How about it?"
  "Maybe," assented Tom, who was occupied just then in
making a good landing. "I am interested in airships, but I
never thought I could build one."
  "Easiest thing in the world," went on Mr. Sharp...
  Their first airship took several months to build, apparently, and in the process they solved some relatively major
problems. They had nine explosions trying to get the right
gas mixture and Mr. Swift had to design and build a special
engine for it. The machine was a biplane with two propellers, one in front and the other at the rear. In addition
to the wings there was an aluminum tank, shaped like a
cigar, filled with a special gas that would keep the plane
afloat without the engine. The Swift engine had 20 cylinders and the plane could do 80 miles an hour against a
moderate wind. The cabin of the airship contained a galley,
berths and even easy chairs, "where the travelers could rest
in comfort while skimming along high in the air."
  The Red Cloud performed so well in trial tests, having
won at the Blakeville air meet, that Tom, along with Mr.
Sharp and Mr. Damon had no concern about heading for
Atlanta, Georgia. Mr. Swift was unable to go, partly because of a new submarine invention on which he was working

and partly because of his health. "Mr. Swift was getting
rather along in age, and his long years of brain work had
made him nervous." As it turned out, they had to return
after reaching North Carolina when they learned they had
been accused of robbing the Shopton bank but the Red
Cloud, in general, performed beautifully--although the
engine refused to start when they needed to rise above a
forest fire, a cylinder broke on the return trip and the ship
was struck by lightning. The Red Cloud proved her worth
in finding the Diamond Makers and had many successful trips
before it was crushed in the Caves of Ice in Alaska.

Meanwhile, Tom had turned his attention to more conventional aircraft. He built the Butterfly, "a trim little
monoplane--one of the speediest craft of the air that had
ever skimmed along beneath the clouds." Tom Swift had not
only built this monoplane himself, but was the originator of
it, and the craft contained many new features. This was
the machine in which Tom took Eradicate Sampson for a ride,
thoroughly curing him of any further desire for riding in an
airplane. Tom had now graduated from following other's
plans to bold and original designing of his own.

About six months after his return from Alaska he was
asked to enter the Eagle Park aviation meet to compete for a
prize of $10,000. He determined to build a small monoplane
with a light engine, yet powerful enough to make over 100
miles an hour, if necessary, a fantastic speed at that time.
He had three months in which to build it, which was ade-
quate for Tom. The final machine, which Tom named the
Humming-Bird, had wings shaped somewhat like those of a
hummingbird while the body was shaped like a cigar, "with
side wings somewhat like the fin keels of the ocean liners, to
prevent a rolling motion." The engine, built by the Swifts,
was a wonder for lightness and power. Athough the Humming-Bird was designed as a small racing machine, it could
carry a passenger and Tom saved his father's life by bringing Dr. Hendrix to his aid after a railroad bridge collapsed
and the trains were cut off from Shopton.

In the great race at Eagle Park, Tom's machine registered an incredible 130 miles per hour. So superior was
the Humming-Bird that when Tom suffered a temporary
engine failure with just three miles to go in the race he was
still able to catch up with the other contestants and he beat
Andy Foger by a good length to win the prize. After the
race he "made a most advantageous deal with the United
States officials for his patents."

Tom's career in aerospace expanded rapidly in the
following years. He built the Black Hawk, which he took to
Africa and used successfully to hunt elephants and rescue
missionaries. He then built the Falcon, also a combination
airplane-dirigible, but larger than the earlier models. This

was the airship Tom flew to Russia, carrying the air glider he had invented to search for the lost platinum mine in Siberia. The Vulture, as the glider was called, could remain motionless in the air when the wind, "as evidenced by the anemometer, was howling along at 120 miles an hour!" By means of the Vulture, Tom and his associates found the lost platinum mine and in three days collected platinum worth a king's ransom, following which they flew back to Shopton.

Still another combination airplane-dirigible was the Flyer, which Tom designed and built for use in his "Wizard Camera" expedition of 1912. Tom and his friends flew over India, Europe and a good part of South Africa in it although it had to be shipped to Calcutta and reshipped from Europe to Peru.

Tom used both the standard airplane concept and the combined airplane-dirigible idea in his designs and, in addition, on several occasions built straight dirigibles. For his "City of Gold" trip Tom designed a small dirigible which he used successfully to make his way to the ruined temple. In the bag he used a new gas which was much more powerful even than hydrogen and which he made from chemicals that were carried in the airship.

His Aerial Warship, invented about 1915 for the protection of his country, was much larger. "In brief, Tom's aerial warship was a sort of German Zeppelin type of dirigible balloon, rising in the air by means of a gas container, or rather, several of them, for the section for holding the lifting gas element was divided by bulkheads...." "Tom's aerial warship contained many new features. While it was as large as some of the war-type Zeppelins, it differed from them materially." The Mars was about 600 feet long and the three double-bladed propellers would give a maximum speed of about 75 mph. Tom's biggest problem was compensating for the recoil of the guns mounted in the dirigible. When Ned Newton's door-check recoil did not work properly he was forced to copy the method used on some of the German Zeppelins and make double guns to fire in opposite directions at the same time.

Tom's last major lighter-than-air design was the Silver Cloud, built in 1930. This mammoth dirigible was all metal with some radical departures in construction including the novel stabilizing fins. It was larger than the Graf Zeppelin and was designed to go 10,000 miles and have a speed of over 200 miles an hour. Tom designed it under contract with the Jardine company and it eventually became their property.

Although the Swifts produced a number of dirigibles through the years, Tom always preferred airplanes to balloons and his inventions in the heavier-than-air field have been well-chronicled. The Air Scout was the first silent airplane ever built and was developed by Tom in 1918 to be used in the World War. "Those of you who have read of its work against the Boches, and how it helped Uncle Sam to gain the mastery of the sky, need not be reminded of this." A few years later he perfected a flying boat. The Winged Arrow was 60 feet long, was driven by two engines of 400 horsepower each and could carry 10 or 12 passengers. Her air speed was over 100 mph, which was exceptional for a flying boat of that type. A new equilibrator principle permitted level flight under all conditions and, even in rough water, the flying boat "floated like a well ballasted sailing craft." With it Tom, Ned Newton and Koku flew to Iceland in less than three days and rescued Mr. Damon and Mr. Nester from an iceberg.

It was in 1926 that Tom inaugurated his celebrated airline express. It ran from New York to San Francisco, a staight-across-the-continent flight in 16 hours. Since no plane could reliably fly across the country in a day, Tom came up with a unique solution. The passengers took their places in a pullman-type coach which was fastened to an airplane by clamps. This plane then flew to Chicago and landed. There a fresh plane was attached to the coach and the flight continued to Denver. At Denver a third plane took over and flew the coach to San Francisco. The fare was $1000 each way, the odd machine met with much favor and the venture was a financial success for the Swifts.

The following year Tom circled the globe in a little over 19 days to win a prize of $100,000 and, incidently, $20,000 in bets his father had made. He made the trip in his Air Monarch, an advanced design that was a combination automobile, motor boat and airplane. In his research for this creation he developed a more powerful gasoline engine since his initial model was not speedy enough to suit him.

By the early 30's Tom was successfully building commercial planes of many types. One of his most novel inventions was the Sky Train, in which a powerful airplane picked up gliders filled with passengers at flying fields in cities across the country and dropped the gliders off as a railroad train "drops off coaches at local points." The Sky Train became a coast-to-coast express without stops. At intermediate points the gliders, loaded with passengers, were hauled into the air by an auxiliary motored plane and coupled to the rear of the Sky Train while in full flight.

One of his last major inventions in the aerospace industry was the ocean airport, designed as a floating landing field for airplanes flying between Europe and the United States. It contained provisions for spare parts, mechanics and relief pilots and went far to make air travel over the Atlantic practical and safe. After its inauguration in 1934 Tom turned his energies in other directions.

Tom's inventions were by no means limited to the aircraft field and the amazing thing is that with all his adventures he found time to do as much creative engineering as he did. In the field of surface transportation he developed improved versions of an electric runabout, electric locomotive, house trailer and army tank. He invented an electric rifle, an improved movie camera, the photo telephone, talking pictures, a television detector and giant magnet. His giant searchlight pre-dates the laser by many years. His giant cannon, which he invented to protect the Panama Canal, established new records for distance. He was involved with submarine development from the time he built his first submarine boat about 1910 until he raised the sunken U.S. Navy submarine S.V.J. 13 in 1932.

Who was Tom Swift? In a sense Tom was all of the rugged individualists of the time who dared to dream and plan and struggle and create. He was Edison and Steinmetz. He was Walter Brookins who at 21 set a world's altitude record after being interested in flying for only six months. He was Lindbergh and Byrd and the crew of the NC4. He was what many of us wanted to be and knew we could be when we grew up. His early career closely parallelled that of Glenn Curtiss. It was Curtiss who also started with bicycles, graduated to motorcycles and set a world's record of 136 mph in 1907 using an engine he had personally designed. It was Curtiss who, in 1911, built his Golden Flyer in less than two months and won the first international air meet at Rheims, France. And it was Curtiss who was responsible for almost as many developments in aviation as Tom himself.

Tom's name came from an 1894 Stratemeyer serial, Shorthand Tom. Howard Garis, creator of Uncle Wiggily, did much contract writing for Stratemeyer and apparently was involved in about 36 of the 40 books in the original Tom Swift series. Volume 38, the last of the hardcover books, appeared in 1935 but two "Better Little Books" were issued in 1939 and 1941. After this, Tom and Mary Nestor, whom he had finally married in a somewhat less than whirlwind courtship, seemed to devote their time to bringing up their two children.

Tom Swift Jr. has benefited from the scientific training of his father and grandfather and is becoming an eminent engineer in his own right. His inventions and adventures are now being recorded in the Tom Swift, Jr. series. But best of all in the new series is to find that our friend, Tom Swift, is still alive and active and helping his son solve the engineering problems of today.

Chapter V

SHOPTON, HOME OF THE SWIFTS

I have always wondered where Shopton, New York is. It is an elusive village in "central New York." The following notes may be helpful to those engaged in detective work of their own aimed at pin-pointing its exact location.

The Brungarians know where Shopton is. Their agents have spent countless hours there in nefarious plotting against the Swifts. Ivan Barsky had no trouble finding Shopton. Neither did Happy Harry alias Jim Burke, nor the agents from Verano. The scientists from Hemispak and the top brass in the Army know how to reach Shopton. Their friends in outer space are able to land projectiles on the very grounds of Swift Airfield. It sometimes seems that every major malefactor of the century has either visited Shopton or sent agents there.

Why then is it that letters addressed to the Swift Construction Company in Shopton, or to its subsidiary the T. Swift Boat and Engine Works, are returned marked "Address Unknown." And why is Shopton not shown on any known map of New York State? It seems obvious to this observer that high government officials are taking all possible precautions for the security of the Swift companies. This would be highly desirable if it served a real purpose. We are all familiar with the contributions of the Swifts, including Barton, Thomas and Thomas, Jr., to national security and welcome reasonable regulations. Since, however, both national and international criminals are thoroughly familiar with the location of the Swift companies in Shopton it seems the height of bureaucratic stupidity to pretend that Shopton does not exist.

Of course Shopton exists. Not only is this obvious from the actual developments of the Swifts, fantastic though they may seem to the uninitiated, but Appleton and his nephew give a great many clues to the location in their series of historical reports of the Swift enterprises. The purpose of this chapter is to sift the clues, conflicting and confusing as they sometimes appear to be, and present to their admiring public the true location of Shopton, home of the fabulous Swifts.

The Misters Appleton have been recording the Swift

history only since 1910 although the name is an old and honored one. An uncle of Thomas and brother of Barton was immortalized by Edward Stratemeyer in Shorthand Tom, the Reporter. This Tom, for whom the more famous Tom was named, was a noted editor on a New York newspaper. Benjamin Swift, uncle of both the senior Tom and Barton, was noted as a wealthy explorer and it is on record that he died in Africa in the 1890's leaving his wealth to his nephew Tom.

Arthur Winfield in The Schooldays of Fred Harley mentions a Billy Swift who was matriculated at Parker Academy, Maplewood Center, New York. This particular youth appears to have been a bit of a cad and an insufferable snob and it is perhaps fortunate that there is no proven connection with the Shopton Swifts. It is believed that the Swift family was related through the maternal side to both the Porter and Rover families, well known in central New York. It is interesting to note, in passing, that Messrs. Stratemeyer, Winfield and the elder Appleton were extremely good friends and that both Stratemeyer and Winfield corresponded with Appleton on the Swift series.

At any rate the Swifts have been established in Shopton for many years. Appleton notes, "Shopton, the suburb of the town where Tom lived, was named so because of the many shops that had been erected by the industry of the young inventor and his father" (Tom Swift among the Fire Fighters, 1921, p.9). It is perhaps significant that details are more plentiful in the earlier books than in the more recent ones. As the importance of the Swifts has increased, more and more emphasis has been placed on preserving their privacy. In Tom Swift and His Motor-Cycle (1910, p.9) there was no question: "Mr. Swift and his son lived in a handsome house on the outskirts of the village of Shopton, New York State. The village was near a large body of water, which I shall call Lake Carlopa...."

Much later, in Tom Swift and His Sonic Boom Trap (1965), the location was not specified but even here could still be determined, at least roughly: Leaving Shopton, "In a few minutes the sleek silver sky giant roared upward westward toward the Great Lakes.... Twenty minutes later the supersonic jet was swooping down toward Detroit's Metropolitan Airport."

A detailed examination of the 73 books comprising the canon has produced so much information that only the most important clues can be considered in this chapter. The research was based on the following items: (1) distances and directions specifically given, (2) identifying characteristics of cities, lakes and general terrain, (3) inferences drawn from known times and speeds between Shopton and related points, and (4) miscellaneous references from which reasonable inferences could be drawn. In preparation for the study, several large maps and atlases were obtained as well as railroad time tables of 40 years ago covering all known railroads in New York State. The obvious references were first plotted by drawing arcs with minimum and maximum values from a known starting point. As reasonable inferences were drawn, additional arcs were plotted. Eventually a pattern began to emerge.

Early in the study a startling suggestion presented itself. The evidence became so strong that the suggestion became a hypothesis and the accumulated data was tested against it. The thought was this. Shopton was actually Hammondsport, New York on Keuka Lake. The reasoning was as follows: Hammondsport was the home of Glenn Curtiss, famous inventor, aviator and manufacturer. Tom Swift was the boyhood hero whose career Curtiss attempted to follow. The early careers of Curtiss and Swift were just too identical to be a coincidence. Both were ardent bicyclists who moved on to motorcycles. Both improved on existing motorcycles and went into business manufacturing them. Curtiss invented the motor which powered the Baldwin dirigible and Swift collaborated on the Red Cloud. Swift planned and built the Hummingbird in three months and won the Eagle Park Air Meet. Curtis built the Golden Flyer which won the first International Air Meet at Rheims, France, in about a month. (See John W. Donahey's "Tom Swift and His Magic Typewriter," Concept, vol. 1, no. 1 [1963], p. 23.) Anything that Swift did Curtiss tried also. So closely did he follow Tom Swift's ideas that he must have had ready access to the Swift Construction Company. The suggestion even presented itself that Curtiss was the model for Andy Foger, but both his reputation and successful inventions, independent of Tom Swift, indicate that this is doubtful. Looking again at the canon in light of these truly remarkable coincidences it seems that many of the Appleton comments were obviously referring to Hammondsport.

Let us now turn to the actual sources. At one point Mr. Damon commented that it took the train over five hours to go from Shopton to Philadelphia. In the Butterfly Tom expected to take only three hours. "Yes, I know, but we're going direct and it's only about two hundred and fifty miles" (Tom Swift and His Wireless Message, 1911, p. 46). The "about" may be a flimsy attempt at camouflage or it may show the inaccuracies in the maps of that day. It is easily seen that a 250 mile arc from Philadelphia does not pass through any lake large enough to qualify as Carlopa except Lake George, and since, from other evidence, Shopton is definitely in central or western New York, Lake George has to be eliminated.

A 225 mile arc includes Oneida Lake and a 200 mile arc

includes all of the Finger Lakes. Since we know it took the
train a certain time, it shows that Shopton was on a railroad
line. Unfortunately, "over five hours" is a bit indefinite.
The Lackawanna railroad time table does little to help. Utica
(the closest main station to Oneida Lake) to Philadelphia took
over 10 hours which leads us to question whether Oneida
Lake was intended as Lake Carlopa. Ithaca, at the end of
Cayuga Lake, was eight hours and 22 minutes from Philadelphia, and thus also farther than indicated. Of the remaining
lakes large enough to fit the description of Lake Carlopa and
which also had rail connections to Philadelphia, the one
which seemed to be the best possibility was Keuka Lake.
The village of Hammondsport has a rail connection to Bath, a
few miles distant (Mansburg?) and the running time from
Bath to Philadelphia on No. 6, the Lackawanna Limited, was
eight hours and 38 minutes. It was also made clear that
Tom would have had to change cars since he states, "It's
quite a little run from Shopton, because I can't get a
through train" (...Wireless Message, p. 10). It may be
noted that no village in New York State within a 250 mile
radius of Philadelphia had a train that took less than eight
hours. The suspicion here is that Mr. Appleton was being
cagey and deliberately increased the mileage and decreased
the train time for his own purposes.

In an early adventure Tom was required to ride his
motorcycle to Albany. It was to be a one-day trip and he
planned to eat lunch in Centreford and arrive in Albany
before dark (...and His Motor-Cycle, 1910, p. 84). His
dad's comment was, "Don't try to make speed, as there is no
special rush" (p. 85). Tom, in a discussion with Happy
Harry, a vindictive tramp, told him the machine would do
"two hundred miles in a day, easily" (p. 93). Even after he
had been delayed by the tramp, he took time for a good
dinner in Centreford, feeling no urgency. He did realize he
would have to do some night riding, but it didn't bother him
since "the roads from now on are good. The highway leading to Albany was a hard, macadam one..." (p. 106). This
was in 1910 and the implication is clear that Tom had picked
up either the old Cherry Valley Turnpike, now Route 20, or
the Utica-Albany road, now Route 5. During the afternoon
Tom came to grief when he was mugged in a church stable
as he was waiting out a rain shower. He had just solilo-
quized that "if I get to Fordham by six o'clock I ought to be
able to make Albany by nine, as it's only forty miles. I'll
get supper in Fordham..." when he was knocked unconscious
and carried to Dunkirk.

"Am I near Albany?" he asked when he regained con-
sciousness.

"Albany?" You're a good way from Albany," replied
the farmer. "You're in the village of Dunkirk."

"How far is that from Centreford?"
"About seventy miles" (p. 123).
In terms of 1910 a "good way" might be anything from 20 to 50 miles. Assuming that Dunkirk was on the way to Albany, which is indicated by internal evidence, Centreford to Albany might be 90 to 120 miles. Shopton to Centreford would seem to be a little less than half the total distance to Albany, or about 80 miles. The total would be roughly 170 to 200 miles, which is in agreement with Tom's statement to Happy Harry. My personal experience in riding a 1917 one-cylinder Indian motorcycle some years ago leads me to believe that Tom was bragging a bit and that while he might do 200 miles a day over 1910 roads, he wouldn't do it easily.

Referring again to the map and examining the evidence, we note that Oneida Lake to Albany is about 125 miles, or considerably less than our figures. Hammondsport, on the other hand, is about 190 miles. Several other villages in the Finger Lakes region would also possibly qualify.

After Tom had failed miserably in his trip to Albany, his father found it necessary to take the train there to salvage what he could. "I'll take the night train, Tom" (p. 144). The next day, "He got a telegram from his father that afternoon, stating that Mr. Swift had safely arrived in Albany..." (p. 156). If he had taken the No. 10 Lackawanna from Bath at 9:18 p.m. and changed at Binghampton to the Delaware and Hudson No. 305, he would have arrived in Albany at 11:50 a.m. The evidence accumulates.

We now have distances from two points and apparently have reduced the possibilities to the area of the Finger Lakes. Turning to Tom Swift and His Big Dirigible (1930), we find Tom occupied with vacation plans at Mt. Camon. "Wonderful hotel there, but in the middle of a great wilderness" (p. 6). "Mt. Camon was the summit of a series of big hills, about two days' journey by automobile" (p. 38). "The Mt. Camon Hotel was situated on a mountain top, girt around by immense forest stretches in every direction" (p. 75). Mt. Camon must be in the Adirondacks, in northeastern New York. It is also close to a railroad. Mr. Damon comments, "The bus brought me here from that little jerkwater station shaped like a mushroom." Railroads were never over-plentiful in the north country but Lyon Mountain had both a railroad and the requisite wilderness. It fits the description almost exactly.

Meanwhile Tom was working on his dirigible, the Silver Cloud. In trying it out around Shopton, Ned Newton commented, "You know the Moochie range of mountains lie south and there are some pretty tall peaks." This again points towards central New York. A few chapters later Tom had to run the Silver Cloud at full speed for about two hours to reach Mt. Camon. Thus the speed was at least 125 mph,

which would give 250 miles by air from Shopton to the resort
hotel.   By air the distance from Lyon Mountain to Hammondsport is 230 miles.

When Tom was getting ready for the big race in Tom
Swift and His Electric Runabout (1910) he commented, "It
will be quite a trip to Long Island, and I think my best plan
will be to go direct to the cottage we had when we were
building the submarine and from there proceed to the track"
(p. 188).   They had planned to spend two days and one
night on the road, and did reach the shore cottage near
Atlantis, New Jersey, in two days (p. 201).   The car was
good for 100 mph but the roads were not, and in addition
the batteries had to be charged.   "He hoped to be able to
make the entire distace to the shore cottage on the single
charge" (p. 188).   Some juvenile delinquents had short-
circuited the battery and Tom had to borrow juice from a
trolley car line in order to make it to New Jersey.   Since it
took two days from Shopton to both Mt. Camon and to the
New Jersey coast the supposition is that the distances should
be similar.   Examination of the map shows that from Hammondsport to Lyon Mountain and from Hammondsport to the
New Jersey coast are indeed almost exactly the same.

The mind begins to boggle from the plethora of clues.
We find Shopton was on a government airmail route.   West of
Shopton were open places with widely scattered cities.   They
flew to Iceland in three days, steering north of east from
Shopton (Tom Swift and His Flying Boat, 1923, p. 135).
Our general location is quite definitely determined.   The
remaining problem is to identify Lake Carlopa.   This is
doubly difficult since it changes in size periodically.   At one
time Tom discussed taking a week's tour of Carlopa by boat
(Tom Swift and His Motor-Boat, 1910, p. 9) and some time
later is taken by a hidden tunnel from Shopton to the end of
the lake (Tom Swift and His Airline Express, 1926, p. 23).
Either someone did a lot of digging or the lake had dried up
some.

Again, let us examine the evidence.   Mr. Damon "was
traveling along a road that bordered the lake, about fifteen
miles above here" (...and His Motor-Boat, p. 146).   Keuka
Lake measures about 20 miles in length.   "Lake Carlopa was
a large body of water and it would take a moderately powerful boat several days to make a complete circuit of the
shore, so cut up into bays and inlets was it" (p. 10).
Keuka would certainly fit this description.

Several villages bordered Lake Carlopa, including
Lanton, Sandport, Daleton and Waterfield.   Urbana, Keuka,
Catawba, and Penn Yan could easily be the ones described.

Occasionally Mr. Appleton seems deliberately confusing.
The General Harkness mansion was "away up at de head ob
Lake Carlopa," according to Eradicate (...and His Motor-

Cycle, p. 171). "The Lake was a large one, and Tom had never been to the upper end" (p. 176). Technically, the upper end of Keuka is the southern end since it flows north and since Shopton is near the southern end this description seems questionable. Then, however, Mr. Appleton gives away his deception by quoting Tom, "I'll circle around, and reach the mansion from the stretch of woods on the north" (p. 176). He later gives the game away completely when he notes, "It was getting well on in the afternoon, and the sun was striking across the broad sheet of water. Tom glanced up along the shore...." "It was the chimney of a house" ... "the sun striking full on the mysterious mansion..." (p. 178). The Harkness Mansion was obviously at the north end and Shopton towards the south end of the lake.

Need we continue? Some may carp that Keuka is too small for the description. It is true that it took Tom about seven hours to go from Sandport to Shopton in his boat the Arrow, but the boat, which was 21 feet long with a 5½' beam, had only a 10 HP motor. A speed of 10 mph was claimed for it but this had to be under ideal conditions. In addition, Tom had to stop for a burning balloon, which took a few minutes.

Others may claim that Keuka is too large. As noted earlier, in Airline Express Tom walked the length of a tunnel from the Swift Works and found himself on Barn Door Island. "The Island was at the end of the lake farthest removed from Shopton and the Swift plant" (...and His Airline Express, p. 23). A 20 mile tunnel is just too much--unless of course Tom himself had dug it (which he hadn't). This occurs in series volume 29 and it is apparent that by this time Victor Appleton was deliberately throwing red herrings across the paths of future investigators.

The temptation exists to overwhelm the gentle reader with additional deductions. Further evidence, however, seems unnecessary. We could prove that a river ran through Shopton, that there was only one hotel in the village, that there was a trolley line and that Grandyke University was located nearby but this is unnecessary. Let us close by simply saying that we do not claim to have proved that Hammondsport, New York, is the home of the vast Swift enterprises or that Keuka Lake is indeed Lake Carlopa. We offer the evidence only and let the readers make their own deductions.

Chapter VI

TOM AND SCIENCE FICTION/FACT

Part IV, toward the end of this book, deals with Stratemeyer's earlier (pre-Swift) contributions to the juvenile science and adventure field. Popular as these books were at the time, they are largely unknown today. Tom Swift, on the other hand, is still recognized by any red-blooded American youth and indeed has just recently had an electric rifle named after him.

The Tom Swift saga made an indelible imprint on youthful mechanical minds from 1910 on. My son was asked in an engineering class at Purdue, not too long ago, where a major source of the world's platinum was. "In Siberia," he answered properly, somewhat to the amazement of professor and class. He neglected to add that Tom Swift and His Air Glider describes the source in detail. All sorts of useful information are available in both the first series and the Tom Swift, Jr., series.

The first series was written from 1910 to 1941 and includes 38 hardcover books and two "better little books." The two "better little books" were written by Harriet S. Adams, Stratemeyer's daughter, and are therefore included in the canon.

In 1954 Tom's son, Tom, Jr., became active. The series recording his inventions and adventures (and some of his father's) includes 33 books and was written from 1954 to 1971.

To digress briefly, it was not uncommon when a series was particularly successful to continue with another generation. When Frank Merriwell had spent an embarrassing number of years at Yale, Gilbert Patten discovered a brother Dick Merriwell to carry on. Later, about 1915, Frank Merriwell, Jr., or "Chip" also went to Fardale Academy, Frank's prep school. To complicate the Merriwell genealogy a modern version of Frank, Jr., appeared in the mid 1960's with Mike Frederic as the author. Logically the series should have been about Frank's grandson.

The Stratemeyer series were similar. The Rovers had seen all and done all in 20 volumes and the last 10 books of the 30 in the series were accounts of their offspring. Again, the chronology is confusing, as it often is in a long

series. The Rovers were married and had children old
enough to attend prep school at the time of World War I but
all three of the older Rovers enlisted in the army and,
despite their age, saw considerable action.

Tom Swift had a long but tepid romance with Mary
Nestor. After 32 books he stopped inventing long enough to
marry her in Tom Swift and His House on Wheels. The
courtship lasted some 19 years, as closely as can be determined. When Victor Appleton II started recording Tom,
Jr.'s adventures in 1954 Tom was 18 and his father was
middle-aged so this chronology is reasonably accurate.

Fortunately it is both possible and necessary to arrest
the aging process indefinitely in series books. It comes as a
shock to realize that Bert and Nan Bobbsey should be 84
(they were 8 in the first Bobbsey Twins of 1904) but they
have not aged appreciably in the current books.

The Tom Swift canon now contains 73 books. No books
have been issued since Galaxy Ghost, no. 33 of the Tom,
Jr., series. The budding romance between Tom and Phyllis
Newton should result in another wedding and hopefully the
continuation of the line. In a few years we may read of Tom
Swift III.

The start was probably 1909. At that time a number of
Stratemeyer series were doing well including the Motor Boys,
Old Glory Series, Rise in Life Series, Bobbsey Twins, Boys
of Business, the Rover Boys and Great Marvel Series to
mention just a few. The earlier Motor Boys series was a
combination of action, adventure and speed. Starting with
bicycles the boys worked their way up to motorcycles, auto-
mobiles and flying machines. The theme proved exceedingly
popular. The Speedwell Boys and Dave Dashaway, both of a
few years later, also used exciting mechanical aids for their
adventures. The time seemed ripe for a young inventor
series that could combine science and adventure and appeal
to the technically-oriented juvenile reader. The Motor Boys
was a Stratemeyer series with Howard Garis doing much of
the writing. The formula was a good one. Why not continue it with the new series?

George T. Dunlap of Grosset & Dunlap writes, "I well
remember the time Stratemeyer came into our office over on
West 26th Street with a scheme for publishing a series of
boys' books that would have to do with things mechanical,
aviation, submarines, marvelous mechanisms of all sorts....
Out of this idea grew the 'Tom Swift' series, of which,
millions have been sold" (The Fleeting Years, privately
printed, 1937). He stated later that Tom Swift had sold a
total of 6,566,646 copies. His autobiography was printed in
1937, close to the end of Tom's printed career. The figure
should be fairly accurate since Grosset & Dunlap published
all of the books except for the reprints.

Millions of boys have read of the adventures and inventions of Tom Swift and his famous son. Call them science and adventure if you wish, science fiction, at least in the Jules Verne sense, is equally fitting. In the 33 books of Tom Swift, Jr., are a space trip to other planets, communication with beings from another world through the use of mathematical symbols, a "jetmarine" which Verne would have envied and an atomic earth blaster. The 40 books that chronicle his father's inventions generally include more mundane inventions--a great search light (prototype of the laser?) an effective airplane engine muffler (which we still need), an improved army tank and a host of others. Tom, Sr., also discovered life on Mars. Both series were based on an extension of existing scientific knowledge of the day and, as Verne's tour of the Nautilus is now commonplace, so are many of the Swift inventions, so rapidly has our technology changed. If nothing else, the Swift saga shows a fascinating picture of 70 years of American invention from the early airplane to the rocket ship--and beyond.

"It is the purpose of these spirited tales to convey in a realistic way the wonderful advances in land and sea locomotion, and to interest the boy of the present in the hope that he may be a factor in aiding the marvelous development that is coming in the future." This is the somewhat wordy blurb on the old Tom Swift dust jackets. The dust jacket of the first Tom Swift, Jr., book, describing the series as "thrilling stories of new inventions in the world of tomorrow," notes that "each scientific detail of this fascinating story has been carefully checked. Tom Swift's inventions may be years ahead of the time, just as his father's were in their time, but they are all plausible and some day you may see them in use."

Andrew E. Svenson, late partner in the Syndicate, put it a little differently (in an October 25, 1963, letter to the author): "Certainly youngsters interested in science and invention realize that Tom Swift Jr. books are based on scientific fact and probability, whereas the old Toms were in the main adventure stories mixed with pseudo-science."

Tom Swift has a nice ring to it. Stratemeyer borrowed the name from his 1894 serial, "Shorthand Tom, the Reporter," which was also published in hardcover in several editions. The name of his friend Ned Newton was quite possibly taken from the 1887 Alger story, "Ned Newton; or, The Fortunes of a New York Bootblack." Bumbling, eccentric Mr. Damon has a lot in common with Garis's Uncle Wiggily, and Eradicate Sampson bears a marked resemblance to the portayal of Washington White in the Great Marvel Series. The author of Tom Swift was given as "Victor Appleton."

The action takes place in Shopton, in central New York on Lake Carlopa. Tom's father, Barton Swift, is a success-

ful American inventor. He has done well enough to move to
Shopton and set up his labs near town. Tom is motherless
and Mrs. Baggart is their housekeeper.

Tom started off in a modest way in the first book,
riding a bicycle while Andy Foger, the rich bully of the
village, drove a high-powered automobile. "Bicycles are a
back number," growled Andy. This situation couldn't continue and after eccentric Wakefield Damon tried to ride his
motorcycle up a tree he sold it to Tom for $50. Up to that
time Tom's only invention on record was "the egg-beater I
was telling you about. But I'm working on some things."
He had "planned some useful implements and small machines"
(p. 10).

Mary Nestor, who was responsible for perpetuating the
Swift dynasty, was introduced on page 22 of the first book
when Tom's bicycle frightened her horse, the horse ran
away, and Tom had to rescue her. His first love, sad as it
may seem, appears to have been his inventions. Mary was a
patient soul but Tom was worth waiting for and they were
finally married as already noted.

"Tom had graduated with honors from a local academy,
and when it came to a question of going further in his
studies, he had elected to continue with his father for a
tutor, instead of going to college. Mr. Swift was a very
learned man..." (p. 54). He had a B.S. in electrical engineering.

The motorcycle was a challenge to Tom: "...it was not
such as easy task as he had hoped to change the transmis-
sion. He had finally to appeal to his father, in order to get
the right proportion between the back and front gears, for
the motor-cycle was operated by a sprocket chain...." "Mr.
Swift showed Tom how to figure out the number of teeth
needed on each sprocket, in order to get an increase of
speed..." (p. 55). Fortunately Tom was a fast learner and
his later inventions showed a marked improvement in engineering ability.

During 1910 five books appeared. Tom followed up his
motorcycle with a motorboat. In both of these books he
rebuilt an existing mechanism, improved on it somewhat but
created nothing radically new. The technical approach of
the first Tom Swifts seemed reasonable to the juvenile audience. They could do the same things with an engine and
some probably had. The adventures were exciting and the
love interest innocuous. The kids bought Tom Swifts like
wildfire. Volumes 3 and 4 introduced an airship and submarine boat but throughout the entire series the technical
explanations were reasonable and comprehensible to a boy.
Even after Tom shortly passed the technical level of his
readers he wasn't too far ahead. Under the right circumstances they could have done the same. And always they

could identify with Tom and share in his exploits. This was
a major key in the success, not just of this series, but of
most of Stratemeyer's productions. He probably knew the
juvenile mind, its interests, aspirations and dreams, better
than any writer of his time. This "empathy" is still very
much a feature of the Stratemeyer Syndicate.

Tom's airship, the Red Cloud, was designed by John
Sharp the Aeronaut and built by him and the Swifts. It was
a combination dirigible and airplane as were several of the
early Swift machines. The submarine Advance was an advance even on current technology. The negative and positive plates which propelled it were probably superior to our
atomic propulsion systems. These plates were invented, not
by Tom, but by his father, Barton Swift. In the Advance
the Swifts salvaged $300,000 from a sunken ship, the Bol-
dero, at a depth of two and a half miles and could have
worked at depths of three miles.

Volume 5 introduced an electric runabout which Tom
used to win the big race down on Long Island and also to
bring urgently needed cash to save an ailing bank. Back in
the 30's when I first read this book it seemed quite dated.
Nowadays it appears that Tom was just further ahead of the
times than we realized. It is true he would have trouble
today finding trolley lines to recharge his batteries as he
did at one time, but this battery design seems to be as good
as anything in the field today. It used lithium and potas-
sium hydrate as an electrolyte. This seems to be the first
major invention exclusively by Tom, and the new feature was
the battery, not the car.

The next volumes contained more adventures than
inventions. Tom perfected an airplane for an acquaintance
of his father since "inventors should be mutually helpful."
This airplane was also a combined dirigible-airplane since
Victor Appleton seemed to be partial to that design. In it
they took a trip to Earthquake Island that ended in near
disaster. Only at the last possible moment was the party
saved.

When Tom went looking for the Diamond Makers he
threw his inventing to the winds and spent the entire book
adventuring. After a routine trip to the Rockies in the
Red Cloud marked only by finding a stowaway they discovered the mountain and cave where the diamonds were made.
An electric storm destroyed the cave and mountain and
almost destroyed our friends but they escaped with a double
handful of diamonds. When they returned to Shopton Tom
and his friends tried to make diamonds using an electric
current instead of lightning but were unsuccessful.

The hiatus in Tom's inventing continued in Caves of Ice
although the electric rifle made its first appearance in this
book. In fact the major invention was a tri-plane built by

the thorough rascal, Andy Foger, and he personally did little or no inventing himself, hiring most of the construction. The Swift expedition to Alaska shipped the Red Cloud to Seattle, where it was reassembled. The Fogers, who were after the same gold as the Swifts, shipped their plane to Sitka. From then on it was nip and tuck between the rivals until the Fogers broke two of the wings of their plane, the Anthony.

Tom's radically new electric rifle was introduced at a very trying time in Caves of Ice. As the adventurers were being charged by musk oxen Tom appeared with a peculiar-looking gun. "It's my new electric rifle.... I don't know how it will work, as it isn't entirely finished, but I'm going to try it" (p. 163). It worked fine, much to the detriment of the musk oxen. Somehow Tom had "put some finishing touches on it since undertaking the voyage to the Caves of Ice." He kept busy. But the electric rifle was quite incidental to the adventures in the search for the gold fields. The outcome included the demise of the Red Cloud, the accumulation of considerable gold by the Swift party and additional unpleasant experiences by the Fogers.

Tom's inventive genius came to the fore in volume 9, Sky Racer, published in 1911. Heretofore, as far as we can tell, he had been a collaborator with John Sharp or his father. However, "Is this Tom Swift, the inventor of several airships?" asked James Gunmore, secretary of the Eagle Park Aviation Association at the beginning of Sky Racer. Apparently Tom had been doing some inventing unrecorded by Mr. Appleton. Tom mentions a small monoplane, the Butterfly, which he has built. He agrees to build a plane for the Eagle Park contest if his father will help him. Barton is working on a wireless motor and is still the inventive genius of the family until he is taken seriously ill. Even Tom's Sky Racer had an engine "modeled after one his father had recently patented" (p. 26). The plans for the airplane were entirely Tom's and, while his father discussed the plans with Tom, he made few significant suggestions. Needless to say Tom finished the plane well within the two months allowed, won the race with an astounding speed of 130 miles an hour and carried home the $10,000 prize.

Although Tom's plane, the Humming-Bird, was his original design it is still interesting to note that "it was to be a cross between the Bleriot and the Antoinette, with the general features of both, but with many changes or improvements" (p. 45). It also included "a new principle ... not yet patented" (p. 34). It can be seen that Tom, while rapidly advancing in his engineering ability, was still leaning heavily on earlier developments. However the airplane was most successful and "with the money received from winning the big race, and from his contracts from the Government,

Tom Swift was now in a fair way to become quite wealthy" (p. 207).

The number of really new and original inventions entirely the product of Tom's imagination is limited. He had an unusual ability to take an existing mechanism or device and improve on it. He was able to develop special materials to resist extreme pressures and temperatures, special gases to produce more lift than hydrogen, and so to improve on existing creations. He improved on the existing aeroplanes, air gliders, moving picture camera, fire extinguishers, dirigibles, war tanks, oil drilling equipment and house trailers. The majority of the 40 books are stories of such improvements. However there are several original creations which apparently came almost entirely from Tom's genius. The first was the electric rifle and the list certainly includes his photo telephone, his great searchlight, his sky train, his television detector, his planet stone, giant telescope and magnetic silencer.

The electric rifle had its baptism under fire in the musk-oxen incident. Tom later improved it so that "I can calculate exactly, by means of an automatic arrangement, just how far the charge of electricity will go. It stops short just at the limit of the range, and is not effective beyond that" (Electric Rifle, p. 18). This feature has never been duplicated. It had the slight disadvantage that the range had to be set and a mistake could cause problems as Tom found out when he accidentally shot the town skinflint. The range had been set for 2000 feet instead of 200. The skinflint was annoyed but not hurt and Tom bought him off for $12.

Tom was quite detailed in his description of the gun. "There was no sound, no smoke, no flame and not the slightest jar," with the rifle (p. 19). "Strictly speaking, it is a concentrated discharge of wireless electricity, directed against a certain object. You can't see it any more than you can see a lightning bolt, though that is sometimes visible as a ball of fire. My electric rifle bullets are similar to a discharge of lightning, except that they are invisible" (p. 34).

In Tom's trip to Africa with their new plane the Black Hawk, he used the electric rifle to real advantage. In short order he disposed of a whale (p. 81), sharks (p. 84), wild buffalo (pp. 93, 140), two pythons (pp 98-99), numerous elephants (pp. 118, 124, 136), lions (p. 129), two rhinoceroses (p. 149), some birds (p. 155), numerous pygmies (p. 166), and also hostile natives, "black, half-naked forms" (p. 207). We should note he disabled the pygmies and natives and did not kill any of them.

Tom's African safari was most successful as it included rescuing a brace of missionaries and the Foger party, and securing a large number of elephant tusks from unwilling elephants. "A division was made of the ivory, and Tom's share was large enough to provide him with a substantial amount."

When Tom rescued Andy Foger and his party in the wilds of Africa he partially ruined a perfectly good villain in so doing. Andy told Tom, "...but first, Tom, I want to ask your forgiveness for all I've done to you, and to thank you, from the bottom of my heart, for saving us" (p. 197). One would think he could never be the same after a speech like that, but he didn't really change too much.

Tom's Great Search Light (1912) might seem at first glance more like a moderate improvement on an existing device rather than a futuristic invention. It is probably both. The evidence shows that the light was an accidental discovery caused when Koku accidentally crossed two wires. Tom was trying to catch a chicken thief when Koku had his mishap.

"Look, father!" he cried. "The alternating current from the automatic dynamo has become crossed with direct current from the big storage battery in a funny way"; "it has given a current of peculiar strength and intensity--a current that would seem to be made especially for searchlights. Dad, I'm on the edge of a big discovery" (p. 70). As Tom thought out the problem he added, "With larger carbons, better parabolic mirrors, a different resistance box, better connections, and a more powerful primary current there is no reason why I could not get a light that would make objects more plainly visible than in the daytime, even in the darkest night, and at a great distance" (p. 72).

It was noted that the light had a range of several miles but, since it was portable, it had much less candlepower than an existing lighthouse light of 95,000,000 candle power which could be seen 50 miles. Nevertheless it seems to have been a major discovery and well may have been the prototype of the laser.

With the light and his noiseless plane, incidentally still a combination aeroplane-dirigible, Tom tracked down smugglers from Canada. He also rescued from a watery grave on Lake Ontario the same missionaries he had saved in Africa. Tom's preventive maintenance was obviously lacking, as he admitted, when his gas pressure went to 775 psi and almost blew up the plane. Finally on a night cruise after the smugglers, Tom caught one in the searchlight beam and then shot it down with the electric rifle. The smugglers included both Fogers, since the elder Foger had lot most of his money. Andy's reformation had been quite temporary. The searchlight makes appearances in later books in both old and new series and is a classical example of the Swift genius for discovering and applying new technical principles.

"'What do I care for principles of science?" cried Tom."
He and his father were arguing about the possibilities of
"sending light waves--one of the most delicate forms of motion in the world--over a material wire." It was 1914. The
book was Photo Telephone. Tom was convinced he could
transmit both light waves and electrical waves on the same
conductor and so have a visual picture of the telephone
caller. It was a radical thought for the time. Scientists
said it was impossible. Tom had many failures. He selected
selenium in several forms to coat the plates. He tried "an
alternating current on the third wire," to see if that would
make it any better. Nothing worked. Eradicate Sampson
was the actual inventor of the successful photo telephone,
quite by accident. He was attempting to scare Koku, so he
connected the photo telephone and its amplifier. Then he
plugged in by mistake the wire to the arc light circuit which
carried over a thousand volts. He got thoroughly shocked
in the process but Koku's image appeared on the selenium
plate so it was worth it. As Tom put it, "I understand it
now, Rad; but you did more than I've been able to do. I
never, in a hundred years, would have thought of switching
on that current" (p. 123). As Koku found the principle of
the great searchlight by accident, so did Rad discover the
missing element in the photo telephone.

With a good deal of improvement on "Eradicate's Angel
Gabriel system," as Tom called it, the photo telephone became a practical development. He made several interesting
variations on the basic theme. He arranged it so that a
picture could be taken of a caller without his knowledge.
He arranged it also so that the plate was like a mirror so
"he can see his friend as well as talk to him" (p. 131). The
question of violation of privacy was not considered in Tom's
inventions. He even added a dictaphone to record the
messages. Mr. Damon was kidnapped by scoundrels after
they had bilked him of most of his fortune. Tom was able to
bug the telephone booth the villain used to talk to Mrs.
Damon about additional loot. Tom recorded the villain's
voice, also took a picture of him and got him dead to rights.
It turned out to be Peters, the unscrupulous promoter who
had swindled Mr. Damon. After getting a warrant on the
basis of the photo telephone picture Tom went after Peters
and eventually captured him. Peters was convicted on the
basis of Tom's recorded messages and the photography from
the photo telephone. Mr. Damon got most of his fortune
back.

Tom's Airline Express is an example of an idea that
never really got off the ground. It is neither science fiction
nor even good engineering. The idea has superficial merit.
In 1926 the idea of transcontinental air travel was quite
visionary and Tom was hard pressed to raise the cash to

finance the trials of the "combination aeroplane and railroad coach." His idea was to have three planes but only one railroad coach. The coach was clamped to the plane in New York and flown to Chicago. "Landing on the Chicago field, the autocar will be detached and rolled, under its own power, to the second aeroplane which will be in waiting" (p. 115). Then on to Denver and a new plane and finally to San Francisco, all in one day of about 16 hours. "Figure five hours to a lap, that would mean a flying rate of two hundred miles an hour--not at all impossible. We'll charge a fare of one thousand dollars each way" (p. 116). Tom made the flight in 15 hours and 46 minutes to win the financing he needed and all was well. This was not one of his greatest inventions, however.

Sky Train (1931) is a little different. This invention was both imaginative and practical. The opinion has been expressed that this concept was used in the glider landings of World War II. As a commercial venture it never really proved itself and Tom did not make too much use of it, at least according to later writings. It does appear in Planet Stone where Tom towed his private lab car Metalanthium to South America in his search for the mystery of the meteorites. Briefly, the technique was this: A powerful airplane towed two or more gliders behind it in the manner of an aerial freight train. The unusual characteristics were that the plane could unhitch and hitch up to the gliders in mid-air. Not only that, but the gliders in a later improvement contained a gas, lighter than hydrogen, which supported them so they could not crash. In the later books Tom was often over-extended financially. This was true in Sky Train but all turned out well, Tom won a $25,000 prize and "the sale of the world rights was put at a sum sufficient to clear off all the Swift plant debts and leave a big margin" (p. 215).

Television Detector was written in 1933, presumably by Mrs. Adams. It contains more elements of science fiction than many of the series. Both Tom's photo-telephone and his talking pictures embodied features of television but this invention was much more advanced.

It all started when Tom's formula for a deadly gas was stolen. (It was not his invention--he had bought it from a foreigner). Tom had found the gas useful to kill rats but it had other undesirable qualities and he was eager to recover the formula. To do so he invented a television detector. This television detector had a number of radical new ideas. It embodied "a double anode, high vacuum, cathode ray oscillograph tube" among other things (p. 54). In 1933 even Tom hadn't invented solid state components. He had to "generate not only the power by which I see but also the power that will enter the building and transmit the images"

(p. 56).   A worthy task, even for Tom.   With this invention he expected to catch the thief of the gas formula. Along with the television detector Tom invented a "walkie talkie," which was a portable sending and receiving radio to transmit by means of the Morse Code.   Ned had hoped Tom could make it work by voice "but that was a little too much to expect" (p. 68).   Tom finally made a major break-through on his detector when he solved the problem of concentrating the television beam and decreasing the size of the phosphorescent spot where the electrons struck the end of the glass cathode tube.   And it worked.

"When I point this gadget ... at a brick wall, or at a wooden or stone one for that matter, the rays in my machine penetrate through the barriers, bombard the objects beyond with electrons, flash back to me and show themselves on a screen" (p. 95).   The device would penetrate for several miles through brick and wooden walls.   It had to be focused but this was no problem.   Tom even added a radium tube that would "shoot out any distance and will illuminate the persons I want to see without their knowing it.   Then I can see them in the dark" (pp. 99-100).

The upshot of this futuristic invention was that Tom located a missing anarchist for whom the Secret Service was urgently looking and also located the Black Leopard Gang who had stolen his deadly gas formula.   The invention of a device which would see through walls of all types and permit the viewer to examine all activities within the range of the instrument has some obvious implications.   Even though the United States Secret Service was delighted with the results they should have raised some objections to the legal and moral aspects of this invention.   Even Tom was not disturbed, probably since he was using the invention in the service of his country.   This is one invention of Tom's which has not been duplicated and which should not be, even in our current "Big Brother" atmosphere.

A late adventure in the original series involved life from outer space and a miraculous health lamp, as well as a return to Giant-Land.   In Planet Stone; or, Discovering the Secret of Another World (1935) Tom had been designing a metalanthium health lamp which was only partly successful. Meanwhile a letter to Koku, Tom's devoted giant, informed him that the king of giant land had died, and Koku and his brother were next in line for the throne.   Ned Newton, Mr. Damon and Tom organized an expedition to return Koku to South America.   The trip had to be postponed while Koku recovered from an accidental overdose of Tom's "XYZ" mixture.   There seemed to be malpractice problems even then since Tom gave the injection which saved Koku's life and "Dr. Bane," current villain of this book, did his best to have Tom arrested for practicing medicine without a license.

Since Koku recovered, the incident blew over.

The trip to Giant Land by Sky Train was relatively uneventful. The craft weathered a routine fierce storm and landed safely in the midst of an antisocial tribe of savages. Mr. Damon, who was the proud possesor of a wig, inadvertently used this fact to impress the Wabawaba tribe. Anybody who could scalp himself and then replace his scalp was too much for them and they were properly impressed and also subdued. The wig played a prominent part in the success of the expedition. The party found a meteorite which Tom blew to pieces for scientific investigation and work proceeded satisfactorily, interrupted by the need to kill a jaguar and a python with the electric rifle. The "sky stone" proved to be a dud but fortunately a severe thunderstorm brought another meteorite. After some strenuous activity in which Mr. Damon had to subdue the natives with his "usual wig medicine business" the giants dug up the second meteorite and hauled it to Pabalo, the main village. Tom blew the second meteorite into pieces. His scientific methods remind us somewhat of Heinrich Schliemann. Tom was excited. "We're on the verge of something big and important. Here is an inanimate object from another world than our own--a sky-stone as the natives call it--and it glows with a strange light. Ned, maybe I can prove life on another planet!" (p. 140).

The stone contained "a strange irridescent powder and an inner asbestos core which was like a nut." The nut, in turn, contained six small seeds. One thing led to another and Tom and his friends aided the giants in a campaign against the Wabawaba and the nefarious Dr. Bane. Amo, Koku's younger brother, finally settled the conflict by killing three of the enemy in single combat and earned the right to be king since his brothers had abdicated.

After numerous discouragements Tom finally grew two plants from the meteorite seeds (one of which Mr. Damon had found in his wig). The "flowers bloomed and expanded into beautiful white blossoms with a blood-red centre" (p. 192). The flowers were ground to a white powder and in conjunction with the metalanthium light "never once failed to restore health to the afflicted subjects" (p. 197). Swatem Goth, baseball hero of all America, was stricken by a baffling disease and saved by Tom and his new discoveries. "A solution of the crushed seeds, strangely glowing, was forced between the blue lips. An injection was also hypodermically administered" (p. 200). Tom presumably let a licensed physician make the injection. Mr. Goth lived and Tom was a hero. Dr. Bane, himself, was later arrested for practicing medicine without a license. The planet from which the meteorite came is still unknown. "Where that world is remains yet to be discovered. But Tom Swift has proved that plant life exists on it--life that came to him most marvelously in a meteorite" (pp. 201-202).

The meteorite formed part of another scientific break-through in 1939, in Tom Swift and his Giant Telescope, a Whitman Better Little Book. This was roughly the time when Corning Glass was casting the mirror for the Mount Palomar telescope and there was considerable interest as to what their telescope would show. Tom's telescope was set up in the Adirondacks but the magnifying properties were supplied by "the wonderful green substance from the Planet Stone." It developed that much of the planet stone was still imbedded in giant land in South America but through the help of Tom's giant friends it was removed and shipped to the United States. On the way it was jettisoned during a storm and Tom had to assist in recovering it from the ocean depths. In the process he used his electric rifle to shoot a big fish which was holding two divers on the ocean bottom. The electric rifle probably holds the world's record for variety of types of game shot. Tom had also been spending his spare moments in inventing a bendable glass which was flexible but hard as glass. It was also fortunate since Tom had a habit of spending the company money rather profligately when involved in a new project.

The telescope was set up and far outshone anything Palomar could produce. "Before his eyes were revealed a great city, nearly seventy-five million miles distant! Pecu-liar people surged along the avenues, weird aircraft thronged the upper atmosphere, and gigantic buildings and palaces dotted the place. All on far-distant Mars!" (pp. 423-424). Into the eyes of Barton Swift came tears as he said: "Tom, my son, you have performed the greatest miracle of the Age!" (p. 424). Who are we to question it? The only surprising thing is that no Swift expedition, as far as is recorded, ever visited this great city of Mars. This may be a project for Tom Swift III.

Tom's last chronicled invention in the original series was the Magnetic Silencer, also published as a "Better Little Book" by Whitman in 1941. Purists sometimes question why either Giant Telescope or Magnetic Silencer are included in the canon. The answer lies in the fact that both books feature Tom Swift and his friends but more importantly that both were products of the Stratemeyer Syndicate. Harriet Adams informed me (in an April 2, 1975, interview) that she personally wrote all of the Tom Swifts after her father's death, including the "Better Little Books." At any rate Magnetic Silencer has one most interesting reference: "Tom Swift had been gone for hours to test his latest experiment with a secret bomb" (p. 12). Whether this is an actual reference to the atomic bomb is not clear but it was probably not beyond Tom's capabilities at this time. The book refers

to the bomb as being a "controlled bomb-planter" for use by
farmers in distributing seed or insect killer but this may be
camouflage. When Ned Newton suggested military uses for
the bomb, Tom replied, "Scientific developments have already
been misused too often by war-crazy men! They'll never kill
men with my ideas!" (p. 78). However, he admitted he was
giving the War Department full details of the invention. He
seems to have forgotten that a good part of his fortune was
founded on his sales to the government of such devices as
his war tank, air scout and aerial warship. Another thing
he seems to have forgotten is that back in 1912 he invented
an airplane silencer which seemed most effective; "save for a
soft whirr, such as would be made by the wings of a bird,
there was absolutely no sound" (Great Searchlight, p. 36).
However, apparently this wasn't good enough so Tom started
over.

The main plot of Magnetic Silencer concerned a new
magnetic ore which had an attraction for sound waves. It
"attracts and absorbs the whir of the propellor as well as
the roar of the engine" (p. 180). After many trials Tom
was able to adapt the material for his uses and developed a
most advanced silencer. "To the critical examining board he
showed that even the most sensitive audio locator could not
pick up a sound from a plane equipped with his device, even
when flying comparatively low" (pp. 423-424). "'You have
made a very great contribution to your country's defense,
Mr. Swift!' declared Colonel Brooks, after formally accepting
the use of the magnetic silencer on behalf of the United
States" (p. 424).

Tom had now appeared in forty books. (See the Appendix.) His active career as an inventor had covered
thirty years. He was a wealthy man from his inventions and
adventures. Unlike Jules Verne, his capacity for invention
did not appreciably diminish as he grew older. His son,
however, as will be shown later, far surpassed him in the
scope of his creations.

Tom certainly does not fall under the usual umbrella of
"science fiction" in the modern sense. Ignoring the ten-
dency both to pedantry and sophistry in modern critical
writing about science fiction, compare Verne and Swift. As
previously noted, the writings of both were extensions of
existing scientific knowledge. Verne developed a flying
machine which anticipated modern techniques. So did Tom.
Tom's submarine was fifty years ahead of actual developments. Some of Tom's developments have still not been
matched. Verne's books on the Barsac Mission combine
adventure in Africa with science. Many of Tom's chronicles
are both adventure and science. In this type of comparison
there is really little difference. The big differences, as I
see them, are these: Verne was a scientific prophet who

attempted to base his books on a sound scientific foundation. His books were seriously considered and generally seriously accepted. The Tom Swifts were written for a juvenile audience. The scientific foundation is much more superficial. As is common in this genre, the books were automatically regarded as entertainment for children and so unworthy of comparison with Verne.

It is quite true that Tom Swift is very good entertainment but he is much more. Without the moralizing of an earlier generation, the books show how a boy from a modest background can, through his use of scientific knowledge. improve the lot of the world and provide a good income for himself. Tom combines the adventures of the Wild West myth, the drive, aggressiveness and moral code of the American boy hero and the concepts of modern applied science and engineering. It is quite true that Tom was generally hazy as to how his inventions worked. It is equally true that Stratemeyer and his writers showed an uncanny prophetic sense. Any comparison of Verne's inventions and Tom's will bear this out. Verne was more specific as to the "how" of his inventions, but no more accurate in his prophesies.

The entire Tom Swift series bears the stamp of Edward Stratemeyer and his attitudes towards science and invention. When he died in 1930, 33 of the series had been published. The remaining seven followed the same strain in general. A case can be made that the last seven by Mrs. Adams have more pure science fiction than the earlier volumes. Millions of American boys read the Tom Swifts not for their implicit moral tone or from a conscious desire to learn more about science, but for fun. The adventure was there. So was the science. The engineering marvels of the next decades were presented for their delight and they loved them. Were these marvels good prophesy? No one knew--or cared very much. Could they follow in Tom's footsteps? You bet. They could and very often did. Consciously or unconsciously, Tom's readers absorbed his beliefs. He reflected American attitudes towards technical creativity, but he also created these attitudes. Ask your older engineers and scientists how many of them read Tom Swift as a boy.

Tom either rested on his laurels for a number of years or Victor Appleton was gagged by the well-known penchant for secrecy in Washington bureaucratic circles. At any rate nothing further appeared concerning Swift inventions until 1954. Tom Swift, Jr., was now 18 and had reached the age where his successes equalled or surpassed those of his father.

Victor Appleton II, nephew of the original Victor Appleton, was the new writer, or so the advertisements said. In fact, of course, the productions, plots and inventions were

the joint efforts of Mrs. Adams and Andrew Svensen, Stratemeyer Syndicate partners, with the writing done by some six
different men over the life of the series. Thirty-three
books were published, the last in 1971. Many volumes are
still available in book stores. A complete list of the titles
appears in the Appendix, section B.

The Tom Swift, Jr., books have a different flavor from
the original series. The thought may be that today's youth
are more precocious, more worldly and more advanced.
Therefore, the books should also be more worldly and advanced so as to attract the young reader. The result
doesn't quite come off. My unproven belief is that the more
a child can identify with a situation the more believable it
becomes to him and the more he becomes personally involved
with the life of the hero. When a book adds stress situations where the hero overcomes the opposition--but only
after a major and sometimes desperate effort--along with
vivid but relatively realistic action, the child's involvement
becomes even more complete. The hero succeeds. The child
reader can also succeed. In all the books issued by Stratemeyer and the Syndicate, we find this theme. We also find
hard work encouraged and rewarded. We find honesty,
clean living and the American virtues encouraged and rewarded.

"You Swifts have a reputation for scrupulous honesty,"
sneered the Brungarian villain in The Visitor from Planet X
(p. 121). In the same book, Tom, Sr., also reminded his
son, "Don't forget, Tom, the mind of a human being or any
thinking inhabitant of our universe is based on a divine
soul. No scientist must ever delude himself into thinking he
can copy the work of our Creator" (p. 143).

This wholesome attitude has been a major factor in
American juvenile training for about 90 years. This, it
seems, is why Nancy Drew and the Hardy Boys and the
Bobbsey Twins are still so beloved. Now Tom, Jr., is all of
this also--except he is too competent, too able and too
remote from juvenile reality. It is a good series. It reads
well. There is action and plenty of it. The inventions are
thoroughly researched and there are certainly enough of
them. Years ago on a visit to the Stratemeyer Syndicate I
noted with awe the number of technical journals on the desk
of "Victor Appleton II." The number of inventions--I speak
as a professional engineer--is, I suppose, the crux of the
problem. Just a glance at the major inventions listed in the
33 books would convince any 10-year-old that no one, not
even Tom Swift, Jr., could be that good.

There would be no useful purpose in analyzing all the
inventions from Tom's fertile brain. They ran from his first
major invention, a Flying Lab, to his last recorded invention,
"an ingenious device which can atomize objects, send them

great distances and reassemble the atoms." With this "trans-
mittaton" Tom prevented "a catastrophic invasion of earth by
ghosts from another galaxy" (Galaxy Ghosts, preface). In
between he became the first astronaut to land on the moon,
developed an Outpost in Space, solved the riddle of the
UFO's and saved the earth from a deadly comet. He outwitted the Asteroid Pirates and built a two-man submarine as
a "speed craft for safe sea travel." He was aided by some
special Swift inventions, in particular Tomasite, "a strong,
durable plastic named after the young inventor and his
father. Heat resistant, it absorbed gamma rays much more
efficiently than lead shields which are ordinarily used"
(Jetmarine, p. 9). It also reflected sound waves.

There is a strong undercurrent of both ancient lost
civilizations and visitors from outer space in the series. On
the first page of the first volume a meteorite from an unknown planet landed on the Swift grounds. It was "mechan-
ically made and only beings of high intelligence could have
worked out those mathematical symbols" carved on the side
of the black cigar-shaped device (Flying Lab, p. 3). These
symbols were eventually deciphered and Tom's space friends
played a major part in the series.

At the end of the first book it was announced that Tom
and his Dad had deciphered the strange meteorite symbols as
being from Mars, from a group of scientists who couldn't
determine how to penetrate the Earth's atmosphere. This
group helped Tom at several crucial times with vital information. They warned him of the ghosts from Andromeda who
were invading our solar system, but it was Tom who convinced the ghosts not to invade earth. On another occasion
the "creatures from outer space" moved a small asteroid into
orbit around the earth and sent strange samples of sick
animal life for Tom to cure. He did. They even sent a
"Visitor from Planet X" to gather impressions and data from
earth.

In Tom's diving seacopter Tom discovered a sunken
city, apparently built largely of gold (Spectromarine Selector,
p. 2). The ruins were probably the famous lost city of
Atlantis.

Tom found space symbols carved on Mayan ruins telling
how a spaceship had crashed, and also found similar symbols
on the "Aurum pyramids" in the underwater city of gold.
He discovered a neo-aurium mine used by the original inhabitants. And to top it off, the expedition found an ancient
but advanced spaceship "half buried in the ocean slime" near
the city of gold (Spectromarine Selector, p. 183).

As a general background, at the beginning of the new
series the Swift establishment had grown to several enormous
enterprises. They included the experimental station Swift
Enterprises, which covered four square miles, the Atlantic

outpost on Fearing Island, and the Swift Construction Co.,
headed by Ned Newton, as well as an atomic energy plant in
the west. Tom and Mary Nestor were still happily married
with two children--Tom, Jr., aged 18, and his sister San-
dra, a year younger. Wakefield Damon and Barton Swift had
passed on as had Eradicate Sampson and Boomerang. Shopton was still headquarters for the Swifts, but it seems to
have been moved closer to the East Coast. This may have
just been an impression due to the faster speeds of the new
inventions.

Atomic energy was routine to Tom, Jr. His first major
invention, the Flying Lab, was atomic powered. This airplane, the Sky Queen, had atomic engines and jet lifters and
the "Tomasite" to shield the nuclear reactors. It carried two
baby aircraft, "a small jet plane we call the Kangaroo Kub
and jet-lifted helicopter, the Skeeter." Included in the
plane was a chemistry lab, a physics lab and even a lab for
animal husbandry. One of Tom's first uses of the lab was in
conjunction with his "Damonscope," a revolutionary instrument for locating uranium, with which he uncovered a vast
uranium deposit in South America. The lab was used in
many books of the series, almost always entirely successfully.
Its speed of 1200 miles per hour or more made it most useful.

Tom did everything. He made a great atomic earth
blaster to drill for iron at the South pole. He made an
ultrasonic cycloplane, a deep-sea hydrodome, a spectromarine
selector, an electronic hydrolung, megascope space prober
and an aquatomic tracker in addition to his flying lab and
jetmarine. These are only a sample.

His Sea Hound was a "combination submarine-whirly-
bird--an atomic powered ship able to fly, hover, or speed
through the ocean depths" (Cosmic Astronauts, p. 4).
"Later expeditions had taken him not only into outer space,
but also to the far corners of the globe, including the South
Pole, Africa, and the Yucatan jungles of Mexico" (p. 13).
He even invented a plane that was part jet plane and part
dirigible. It was called a "paraplane." Things had gone
full circle from Tom, Sr. Shades of the old Red Cloud!

The Swift philosphy was this, quoting from Tom. Sr.:
"A true scientist will always find a way to work with whatever tools come to hand" (Cosmic Astronauts, p. 177).
While this is a good engineering philosophy it had probably
also been developed because of the many villainous tricks
perpetrated by the many enemies of the Swifts. As a side
issue in many of the books, Tom had to compete with brilliant but distorted and utterly unscrupulous scientists who
made the Fogers, Tom, Sr.'s old enemies, look like pikers.

There is no question in my mind, but that Tom Swift,
Jr., fits any general definition of science fiction. The
criticisms from purists, perhaps, would be that technical

problems are solved too conveniently by dubious scientific techniques. It may be true, but it does not seem important. In fact, it is difficult to support any contention that science fiction must always show a carefully supported scientific basis of fact. If there is scientific fiction there is imagination and without imagination there is no science fiction.

A point of concern to some is whether the Swifts were scientists, engineers or technicians. I lean to the engineering label. It is noteworthy that the Swift inventions were practical examples based on natural laws. They filled a useful need. Although they apparently discovered a plethora of new scientific principles their interest and purpose was practical application. And this most nearly fits the definition of engineering.

Although the emphasis of this chapter has been on Tom Swift, Sr., and Jr., there are other science-fiction series to consider. A most interesting example is the Rocket Rider series by Howard R. Garis, published in 1933 and 1934 by A.L. Burt Co. Although other series under Garis's own name were marketed by the Stratemeyer Syndicate, it is doubtful if this one was. It is interesting because it shows, independently of the Stratemeyer influence, Garis's own interest in science and adventure. It is common knowledge that Garis was actively involved with the Tom Swift Series until Stratemeyer's death. How much of the writing was actually the work of Garis is not clear. Both men were interested in the field of science. The Tom Swift books were Stratemeyer's creation and his inventions, and certainly reflected his interests.

The Wynn and Lonny racing books by "Eric Speed" are current offerings of the Stratemeyer Syndicate. The last one, Road Race of Champions, was published in 1975. These books, though, follow more the theme of the old Speedwell Boys and Dave Dashaway series with lots of action and things mechanical, but little in the science and invention field.

It is too early to tell about the influence of the Tom Swift, Jr., series. My younger friends give the impression that they like young Tom, but do not identify with him as we did with his father. These books are obviously books of prophesy. They are better researched than the first series and are generally realistic prophesies of what to expect in the applied science world. Indeed, some of the early prophesies have already come true. In this day of giant corporate research, it is more difficult to believe in and identify with, the 18-year-old boy hero who, without formal scientific training, can create these miracles. We can believe in the miracles, but not in the ability of one youth, no matter how gifted, to create them. The logistical support of all the Swift companies, as well as the help of his famous father, still do not bridge the credibilty gap. The books are fun to read, contain much technical information and may be equally successful in creating an interest in science and invention.

Chapter VII

THE BOY ALLIES; OR, WHO WON WORLD WAR I?

The Boy Allies was a popular World War I series that is still avidly collected. Actually there were two series, one for the Army and one for the Navy. Both were written by Clair Hayes and published by A.L. Burt. Neither series had any connection with the Stratemeyer Syndicate.

The Boy Allies were strong on activity but were about as unrealistic and far-fetched as books could get. These books were not as gory as Fitzhugh's Tom Slade series although the enemy was thoroughly decimated by the two sets of Boy Allies. War was a fun game and the Boy Allies showed why in their valiant, intrepid and incredible exploits. Sociologists should read these stories carefully as a complete guide to the beauty and chivalry of modern war.

Many writers credit Generals Pershing, Foch, Haig et al. with winning World War I. Readers of the Boy Allies know better. Certainly the generals had a hand in the war, but supporters of Hal Paine and Chester Crawford, heroes of The Boy Allies with the Army series by Clair Hayes, and Frank Chadwick and Jack Templeton, of The Boy Allies with the Navy Series by Ensign Drake, know who really won the war. In fact, after reading of the expoits of the two sets of Boy Allies the only wonder is that the war lasted as long as it did.

It used to be a matter of some confusion to me as to how there could be two sets of Boy Allies. Either Ensign Drake or Clair Hayes should have objected to the other stealing his ideas. And both series were published by Burt. It seemed that the publisher should have caught on. It wasn't until many years later that the truth was revealed. Clair Hayes and Ensign Drake were, in fact, one and the same. Burt did its best to maintain the fiction of Ensign Robert L. Drake. In their ad for The Boy Allies with the Navy, they state that, "Ensign Robert L. Drake, the author, is an experienced naval officer, and he describes admirably the many exciting adventures of the two boys." But Ensign Drake not only was not a naval officer, he didn't even exist. Clair Hayes, on the other hand, not only existed, his true name actually was Clair Hayes, and he produced a total of 23 Boy Allies books in the five years from 1915 to 1919.

An article about the Boy Allies was written by Larry Siegel and appeared in the January, 1964 issue of Playboy. This is a distinction probably no other series books can claim, and a distinction which might or might not have pleased Mr. Hayes. Siegel's article was a very funny parody of the Boy Allies. He included in his introduction this paragraph:

"Having floated serenely through that conflict (World War I) with the aid of a raft of boys' books which were so popular in the Thirties ('The Boy Allies' series by Clair W. Hayes, among others), I look back vicariously on the struggle as something exciting and supremely glorious. To me it was in essence a war through which clean-cut young protagonists romped heroically, performing fantastic deeds at the expense of a well-meaning but inept foe. In short, to my generation, World War I was basically a fun war."

This is a very pertinent observation and not limited by any means to the Boy Allies, but it must be admitted that the Boy Allies exhibited more heroism, eliminated more enemy, attained higher rank faster and were on a more familiar footing with generals and admirals than the run-of-the-mill hero of the period.

Hal Paine was 17 when war was declared and Chester Crawford was nearly a year younger as described in The Boy Allies at Liege; or, Through Lines of Steel, first book of the Army Boy Allies. Probably the boys had the build and temperament for the army. "Always athletically inclined, the time thus spent among the rough lumbermen had given the boys new prowess. Day after day they spent in the woods, hunting big game, and both had become proficient in the use of firearms; while to their boxing skill--learned under a veteran of the prize ring, who was employed by Chester's father in the town in which they lived--they added that dexterity which comes only with hard experience. Daily fencing lessons had made both proficient in the use of sword and saber. Among these woodsmen, composed of laborers from many nations, they had also picked up a smattering of many European languages...."

By the end of the war they had done well. With that background how could they lose? They survived about every major campaign and emerged more or less unscathed from the great conflict. "Suffice to say that when they reached the shores of America, each wore the United States distinguished service cross--for bravery and valor in action; and when their friends address them now, it is not as major. For out of four years of war emerged Colonel Hal Paine and Colonel Chester Crawford" (The Boy Allies with Marshall Foch).

The complete list of campaigns of the Boy Allies of the Army follows:

1. The Boy Allies at Liege; or, Through Lines of Steel.
2. The Boy Allies on the Firing Line; or, Twelve Days Battle Along the Marne.
3. The Boy Allies with the Cossacks; or, A Wild Dash Over the Carpathians.
4. The Boy Allies in the Trenches; or, Midst Shot and Shell Along the Aisne.
5. The Boy Allies in Great Peril; or, With the Italian Army in the Alps.
6. The Boy Allies in the Balkan Campaign; or, The Struggle to Save a Nation.
7. The Boy Allies at Verdun; or, Saving France from the Enemy.
8. The Boy Allies on the Somme; or, Courage and Bravery Rewarded.
9. The Boy Allies Under the Stars and Stripes; or, Leading the American Troops to the Firing Line.
10. The Boy Allies with Haig in Flanders; or, The Fighting Canadians of Vimy Ridge.
11. The Boy Allies with Pershing in France; or, Over the Top of Chateau Thierry.
12. The Boy Allies with the Great Advance; or, Driving the Enemy Through France and Belgium.
13. The Boy Allies with Marshall Foch; or, The Closing Days of the Great World War.

Meanwhile, their sea-going counterparts, Frank Chadwick and Jack Templeton, were doing equally well and probably for much the same reasons. "Frank had just passed his sixteenth birthday. Always athletically inclined, he was extremely large for his age; and his muscles, hardened by much outdoor exercise, made him a match for many man twice his age, as he had proven more than once when forced to do so." "For a lad of his years, Frank was an expert in the art of self-defense. Also he could ride, shoot and fence."

As for Jack Templeton, "In spite of his youth, Jack was of huge stature. Always tall for his age, he had filled out so rapidly that now at seventeen he was well over six feet and big all through. His strength was immense, and there were no three natives in the village that could stand up against him." "He spoke several languages besides English and one or two native dialects."

By the end of the first book the boys were lieutenants in the British Navy and were under the wing of Lord Hastings, cousin of King George V. In fact they had an audience with King George, who personally promised them commissions in the Royal Navy, for services rendered. These Boy Allies managed to restrict their exploits to ten volumes, but, as the following titles show, nevertheless were reasonably active.

1.   The Boy Allies on the North Sea Patrol; or,
        Striking the First Blow at the German Fleet.
2.   The Boy Allies under Two Flags; or, Sweeping the
        Enemy from the Sea.
3.   The Boy Allies with the Flying Squadron; or, The
        Naval Raiders of the Great War.
4.   The Boy Allies with the Terror of the Seas; or,
        The Last Shot of the Submarine D-16.
5.   The Boy Allies under the Sea; or, The Vanishing
        Submarine.
6.   The Boy Allies in the Baltic; or, Through Fields
        of Ice to Aid the Czar.
7.   The Boy Allies of Jutland; or, The Greatest Naval
        Battle of History.
8.   The Boy Allies with Uncle Sam's Cruisers; or, Con-
        voying the American Army across the Atlantic.
9.   The Boy Allies with the Submarine D-32; or, The
        Fall of the Russian Empire.
10.   The Boy Allies with the Victorious Fleets; or, The
        Fall of the German Navy.

In volume 10 they had several personal interviews with
Secretary of the Navy Daniels who, at one point, escorted
them to the White House for a meeting with President Wilson.
The President, naturally, turned out to be an old friend of
Frank's father.   "So," said the President, "these are the
young officers who commanded the British destroyer Essex,
which accounted for two of the enemy's submarines? They
look rather young for such important posts."

Jack Templeton "had been elevated to the rank of
captain" by this time and commanded the USS Plymouth for a
short time as well as the H.M.S. Brigadier. Frank was his
first officer.   Both boys survived the Ostend and Zeebrugge
expedition in which they sealed off the German submarine
bases. It was at this time that the Brigadier was so badly
damaged that Jack had to be given command of the Essex.
If it had not been for the armistice Frank would probably
have ended up commanding a British ship as well.

Clair Wallace Hayes might be called the mystery man of
boys' series books. Numerous articles about Stratemeyer,
Patten and Garis have been written, but none, to the best
of my knowledge, have been written about Hayes. This is a
little surprising considering the number of books he wrote
and the past and present popularity of his series. It is
probable that most readers assume that Hayes and Drake are
pen names for other writers, if they worry about the matter
at all.

Although Hayes outlived Stratemeyer, Fitzhugh and
Patten, his known boys' books span a brief period. The
entire 23 "Boy Allies" were written in the 1915-1919 period
and all four books of his final series, "The Boy Troopers,"

were copyrighted in 1922. He did not write any boys' books during World War II--apparently, in fact, none after 1922.

Clair Hayes was born October 26, 1887 in Rochester, New York. He was educated in schools in Rochester and St. Louis where he later lived. He spent most of his career as a newspaperman and worked on the Washington Star, the Syracuse Herald-Journal, the Utica Daily Press and papers in Harrisburg, Pennsylvania, and New York City as well. His last position was as copyreader for the Utica Daily Press from 1942 to 1950. He died in Utica, New York, February 27, 1958, at age 70.

An interesting analysis could be made of the number of writers with newspaper training who have written successful series for young people. Howard Garis and Andrew Svenson are two others who come immediately to mind. It may be that newspaper training teaches clarity, brevity and a straightforward, clean style which appeals to young readers. It is also true that this style of writing becomes dated more slowly than most current literary fashions of writing.

It seems surprising that with such a distinguished World War record nothing was heard of the Boy Allies in World War II. It is known that Jack Templeton entered the British diplomatic service and "...in years to come, in all probability, he will hold one of the most important posts in the British Government." Frank remained in Boston and studied law. "He proved an apt student and soon showed signs of talent that undoubtedly will make him famous." Probably Mr. Hayes assumed that their later exploits were so well known that there was no need to record them in books.

"So here we shall take our leave of Jack Templeton and Frank Chadwick, knowing that, in years to come, they will meet again, both famous then, and that through all the years their friendship shall survive, and grow stronger than it was in the days when they fought side by side for the freedom of the world."

Chapter VIII

LAND OF THE HEROES

Where do heroes come from? More specifically, where do the folk heroes of the American series books come from? Before any gentle reader says, "who cares," let me hasten to suggest that this is a significant social concern. For if we accept the premise, as all right-thinking patriots must, that what this country needs is more Tom Swifts, Dick Prescotts and Frank Merriwells, it follows as the night the day that a knowledge of their origins may provide insight on the forces that produce heroes.

At one time it was my contention that the breeding place for heroes--pardon the expression--was central New York. A strong case can be made. Many of James Fenimore Cooper's heroes lived in the Otsego Lake region. If we accept Henry Nash Smith's contention in Virgin Land that fictitional Wild Western heroes were in general modeled after Cooper's Leatherstocking, then all frontier heroes can be claimed, at least indirectly, as New York products. This may be stretching the claim a bit, but more direct concrete examples abound. A few follow:

W.O. Stoddard wrote what is probably his most popular book, Saltillo Boys, about the boys of a private school in Fayette Park in Syracuse.

Oliver Optic found many of his heroes in central New York. Switch Off takes place near "Hitaca" and "Ucayga," anagrams of Ithaca and Cayuga, and other books of the Lake Shore Series have the same locale. The Toppleton Institute and the Wimpleton Institute are prominent in these series.

Richard Grant, hero of In School and Out, also by Optic, came from Woodville, New York, which was located on the Hudson River, but he developed his character at the Tunbrook Military Institute. Since he left Woodville at 9:00 a.m. and arrived before nightfall, it is possible to infer a central New York location for the Institute (p. 108). This reasoning is buttressed by much internal evidence including a description of a summer camping trip of ten days in which the boys covered over a hundred miles in relatively rural country and a comment about "the other end of Tunbrook Lake, distant ten miles by the road" (pp. 161, 163).

We might note in passing that one of the first things the establishment did to Richard upon his arrival at the Institute was to confiscate "several yellow-covered novels." "Can't I have my books?" asked Richard. "No, sir; you cannot. Such trash as that is not fit for boys to read." Poor Richard had his character developed the hard way, cut off from enlightening literature.

Military academies obviously flourished in central New York and one of the most prominent was Putnam Hall. Captain Victor Putnam "purchased a beautiful plot of ground on Cayuga Lake, in New York State, and there he built Putnam Hall..." (Putnam Hall Rivals, p. 3). Meanwhile Anderson Rover had purchased a farm "of two hundred acres in the Mohawk Valley of New York State" and his nephews had moved in with him. They proved too much for the aged agriculturist and he shipped them off to Captain Putnam to be tamed down. Little did he know. The boys took the train from Oak Run, nearest town to the farm, in the morning and arrived at Ithaca by 3 p.m. There they were to "take a small steamer which ran from that city to the head of the lake, stopping at Cedarville, the nearest village to Putnam Hall" (Rover Boys at School, p. 47).

The Swift Manufacturing Company, of course, is located in central New York. Mr. Swift and his son lived on the outskirts of the village of Shopton, in New York State.

Phil Bradley and the "Mountain Boys" came from Brewster, New York. "It lay snuggled among the hills of New York" (Phil Bradley at the Wheel, p. 14). Phil owned a "large mountain estate of wild land" in "one of the loneliest parts of the great Adirondack regions." His home town, though, is "further south, though still in the uplands" (Phil Bradley and the Mountain Boys, p. 200). An interesting incident in Phil Bradley's Mountain Boys finds them rescuing one "John Newton" who admits finally that his real name is Alwyn Merriwell. The connection between this Merriwell and Harton Merriwell, father of the noted Frank, has not been established, but it seems probable that any mother who would name a boy "Alwyn" would be equally likely to name another, "Harton."

Bloomfield, Frank Merriwell's home town, can from occasional references also be placed in central New York. Quoting E.T. LeBlanc, leading authority on Frank, "However in a few cases we can geographically place Bloomfield possibly in central New York State. At one point Frank left New Haven and traveled to Springfield, Mass., to meet a train coming in from the west bringing his guardian, Professor Scotch, to meet him. They evidently met half way. In another story while Frank is in Bangor, mention is made that Bloomfield is 800 miles away. Assuming that 800 miles is by road, this would put Bloomfield somewhere in New York State, tying in with the earlier geographical identification. There are many towns near Bloomfield, including Wellsburg which is tied in to a summer report in the mountains not far away. This could be the Adirondacks...."

Blake Stewart of The Moving Picture Boys (Appleton) lived with his mother's brother "who had a small farm in Fayetteburg, in the central part of New York State" (The Moving Picture Boys, p. 22).

It would seem that if Frank Merriwell, Tom Swift and the Rovers were all from central New York, this area could really be called the "Home of the Heroes." Unfortunately, further research developed that many or even most of our heroes did not come from central New York. Even the Rovers were originally from New York City and moved back there after their retirement from roving. The author's search over many wasted years has turned up evidence about the origins of a number of our heroes which indicates a wide range of backgrounds. In some cases it must be admitted that the hero's homes are notably peripatetic, either by design or by accident. It is often necessary to use an educated inference to determine a logical location. Inferences and geograhical substantiating data for a number of our boy heroes follow.

Although central New York may be too limiting, it is obvious that many heroes have origins in some part of the state or in the adjoining state of New Jersey.

The Radio Boys (Chapman) hail from Clintonia. "Clintonia was ... in an Eastern state, about seventy-five miles from New York City" (Radio Boys First Wireless, p. 21). Newark, New Jersey is "nearly a hundred miles from here" (p. 34). In The Radio Boys Aiding the Snowbound they leave Clintonia to skate up the Shagary River to a lumber camp and "We can make it in a couple of days" (p. 50). The camp is on the Canadian border. "They [the lumberjacks] had come from Canada, as the border was not far away" (p. 93). This would apparently put Clintonia in northern New York. On the other hand, in The Radio Boys at Ocean Point, the ocean resort "was only a pleasant spin of about forty miles" (p. 87) and the ocean is a long way from the Adirondacks. Arcs drawn 400 miles from Pittsburgh, 75 miles from New York City, 100 miles from Newark and intersecting 40 miles from the Atlantic Coast might even lead one to suspect Connecticut. The only unquestionable fact is that the boys came from within a radius of 75 miles of New York City.

The Radio Boys of Clintonia may be a little confused as to where they live but the Radio Boys (Breckenridge) know exactly. "All three boys were sons of wealthy parents, with country estates near the far end of Long Island" (The Radio Boys on the Mexican Border, p. 4). It is nice to find such solid facts.

The Radio Boys (Duffield) on the other hand were Northern New York Staters. "The three boys were seated in Cub's room at the Perry home ... in the City of Oswego, on the shore of Lake Ontario" (Radio Boys in the Thousand Islands, p. 8).

"Don Sturdy ... had been born and brought up in Hillville, a thriving town in an Eastern State, about fifty miles from New York" (Don Sturdy in the Tombs of Gold, p. 12). Here again specifics are lacking, but it is suspected that Hillville is in New York State, north of New York City. In Don Sturdy and the Head Hunters we find our heroes taking a train for Chicago (p. 68). Hillville is apparently on a main train line and they do not have to go through New York City. The supposition is that they were on the New York Central and went North to Albany and then West. On the other hand, in Don Sturdy in the Land of Volcanoes the party took a train to New York City first and then "transferred to a transcontinental flyer," on the way to San Francisco (p. 56). A possible clincher to the New York State argument occurs in Don Sturdy Across the North Pole, where we find this comment: "Cheap sports from the city," remarked Brick. "Wonder what they're doing up here?" (p. 7). "Up" implies that Hillville is north of New York City.

The Mortimer Hamilton family gets around as does their home town of Hamilton Corners, although both seem to be based in New York. Dick Hamilton of the Dick Hamilton Series by Howard Garis is a well-known millionaire, "and the only son of Mortimer Hamilton of Hamilton Corners, in New York State" (Dick Hamilton's Airship, p. 14). In Dick Hamilton's Cadet Days we find he is "of Hamilton Corners, not far from New York" (p. 17), which is pretty definite, but in Dick Hamilton's Steam Yacht "Dick and his bulldog took a train for Hamilton Corners, a fair-sized town in one of our middle western states" (p. 16). Mr. Garis often seems a little vague about geography. In general, it seems to be established that Hamilton Corners is in the northeastern part of New York State. In Dick Hamilton's Touring Car the trip from New York City to his home "was accomplished without accident, an early morning start enabling them to arrive shortly before dark" (p. 67) and on their tour to the West it took four days to drive from Hamilton Corners to Buffalo. An interesting comment or two about Dick Hamilton and his friends' habit of messing up the landscape appears in Dick Hamilton's Touring Car: "'We don't have many dishes to wash,' and he tossed from the window of the car the wooden plates from which they had dined"; "the boys had decided that ... they would use the wooden plates, that could be

thown away after each meal" (p. 107). "They started off
again, leaving a pile of wooden plates behind them as a
souvenir of their stop" (p. 109). Such actions seem out of
keeping for well-bred millionaires but just possibly times
have changed since 1913, when Dick was active.
    The other Hamilton family, as chronicled in the Flying
Boys Series by Edward Ellis, is established in New Jersey.
"The hotel register told me that you are Harvey Hamilton,
from Mootsport, New Jersey" (The Flying Boys in the Sky,
p. 154). "Harvey was the son of a wealthy merchant, whose
business took him to New York every week-day morning....
His elder brother Dick was a student in Yale" (p. 92). He
also had a mother and a sister, Mildred. Interestingly
enough, Harvey's closest friend is Bohunkus Johnson, a
black boy "who was the bound boy of a neighboring farmer"
(p. 28). "The fact that they were of different races had no
effect upon their mutual regard." It must be admitted,
however, that in the matter of intelligence and courage
"Bunk" doesn't come off too well. We know of no connection
between the two Hamilton families although they may well be
relatives.
    Another New York group is the Bungalow Boys (For-
rester), who attended Audubon Academy, which "is situated
on the west bank of the Hudson, not far above historic West
Point" (The Bungalow Boys, p. 6).
    The Outdoor Chums (Allen) seem to have been from
either New York or New Jersey. "Frank Langdon ... having
lived up in Maine knew about all there was to know about
the tricks of campers..." (The Outdoor Chums, p. 12). If
they had been New Englanders they would have known you
always go down to Maine. They plan to "go camping where
muskrats, coons, some mink and even an otter" have been
trapped and are "planning an outing ... back of the lumber
camps at the head of the lake" (p. 2). New York is most
probable.
    Several of Captain Bonehill's heroes have New York
origins: "we had left the Bronxville Military Academy in
Upper New York State..." (When Santiago Fell, p. 1). "He
was going over two hundred miles from home..." (to New
York City), with references to iceboating, Lakeview Academy
and the like which point towards Central New York (Young
Oarsmen of Lakeview, p. 142). Several of the Bonehill
heroes also have other backgrounds as in A Sailor Boy with
Dewey, where the hero, Oliver Raymond, states, "My father,
Samuel Raymond, was a rich merchant of San Francisco" (p.
3), and in Pioneer Boys of the Gold Fields, where Mark
Radley lived in Philadelphia.
    Many of Horatio Alger's heroes come from New York,
some from the city and some from small towns outside New
York City. For just one example, in Tom Turner's Legacy,

our hero lived at "Hillsboro, New York" and "yet we are only thirty miles distant" from New York City (pp. 179, 182).

Bloomsburg, home of the Bird Boys (Langworthy), is apparently also in New York. The boys "travelled down to the trying-out grounds on Long Island" (p. 17). Their father is referred to as "the well-known aviator and balloonist, Professor Bird, once of Cornell" (p. 73). Another famous aviator of a later date, Andy Lane of Fifteen Days in the Air fame, hailed from Hillside, not far from Mineola, Long Island (p. 5). The Boy Aviators (Lawton) Frank and Harry Chester, were "among the most famous graduates the Agassiz High School on Washington Heights had turned out..." (The Boy Aviators in Nicaragua, p. 9). The Dreadnought Boys (Lawton) came from "...Lambs' Corners, a remote village in the Catskill mountains" (The Dreadnought Boys on Battle Practice, p. 6).

Hilton Academy, scene of Barbour's For the Honor of the School, is another of the many fine schools of New York State. We note that the cross-country course "then bore away south along the bank of the Hudson River" (p. 6). This does not mean that Barbour's heroes all lived in New York. Indeed in Four Afoot, which takes place on Long Island, we find that Tom Ferris comes from Chicago, Dan Speede hails from New York, Neilson Tilford lives in Boston and Bob Hethington is from Portland, Maine.

An unsolved mystery, at least as far as is known, is the location of Gridley, home of Dick Prescott and company, heroes of the Grammar School Boys Series, High School Boys Series, Annapolis Series, etc. It is obviously in the north. In The Grammar School Boys Snowbound, this is apparent. It is obviously rural: "we have 16 miles to go to our first camp at the second lake in the Cheney Forest" (The High School Boys' Fishing Trip, p. 36). In Dick Prescott's First Year at West Point, we find the statement, "On their way to New York..." either an indication that they had come from outside the state or a reference to New York City (p. 14). Later on Greg Holmes was allowed three or four days for a "hurried trip home for a ... funeral." Since he went by train, the town of Gridley was obviously quite some distance away. Then in Dick Prescott's Third Year at West Point, one of the "wild Indians" says, "I own a farm on the east end of Long Island," and apparently the implication is that Long Island is well known to his hearers. Later on Dick and Greg leave Gridley by train in the morning and "Late in the afternoon the chums arrived in New York" (p. 96). It becomes obvious that Hancock means New York City when he says New York. Since the boys stayed at a hotel there and took a steamboat up the Hudson, it appears that they came from the west rather than the north. An eight-hour trip logically could originate in northwest Pennsylvania, southwest New York or possibly even Ohio. Just to confuse the issue, however, in The High School Captain of the Team Greg says, "mind my running up there with you?" referring to West Point, and says later, "And we went up to the state capitol yesterday..." (pp. 241, 242). Neither Albany, Harrisburg, nor Columbus fit. It does seem clear that Gridley is in the northeastern part of the country, at least.

A well-known family, apparently from New Jersey, is that of Fenton Hardy, famous detective. The Hardy Boys (Dixon) "lived in Bayport, a city of about fifty thousand inhabitants, located on Barmet Bay, three miles in from the Atlantic..." (The Tower Treasure, p. 2). Internal evidence is conflicting here also, and New Jersey, Long Island and Connecticut are all indicated at various times. In The Secret of the Old Mill, however, "The afternoon express from the North steamed into the Bayport station..." where the Hardy boys were waiting to meet their father, "who had been away ... on a murder case in New York" (p. 1). New Jersey seems pretty definite.

Other New Jersey heroes include Tom Slade, Roy Blakeley and Pee-wee Harris (Fitzhugh), all of Bridgeboro, New Jersey. They spent their summers at Temple Camp in the Catskills of New York and presumably both states could claim credit for their development. Hancock's heroes all appear to be Easterners and several definitely come from New Jersey. In Uncle Sam's Boys in the Ranks, "The place was one of the smaller cities in New Jersey" (p. 9). It was apparently in northern Jersey since it didn't take the boys very long to go from it to New York City to enlist. Royce Osborne, hero of The Aeroplane Express, one of the Aeroplane Boys Series (Lamar), was the son of "George M. Osborne, the highest paid mechanic in Newark..." (p. 22).

Many heroes come from the New England States. Massachusetts and Maine in particular are overrun with them, with the overflow in Connecticut. I have always concurred with the tradition, "In New Hampshire they raise rocks, in Vermont they raise men," but in keeping with strict veracity it must be admitted that not too many heroes seem to come from either of these states. There are a few exceptions. Ephraim Gallup, chum of Frank Merriwell, is a good Vermonter but is awkward, ungainly and uncouth and is not the typical hero. In The Young Acrobat (Alger), Achilles Henderson, the great Scottish giant in the circus, was from Vermont. "It's a good deal easier than working on a farm, especially in Vermont, where I was born and bred" (p. 11).

C.A. Stephens describes in A Busy Year at the Old Squires, the boys' encounter with the Wild Man of Borneo in a travelling show. "Why ... aren't you from the wilds of Borneo?" "Thunder, no!" the Wild Man replied confidentially. "I don't even know where it is. I'm from over in Vermont

--Bellows Falls." What some people won't do to get out of Vermont. Four in Camp, subtitled A Story of Summer Adventures in the New Hampshore Woods (Barbour), concerns New Hampshire but the heroes, as noted earlier, are all from other states. The Woodranger Tales of Browne feature New Hampshire heroes but, in The Hero of the Hills, as an example, which takes place about 1750, the action is considerably earlier than in the better known series books. We should mention the Phillips Exeter series by Dudley in any discussion of New Hampshire, but most prep schools seem to be in other states.

Maine can boast of innumerable heroes. Rex Kingdon of Ridgewood High (Braddock) is an example. Ridgewood lies near the Canadian border and, from the references to the ocean, potatoes and Portland, is without question in Maine though Rex Kingdon himself came from Boston (p. 51). The Ranger Boys (LaBelle) come from Southern Maine. "The three boys live in a small Maine town, only a few miles from Portland..." (The Ranger Boys Outwit the Timber Thieves, p. 7). Rockspur Academy, scene of Patten's Rockspur Nine, Rockspur Eleven, etc., is also in Maine.

The Submarine Boys (Durham) are coastal Yankees. "Jack Benson ... paid for his keep ... by working ... in his native seaport town of Oakport" (The Submarine Boys on Duty, p. 14). Jack and Hal Hastings worked their way into the Dunhaven boatyard, also on the coast, and speedily became proficient at submarine manipulation, Jack at age 16 becoming captain and Hal, engineer, of the Submarine Pollard as well as instructors to Annapolis cadets. Franklin Mathiews, chief librarian of the Boy Scouts, was highly incensed at this, considering it somewhat improbable. Knowing the sterling worth of coastal yankees as we do we can realize that his doubts were unfounded. Descriptions of the weather and general surroundings lead us to suspect Maine as a locale. It took five days of steaming to get from Dunhaven to Annapolis, which also points to Maine, although it does not rule out Massachusetts, Connecticut or Rhode Island.

The Motor Boat Club Boys (Hancock) had a Maine base. Captain Tom Halstead came from the "pretty little Kennebec village of Bayport" (The Motor Boat Club of the Kennebec, p. 8). The Golden Boys (Wyman) came from Skohegan, Maine. Oliver Optic's heroes occasionally came from Maine. Little Bobtail takes place in Camden. The Old Squire series of C.A. Stephens, mentioned previously, have a Maine locale. These are just a few examples of Mainiac heroes.

Frank Nelson, hero of Frank, The Young Naturalist, Frank on the Prairie, etc. (Castlemon), traveled all over the country being heroic but had his origins in Boston and spent some years in Lawrence, Maine, "About one hundred miles north of Augusta" (Frank, The Young Naturalist, p. 11).

The Motor Boys (Young) are Massachusetts products. "Cresville was a pleasant town, not a great many miles from Boston" (The Motor Boys, p. 1). Paul Graham, The Young Bandmaster (Bonehill), had lived in Boston. "At that time ... had lived in the fashionable portion of the town, near the Back Bay..." (The Young Bandmaster, p. 11). Jack Chadwick and his cousin Tom Jesson, famous Boy Inventors, lived "at Mr. Chadwick's handsome home on the outksirts of Boston" (The Boy Inventors' Wireless Triumph, p. 11). Paul Duncan of Little by Little (Optic) came from Bayville which "is situated about seven or eight miles from Boston...." Jack Somers, hero of Optic's The Army and Navy Stories, came from Pinchbrook, not far from Boston. In Optic's The Boat Club we find "Rippleton, the scene of my story, is a New England village, situated about ten miles from Boston."

Crofton Academy may well be in Massachusetts. In Crofton Chums (Barbour), we read, "Gil's home was in Providence, Rhode Island, and Poke's in New York City. The latter had taken an early train and Gil had joined him at Providence and the two had reached ... Crofton well before noon" (Crofton Chums, p. 10). This is either Massachusetts or Connecticut.

It is often difficult to distinguish between Massachusetts and Connecticut academies. Both have a common standard of excellence. "Fardale nestled among the hills which here reached down to the very seacoast" (Frank Merriwell's School Days, p. 12). Fardale Academy, of which Frank Merriwell was the most famous alumnus, was most probably in Connecticut. Merriwell ended up at Yale and all the evidence points to a Connecticut location. Oakdale Academy, home of Ben Stone, was also in New England. In describing life at Nostrand School, Barbour says, "September ... can be extremely warm in New England..." (Tod Hale with the Crew, p. 2). Frank Armstrong was definitely from Connecticut. "You're a credit to the good old nutmeg state of Connecticut," we read in Frank Armstrong's Vacation, (p. 308). His school, Queens, is apparently another fine old Connecticut school.

We can find general references to New England backgrounds in rather unlikely places. Chester Crawford, one of the world-famous Boy Allies (Drake), came from New England. "His father was a well-to-do physician in a small New England town" (Boy Allies on the North Sea Patrol, p. 6). All admirers of Ted Scott (Dixon), first man to fly solo nonstop across the Atlantic, know that he was raised in Bromville, "a thriving town ... in the Middle West on the Rappick River..." (Over the Ocean to Paris, p. 3). It is possibly most significant, however, to find that as a small child "he had been brought from New England to Bromville" and apparently had a New England background (Through the Air to Alaska, p. 14).

The above examples are a random sample of representative boy heroes. Most apparently came from the northeastern part of the country. One can find boy heroes who came from other areas, as we have already shown, but as a percent of the total the number is rather small. A few of the better known ones are: The land-locked Boy Allies (Hayes), Hal Paine and Chester Crawford, who were raised in Illinois; Jerry Todd, Poppy Ott and company (Edwards), who came from Tutter, Illinois; Mark Tidd (Kelland), who lived in Wicksville, Michigan; the Boy Scouts (Fletcher), who lived in an "Indiana town named Beverly" (Boy Scouts Test of Courage, p. 8--in other series we find Boy Scouts scattered all over the country); and The River Motor-Boat Boys (Gordon), who "had been reared in the streets of [Chicago]" (The River Motor-Boat Boys on the Amazon, p. 10).

At this point in our research it might be helpful to take a map of the United States and stick pins wherever a hero from our random sample was born or grew up. The first thing we note is a map full of pins. The next thing, as we suspected, is a preponderance of pins in the northeastern part of the country. A regression analysis of our data informs us that this observation is statistically significant and that there are more heroes born in the Northeast than in any other part of the country. Having carefully and objectively determined this point we can proceed to our next concern, namely, why are heroes more prevalent in the Northeast? More specifically, is it possible to draw any inferences as to genetic backgrounds, climatic conditions or social environments with respect to the development of heroes?

The obvious suggestion is that heroes are born in the Northeast because the recorders of their heroism, or their publishers, or their audience, lived in the Northeast. This suggestion we utterly reject. We admit that the literary virtuosity of Hayes, Garis, Patten, Stratemeyer, Hancock, et al. may have been induced or at least affected by the same influences that produced Dick Prescott, Ben Boltwood, Frank Chadwick, and Tom Swift. More than this we will not admit. The particular influences are possibly not susceptible to scholarly delineation or statistical verification, but in such a pioneering study as this it is proper to project hypotheses and leave others to provide additional data that will either substantiate or refute them.

An interesting consideration and perhaps a pertinent one is the effect of geographical location on physical development but it is first necessary to examine the physical appearance of representative heroes and to determine if there is a dominant pattern that deviates from the population as a whole. Fortunately we have many descriptions available.

We note this description of Frank Chadwick, the sea-going Boy Ally from Boston: "Always athletically inclined, he was extremely large for his age; and his muscles, hardened by much outdoor exercise, made him a match for many a man twice his age." Frank "was an expert in the art of self-defense. Also he could ride, shoot and fence." On the other hand, Hal Paine and Chester Crawford, the land-locked Boy Allies from Illinois, had developed their athletic propensities in "one of the lumber camps owned by Chester's father, in the great Northwest." Ben Boltwood was a clean-limbed, square-shouldered young fellow...." Jack Benson of Submarine Boys fame, "from much practice in boxing, was as agile and slippery as a monkey and an eel combined." Dick Hamilton "was a boy a little above the average height, well built, with curling brown hair and eyes of the same hue." Don Sturdy was "a tall, muscular boy...." A description of Frank Merriwell states, "His face was frank, open and willing ... and the set of his jaw told that he could be firm and dauntless." "Frank [Merrick] was dark, curly-haired, of medium height and slim, but strong and wiry. Bob [Temple] was fair and sleepy-eyed, a fraction under six feet tall and weighed 180 pounds" (Radio Boys--Breckenridge). "Bob [Layton] ... was of rather dark complexion, and was tall and well-developed for his age. He was vigorous and athletic and a lover of outdoor sports. His magnetism and vitality made him a 'live wire,' and he was the natural leader among the boys with whom he associated. His nature was frank and friendly" (Radio Boys--Chapman). We could continue indefinitely. In general our heroes seem to be vigorous and upstanding but not possessed of any abnormal physical superiority. The Boy Allies appear to be the exceptions. This is perhaps fortunate when we consider the vicissitudes to which they were exposed during the war.

In contrast to this we occasionally find a featured hero who is definitely not athletic, clean-cut, frank and friendly. Tom Slade is an example. "He was about fifteen and of a heavy, ungraceful build. His hair was thick and rather scraggly, and his face was of the square type, and his expression what people call stolid. He had freckles but not too many, and his mouth was large and his lips tight-set." Walter Harris, otherwise known as "Pee-wee," was so diminutive as to be a pocket edition of a Boy Scout. Mark Tidd "was the fattest boy I ever saw, or ever expect to see, and the funniest-looking. His head was round and 'most as big as a pretty good-sized pumpkin, and his cheeks were so fat they almost covered up his eyes." We must remember that Mark came from Michigan and this appearance may be common there. To complicate the analysis we often find that the Boy

Chums, Rangers, Inventors, Scouts, and others include an assortment of physical types including quite generally one chubby but good-natured and jolly boy, one small and enthusiastic member of the gang and often one former protagonist of the featured hero, together with the hero himself who stands out because of his natural ability, aggressiveness and leadership, but not necessarily for brute strength.

Summing up the question of physical considerations we can say that there is no dominant pattern among heroes and also that the characteristics of their followers vary as much as the population of the country at large. This would seem to indicate both that physical development itself is not of major importance and that a northeastern location is not significant in the physical development of heroes.

Social and economic environments also do not appear significant. Suffice it to say that northeastern heroes range from impoverished newsboys in New York City and such penniless farm boys as Dave Dashaway the aviator and Blake Stewart the Moving Picture Boy to recognized millionaires such as Dick Hamilton. Many of the boys have sufficient income to do considerable traveling, exploring and inventing as well as to pay their expenses at the academies and prep schools which flourish in the Northeast. It may be significant that they generally seem to be natural gentlemen with good diction and manners, regardless of their backgrounds.

Against the current anti-Wasp tenor of the times it is ticklish business to point out the white Anglo-Saxon Protestant backgrounds of our heroes and suggest it as a basis for their achievements. This background can be accepted without proof by an examination of some of the names already mentioned. Prescott, Grant, Swift, Dashaway, Rover, Merriwell, Bradley, Stewart, Sturdy, Hamilton, Hardy, Osborne, Blakeley are about as English as you can get. Not a Slav, German, or Italian in the lot. We can prove easily and definitely, however, that the ethnic background is not responsible for heroism, simply by noting that almost all of the villains are good old Wasps also. Tom Swift had his Andy Foger, Dick Rover had Dan Baxter and nobody could stand Josiah Crabtree. It seems clear that Wasps are featured as heroes and villains simply because Wasps settled the Northeast and are prominent in that area.

A suggestion raised by some authors is that boys become heroes by trying to live up to their names. This is supposed to account for the success of the Dashaways, Swifts, Rovers, Sturdies and Hardies. Their success seems to be neither more nor less than heroes with less distinguished names and this argument needs more documentation.

What observations can we now make to throw light on why heroes come from the Northeast? A careful re-examination of our data points out a most significant fact. As we noted above, each hero has his villain and not only do more heroes come from the Northeast but so also do more villains. And the villainy of the villains is as deep-dyed as the virtue of the heroes. Leslie Gage was as worthy a protagonist for Frank Merriwell as was Gus Plum for Dave Porter. We have already mentioned Foger and Baxter. As we examine our villains we find that they are generally not as prepossessing in appearance and definitely not as frank and friendly as our heroes but are of about equal or even superior physical development. We question, then, what factors do help them succeed in their villainy. We note that they have a vigor, vitality and aggressiveness which may lead to success in any endeavor and that these characteristics are similar to those noted in our heroes. We may not care to admit it, but a boy of grit, courage, determination and vigor can be either successful villain or hero, depending on his interests and inclinations. So we have apparently isolated basic characteristics of vigor, vitality and determination in both heroes and villains from the Northeast. And with this information we can present a tenable hypothesis as to why so many heroes come from the Northeast. It is the climate of the Northeast, as variable as the backgrounds and abilities of both our heroes and our villains, that is responsible for developing these qualiites. It is the variation in temperature and climatic conditions and the tremendous range of weather experiences that both force the development of heroes and villains and provide opportunities for development.

It takes courage, grit, determination and all the vigor and vitality possible to survive a Northeast winter. No wonder Tom Swift developed the determination to push on with his advanced research in the fields of electronics and aeronautics. He got the practice just in trying to get through the winter. Besides, there wasn't much else he could do anyway in a central New York winter and it kept his mind off the weather. No wonder Don Sturdy headed for the Desert of Mystery, Lion Land and the Head Hunters. Anything to get away from the winter. Anyone who has spent his formative years battling the bleak, inhospitable, punishing winters of the Northeast has to develop determination and vigor or perish.

It seems equally true that while winters develop vigor and determination, summers offer all sorts of opportunities to be heroic. There are lakes by the dozens for canoeing, boating trips or swimming races. There are forests and mountains, caves and islands for sleuthing out ancient mysteries and rescuing miscellaneous damsels from assorted straits. There are simply more heroic things to do in the Northeast. If Rex Kingdon wants to go to the north woods the woods are available. If Tom Swift wants to take a week's cruise in his motor boat, Lake Carlopa is waiting. In the other sections of the country this is not true. There are not as many lakes and woods and mountains to help a boy learn the hero's trade and there is not the weather to force him to become vigorous, aggressive and active. So the hypothesis can be stated in two parts, one, that heroes come from the Northeast because there are more opportunities to practice heroism; second, that the weather is such that the boys have to become heroes to survive.

Chapter IX

STODDARD, SALTILLO BOYS AND SYRACUSE

This chapter throws new light on a long-lived and still popular boys' book. In this book, at least, Stoddard used real life subjects and true incidents. He was an able writer and many of his books still read well. He is currently enjoying a partial revival among collectors.

Original information is highly desirable for anyone doing research in the field of children's books. It is particularly important when it concerns a prolific writer who was at one time well-accepted and influential in the field. W.O. Stoddard was such a writer. No modern history in the field even mentions Stoddard nor do we find as much interest in him among boys' book collectors as, for instance, in Ellis, Optic or Alger, all of whom wrote during the same period. Stoddard is in the unfortunate position of having written books well received during his lifetime but currently not particularly popular with librarians, with historians of the genre or with collectors.

Probably the most popular and enduring book of the more than 75 that Stoddard wrote was Saltillo Boys, which went through numerous printings and editions. Pasted inside the front cover of my 1907 edition is a clipping of an article from a Syracuse, New York, newspaper. The article, entitled "Side Issues: A Story of Syracuse in 1850," is reprinted here:

"The story called Saltillo Boys was published in 1882. The edition now in use in the children's room in the Public Library is dated 1895, and it bears the unmistakable marks of popularity. The copy now before me has been thumbed by scores of eager readers, and succeeding editions will be thumbed by scores of others. W.O. Stoddard's story well deserves this eminence. It is a wholesome lively narrative of boyish experience, each chapter containing an adventure. The recovery of a number of chickens stolen from one of the Saltillo boys by an inhabitant of the Tamarack Swamp, a geologizing expedition in the Valley in which the shortest one of the party narrowly escapes being overtaken by an exasperated bull, a baseball game which a gang from the canal district tries to break up with disaster to the leader of

the gang, a Fourth ˛
is burned down and
climbing down the awnıı. t in which the Whiting Block
excursions afoot to Green La. e Saltillo boys escape by
the visit of Daniel Webster tι from an upper window,
front of the City Hall, describea he Devil's Punch Bowl,
building with butcher stalls in the ᵪ and his address in
mysterious crypts in the basement for old-fashioned brick
of offenders against the law,' an illfated ᵃʳʸ and dark and
one of the salt reservoirs north of the cit ᵢₑf confinement
more are described with vivacity and humor. ᵢng party in
book. ᵪ these and
     ᵧ a bully

"For grown up people a most interesting pass ᵤₑ in
Saltillo Boys is this:
          'The school ceased to exist, and the boys were all
          scattered, as American boys must and will scatter.
          Nevertheless if anybody knew who the Saltillo boys
          really were and would trace in their after years the
          effect of that brief experiment it would be well worth
          while.'
     "Saltillo was Syracuse. The Saltillo boys were the boys
of a private school on Fayette Park. The principal of the
school, known in the story as Mr. Hayne, was [in real life]
James W. Hoyt. The other characters, so far as they have
been identified, were [real names in parentheses]: Charley
Ferris (Charles E. Fitch), Joseph Martin (Rev. Joseph May),
Andy Wright (Andrew D. White), Mr. Ayring (Joseph Allen),
Madame Skinner (Mrs. Smith), Fanny Swayne (Fanny Lawrence), Jim Swayne (James Lawrence), Jefferson Carroll
(Carroll E. Smith), Pug Merriweather (John Butler), Otis
Burr (Otis Burt), [and] Milly Merriweather (Mary Butler).
     "A lady named Huntington was principal of a girl's
school; [she] is the Miss Offerman of the story. W.O.
Stoddard himself, the author of the book, may or may not
have figured in its pages. However that may be, he deserves to be mentioned among the members of that remarkable group of youngsters, so many of whom distinguished
themselves in after life, one as a scholar, another as an
abolitionist preacher, another as ambassador to Germany,
another as a newspaper editor and politician. Mr. Stoddard
himself, now living in Madison, N.J., was born in Homer.
His father was a bookseller and publisher in Syracuse during
William's boyhood. Later William Stoddard became private
secretary to Lincoln and afterwards United States Marshal
for Arkansas. No less than fifty books are credited to him,
verses, boy stories, a life of Lincoln and a Lives of the
Presidents. But Saltillo Boys, the story of Fayette Park
about the year 1850 bids fair to outlive all others.
     "Somebody should ask Andrew D. White whether he did
in fact astound the boys of Syracuse in that year of grace
by sending up a kite with lanterns attached to it. Somebody

should interrogate "Cha... the bull in the pastu... Carroll E. Smith inti... the West Park bon f... several of the le... identified. Ther... who they were... became of Jar... he left Salo... for Saltill... of local...

concerning the episode of
...sk some of those who knew
...ether it was he who set fire to
...nn Derry and Will Torrance, with
...racters of the story, remain to be
...he readers of this column who know
...ere may be those who know also what
... Hoyt, the principal of the school, after
... Such information should be put on record,
...s is more than a juvenile classic; it is a work
...tory of which Syracuse should be proud.--P.M.P."
... article seemed to show conclusively that Saltillo
Boys was based on actual incidents and characters and it
identifies many of the incidents and characters. This is the
exception in boys' books and the more interesting for its
rarity.

With this clipping as a starter, I wrote Carolyn Ann Davis, a researcher and librarian at the George Arents Research Library of Syracuse University. She in turn contacted the Onondaga Historical Association and Gerald J. Parsons, head of the Local History and Genealogy Department of the Syracuse Public Library, asking for further information. The results were amazing.

Parsons dated the clipping as appearing December 20, 1909, in The Post-Standard of Syracuse. It was written by Dr. Paul Mayo Paine. Mr. Parsons stated that "Dr. Paine was a newspaper man, later became a librarian and was director of the Syracuse Public Library 1915-1940." It also developed that after the original story as given above was printed, there were numerous letters to the editor and additional comments by Dr. Paine in The Post-Standard. Copies of all of these were furnished through the kindness of Mr. Parsons. In addition, W.O. Stoddard's own identification of characters as he remembered them on "his seventy-fifth Christmas" appeared in this newspaper.

The identifications in the original article were generally correct, although Stoddard identified Principal Hayne as a Mr. Hazle, Milly Merriweather as Amelia Bassett and Pug Merriweather as Jim Outwater. The newspaper clippings also showed that Saltillo Boys was first published in the magazine St. Nicholas as a serial in 1881 and printed in book form in 1882.

As "One of the Boys" wrote to the paper, "Mr. Stoddard's description of the burning of the first Wieting block, of the Geddes pump house, the Salt works, the Glen at Onondaga Valley, the old City Hall with the butcher stalls on the first floor, are all excellent and entertaining." It is seldom that so many characters and incidents in any book have been so thoroughly authenticated as those in Saltillo Boys.

The number of "successful" graduates of a small school in a village of the 1850's is also rather remarkable. They include a U.S. Judge, a U.S. general and a colonel, an eminent clergyman, banker, the president of Cornell University and a U.S. ambassador, two editors and two authors, counting Mr. Stoddard himself. A mistake in the original article was the identification of one graduate as an "abolitionist preacher." Rather, he was the son of the abolitionist preacher. Stoddard, himself, of course was one of the best known graduates.

The newspaper clippings give a few facts about Stoddard's rather remarkable career. The Dictionary of American Biography gives many more, including a statement about the number of books written, which is at variance with the 50 mentioned in the article: "In all, Stoddard wrote over one hundred books"; "his books for boys, some seventy-six in number, were perhaps his greatest literary successes." (Who's Who in America, 1918-1919, lists 69 books and other lists show 78.)

Stoddard became joint editor of the Central Illinois Gazette at Champaign, Illinois, shortly after graduating from the University of Rochester in 1858. He "worked ceaselessly for Lincoln's election in the Illinois senatorial campaign of 1858 and he was one of the first Illinois editors to suggest him for the presidency."

After the presidential election of 1860 he was appointed by Lincoln as a secretary to sign land patents, then enlisted as a private in the Union army for three months and after being discharged became Lincoln's assistant private secretary. "Stoddard relates the 'queer kind of tremor' that came over him as he copied from 'Abraham Lincoln's own draft of the first Emancipation Proclamation'" (Atlantic Monthly, March 1925, p. 337).

He served as United States marshal for Arkansas from 1864 to 1866 and later "he became engaged in journalistic activities and in telegraphic, manufacturing, and railway enterprises, obtaining nine patents for mechanical inventions. From 1873 to 1875 he served as a clerk in the department of docks, New York City." He spent his later years in Madison, New Jersey, where he died in 1925 shortly before his 90th birthday.

A contemporary and rather reliable source as to his popularity in the late 1800's is Five Thousand Books: An Easy Guide to the Best Books in Every Department of Reading, "selected, classified and briefly described by a corps of experienced editors under the direction of the Literary Bureau of 'The Ladies' Home Journal'." This book was published in 1895 when Edward Bok was editor of the Journal and "the aim has been to choose books of permanent interest and value, and at the same time to provide for all classes of readers, and all healthful tastes."

The section on "Fiction for Young Folks" lists 19 books by Stoddard recommended by the "corps of experienced editors." These include Chris the Model Maker, Crowded Out o' Crofield, Little Smoke, On the Frontier, The Battle of New York, The Captain's Boat, Guert Ten Eyck, Tom and the Money King, Among the Lakes, Dab Kinzer, The Quartet, Winter Fun, Gid Granger, Chuck Purdy, The Red Mustang, The Talking Leaves, Two Arrows, and The White Cave in addition to Saltillo Boys. The editors comment, "Stoddard's books are always wholesome; his boys and girls are real flesh and blood." This was literally true in Saltillo Boys.

But fashions and interests change and by 1920 when Children's Literature by Curry and Clippinger was published, Stoddard was not included. There is no mention of him in any of the currently popular books on children's literature such as Children's Literature in the Elementary School by Huck and Young, A Critical History of Children's Literature by Meigs et al. or in Children and Books by Arbuthnot. This is really a little unfair as well as unscholarly since Stoddard produced a large body of well-accepted boys' books that exerted a significant influence on the youth of his era. He wasn't even tainted with the stigma of writing dime novels!

Although Miller of Dime Novel Authors thought "Major Henry B. Stoddard," who wrote Gordon Lillie, the Boy Interpreter of the Pawnees, and Lillie, the Reckless Rider; or, The Wild Hunter's Secret, was a pen name for W.O. Stoddard, Stoddard's son, W.O. Stoddard, Jr., assured Albert Johannsen that his father never used this name. Johannsen states that "Major Henry B. Stoddard was a pseudonym of Col. Prentiss Ingraham."

Trowbridge and Kellogg, two other contemporaries of Stoddard, seem to be making somewhat of a comeback in certain circles. It is quite certain that anyone really concerned with the history and influence of children's books should also be familiar with Stoddard. These old newspaper clippings shed interesting light on one of his best books.

Part Four. Stratemeyer.

Chapter X

STRATEMEYER AND SCIENCE FICTION

What are the blood lines of juvenile science fiction?
Jules Verne to H.G. Wells to Asimov? Or Ellis to Senarens
to Stratemeyer? A major problem is a definition on which we
can agree. In an interesting 1955 article*, Isaac Asimov
says that "science fiction is that branch of literature which
deals with fictitious society, differing from our own chiefly in
the nature and extent of its technological development."
Gerald Herald, in the same article, says that "Science-fiction
is the prophetic--a better term, the apocalyptic--literature of
our particular and culminating epoch of crisis." Neither of
these definitions fits particularly well either Jules Verne or
the juvenile science and adventure fiction of the century.
Robert A. Heinlein, in "Ray Guns and Rocket Ships"
(Library Journal, 78 [July 1953] 1188-91), says "'Science
Fiction' is a portmanteau term, and many and varied are the
things that have been stuffed into it. ...It would be more
nearly correctly descriptive to call the whole field 'speculative fiction' and to limit the name 'science fiction' to a sub-
class--in which case some of the other sub-classes would be:
undisguised fantasy ... pseudo-scientific fantasy ... socio-
logical speculation ... [and] adventure stories with exotic
and nonexistent locale.... Many other classes will occur to
you, since the term 'speculative fiction' may be defined
negatively as being fiction about things that have not happened."
We have obviously a wide latitude in definition. For
our purposes we are concerned with adventure stories containing a major strand of science and technology, usually
placed in a relatively present day setting with normal,
though technically distinguished characters. The term "science and adventure stories" might better satisfy the purists
but "science fiction" seems understandable and reasonably
appropriate.
The form of popular juvenile science fiction in this
country, particularly in its early days, will surprise many.
The fact is that its origin was in the dime novels and the
"story papers" of the period. The earliest example is considered to be "The Steam Man of the Prairies" by Edward S.

*Webb, Hanor A., "Science Fiction Writers: Prophets of the
Future," Library Journal, 80 (December 15, 1955), 2884-5.

Ellis. This story pre-dated most of Verne's work, particularly the English translation of Verne. The story was first
published as No. 45 of "The American Novels," around
August of 1868. It was reprinted five times through 1904
and was again reprinted in 1974 in Eight Dime Novels, edited
by E.F. Bleiler (Dover). In a December 6, 1968 letter to
me, Denis R. Rogers says, "In my view, 'The Steam Man of
the Prairies' was both before and of its time in that the
demand in the late 1860's was still for the frontier yarn and,
essentially, [this] was an Indian story, with a science fiction element introduced to provide a humorous slant."

As reader's interests changed toward the "technical" or
"scientific," other writers and publishers entered the field.
Frank Tousey copied Ellis's creation with "Frank Reade and
His Steam Man of the Plains" in 1876 and the science fiction
battle among dime novel publishers was on. Luis P.
Senarens created "Frank Reade, Jr.," for Tousey and,
writing as "Noname," created a fantastic array of scientific
marvels. Not only did Verne write a congratulatory letter to
Senarens but according to Sam Moskowitz, he paid him the
ultimate compliment of "borrowing" his material*. Street and
Smith competed with such stories as "Tom Edison Jr.'s Electric Sea Spider" in the Nugget Library of 1893 and Emerson
Bell's serial "The Electric Air and Water Wizard" in Good
News, 1893-1894.** The youth of America devoured the
stories of science and adventure. This was their introduction to science fiction.

The American writers were particularly influenced by
the American growth in science and technology and by
American scientific heroes. Street and Smith helped themselves to Edison's name. Even Edward Stratemeyer used the
pen-name "Theodore Edison" for his serial, "The Wizard of
the Deep," published in Young Sports of America in 1895.
The youthful readership may have later read Jules Verne
and H.G. Wells but their initial exposure was mainly to
native American science fiction.

For librarians and educators the American writers do
not exist. Children's Literature in the Elementary School
(by Charlotte S. Huck and Doris A. Young; Holt, Rinehart
& Winston, 1961, p. 56) has this statement: "The beginning
of science fiction and adventure can surely be found in Jules
Verne's Twenty Thousand Leagues under the Sea (1870),
and Around the World in Eighty Days (1872). Modern
readers may be surprised to note the early dates of these
books." How Edward Ellis and Lou Senarens would have
hooted, not to mention the generation brought up on "Jack
Wright" and "Frank Reade Jr."

---

*Sam Moskowitz, Explorers of the Infinite, Cleveland: World,
1960; p. 115. **Emerson Bell was Edward Stratemeyer.

Cornelia Meigs, in A Critical History of Children's Literature (rev. ed., MacMillan, 1969, p. 223), under a section entitled "Jules Verne Conducts Excursions to a Hidden World," says, "To the many nineteenth century milestones along the road of children's literature must be added one more, the rise of the scientific adventure story. Jules Verne (1825-1905), its progenitor, was a Frenchman...."

To these statements one can only say, "hogwash!" If these writers had said instead, "among the writers of whom we approve, Jules Verne was an early and influential figure in science fiction," no one could have objected. The plain facts are, and they have been plentifully documented by numerous writers including Sam Moskowitz, Denis Rogers, Quentin Reynolds and Charles Bragin, that Verne did not originate science fiction or the scientific adventure. In addition he was certainly not as popular among the American boys of the period as Ellis or "Noname." The mainstream of the popular boys' scientific adventure in this country has been much more influenced by Ellis, Senarens and later, Stratemeyer, than by Verne.

Even J.O. Bailey's classic Pilgrims Through Space and Time (Greenwood, 1972, p. 96) contains misleading statements about the dime novel and story paper era. He states: "Before 1900 scientific fiction, made popular by the romances of Jules Verne, branched out into juvenile literature." "A typical series is the 'Frank Reade' stories. Noname (pseud. for Lu Senarens) published weekly adventures of a boy-hero in his 'teens...." "Details of the machine are always vague, but it is usually something made familiar by Verne or other writers of scientific fiction." Not only is the dating inaccurate but the implication that the dime novel authors were sterile hacks who lifted their material from better writers is completely erroneous. There was certainly some plagarism --on both sides as Moscowitz has pointed out--but the one criticism that is seldom seriously made of dime novel writers is a lack of imagination!

It is possibly reasonable to ask why Verne gets such a good press by the writers of histories of children's literature while writers like Ellis, Senarens, Patten, Stratemeyer and Garis do not receive passing mention for their science fiction writings. The unfortunate answer is that these writers of "history" do not generally acknowledge the existence of the "subculture" of popular children's literature, including the dime novel, story paper and hardcover series books. Not only does this attitude give the student who may soon be teaching or working in the library field an unbalanced presentation, it gives an inaccurate one. As important as Verne was, he was only one of a host of writers in the field.

Continuing our examination of the blood lines of juvenile science fiction let us briefly note two modern series. "Lucky Starr" (Lucky Starr and the Oceans of Venus, Lucky Starr and the Moons of Jupiter, etc.) is the hero of a series by "Paul French." Paul French is better known as Isaac Asimov. The books are well-written and entertaining. They contain a cast of characters from various planets and take place at least a thousand years in the future. The adventures are, to date, somewhat implausible. This series might be considered the "classic" evolution of the Jules Verne-Wells prototype.

The second example is "Tom Swift, Jr." As noted in some detail in Chapter VI, Tom is a modern earthling, quite scientifically advanced for an 18 year old. His adventures and inventions are in the realm of the near-future. These books are also well written and entertaining and well researched. They can be classified as the offspring of Tom Swift (literally) and the story papers of the 1890's (figuratively). Of the two series, "Tom" has been unquestionably the more widely read and influential. And Tom is only the latest "science fiction" series creation by the Statemeyer Syndicate.

Edward Stratemeyer's importance and influence in the juvenile field have been so thoroughly discussed in numerous articles that it is redundant to mention them. His interest in science and invention and his own writings in the field are less well known. The interest was an early one. His second published serial was "Jack, the Inventor; or, The Trials and Triumphs of a Young Machinist." It appeared in Edward Ellis's The Holiday from April 25 to June 3, 1891 (see Chester G. Mayo, "Bibliogaphic Listing of 'Good News'," Dime Novel Round-Up, September, 1960). The magazine expired and it is uncertain whether the entire serial was published. It was published in its entirety, however, in Street and Smith's Good News, vol. 4, nos. 90-100, January 23 to April 2, 1892. It made a third appearance in Stratemeyer's own Bright Days as "A Young Inventor's Pluck; or, The Wellington Legacy," nos. 30-31, February 20 to February 27, 1897, and again was unfinished as the magazine folded. The same story, slightly revised, was then printed in hardcover by Saalfield in 1901 as A Young Inventor's Pluck, or, The Mystery of the Willington Legacy and went through various printings by Saalfield and others. The author was "Arthur M. Winfield" in the book form but Stratemeyer in the earlier serials.

There is more of adventure than science in this story. Jack is "a wide-awake American lad of a mechanical turn of mind." He "is an inventor and has almost ready the model of a useful and valuable invention...." The invention was a planing machine attachment and was sold for $4000, a good

sum in 1891. At the end of the story "Jack is now superin-
tendent at the tool works, and besides his salary, draws a
handsome royalty from his father's and his own inventions."
The pragmatic emphasis is somewhat reminiscent of Tom
Swift and His Motor-Cycle where Tom had to have his father
show him how to gear up his motor-cycle properly.

"Joe the Surveyor; or, The Value of a Lost Claim," is
another engineering-oriented serial published in Good News
from May 5 to July 21, 1894. Here, again, the science plays
a subordinate part to the adventure. It is a good story,
however, was printed in hardcover in 1903 by Lee & Shepard, and later became volume No. 6 of Stratemeyer's "Popular Series."

This is not to imply that Stratemeyer was either unaware of or uninvolved in more exotic science fiction. As
editor of Good News in the early 1890's, as assistant editor
and later editor of Young Sports of America and as editor-
publisher of Bright Days, he was competing with the leaders
in the field. Recent research in the S & S files at Syracuse
University has established that Stratemeyer, himself, wrote
"The Electric Air and Water Wizard," which ran from November 18, 1893 to February 3, 1894; R.Y. Toombs wrote "Beneath the Waves," which started March 10, 1894, and Gilbert
Patten wrote "In the Heart of the Earth," commencing October 20, 1894. All of these stories used the pen name "Emerson Bell." Another Emerson Bell story, again written by
Stratemeyer, was "Overhead Steve," which is more engineering than science fiction. The writer of the "Lad Electric"
stories in Good News has been identified from the S & S files
as "Smith." By that time, however, Stratemeyer had joined
Frank J. Earll of Young Sports of America.

Although Young Sports of America (later Young People
of America) had a strong sports emphasis, Stratemeyer wrote
two science and adventure stories for this periodical. The
first was the serial, "Nat Donald, King of the Air; or, The
Marvelous Adventures of a Young Balloonist," by "Roy
Rockwood" (July 20 to August 24, 1895). "Roy Rockwood"
was a pen name for Stratemeyer at this time, though later
used as a "house name" for Syndicate series. The following
month "The Wizard of the Deep; or, Over and Under the
Ocean in Search of the $1,000,000 Pearl," by "Theodore
Edison" appeared. It ran from August 10 to September 14,
1895. This serial was published by Mershon in 1900 as
The Wizard of the Sea; or, A Trip under the Ocean with
"Roy Rockwood" as the author.

As publisher of Bright Days, Stratemeyer continued to
give his readership a wide choice of topics. In the science
line was "Bound to Be an Electrician; or, A Clear Head and
and Stout Heart," April 1896 to August 1896 by "Arthur M.
Winfield." Another example is "The Land of Fire," with its

secret underground mines complete with underground village
lighted by arc lights. This serial, first published from
September 26 to November 14, 1896, was printed in hardcover by Mershon in 1900. The author, "Louis Charles,"
was Louis Charles Stratemeyer together with Edward Stratemeyer, according to Harriet S. Adams in an April 2, 1975
interview.

In the same year appeared "Balloon Boys; or, Adventures among the Clouds," by "Capt. Ralph Bonehill" and
"The Young Civil Engineer; or, Perils of the Backwoods,"
by Edward Stratemeyer. It is stretching it considerably to
consider "Joe the Surveyor" and "The Young Civil Engineer"
as science fiction, but it shows Stratemeyer's interest in the
technical. This civil engineering interest also appeared in
another serial called "Building the Line," a railroad story,
which appeared in The Popular Magazine of July and August,
1904.

Three unusual Stratemeyer serials appeared in Norman
Munroe's Golden Hours. The first was "Holland, the Destroyer; or, America Against the World," by "Hal Harkaway." It ran from November 24, 1900, to January 12, 1901.
It was first printed in hardcover as The Young Naval Captain; or The War of All Nations by Thompson and Thomas in
1902. The author was given as "Capt. Ralph Bonehill." It
was later reprinted by Donahue as Oscar the Naval Cadet.
The second to appear was "Lost in the Land of Ice; or Bob
Baxter at the South Pole," by "Roy Rockwood." It ran from
December 1, 1900, to January 26, 1901. Wessels published
this serial in hardcover in 1902 with "Capt. Ralph Bonehill"
as the author. The third was "Rival Ocean Divers; or, A
Boy's Daring Search for Sunken Treasure," by "Roy Rockwood" which appeared January 5 to February 23, 1901.
Although it was not published in hardcover until Stitt
brought it out in a revised form in 1905, it had a long life
and appeared in "The Deep Sea Series," "The Dave Fearless
Series" and "The Sea Treasure Series."

Two of Stratemeyer's books, First at the North Pole
(1909) and Over the Ocean to Paris (1927), would have
qualified as science fiction if they had been written a few
years earlier. The first was written at the time of the Dr.
Cook-Peary controversy and the second after Lindbergh's
flight so that both are current science and adventure.

If we insist on a minimum of science, Lost in the Land
of Ice would fail to qualify. Even though the boys reached
the South Pole in 1900 they did it by conventional means.
They went by boat and outside of a few difficulties with ice-
bergs, polar bears (at the South Pole!) and giant condors,
which carried off one of the party, they had a routine expedition. They used no special scientific devices or aids.

The three early books written entirely by Edward

Stratemeyer that come closest to juvenile science fiction are The Rival Ocean Divers, The Wizard of the Sea and The Young Naval Captain. The Rival Ocean Divers concerns a voyage to the Pacific in search of a treasure in the sunken ship Happy Hour. The expedition uses a "Costell diving bell."

"You mean one of those glass cages which they can lower to the bottom of the ocean and then walk around on big steel legs, like an artificial crab?"

The Happy Hour is 12,500 feet down in the middle of the ocean. In spite of this the salvage party found it with relative ease, as did their enemies. The divers were lowered to the bottom in the diving bell. They were able to leave the bell in "those new steel-ribbed diving suits we had made in Washington especially for this trip...." The treasure had disappeared from the ship.

Since this is also a scientific expedition the divers captured a "linophyrne lucifer," or electric-light fish and a "ray of fire" fish. Another "ray of fire" fish almost finished off Amos Fearless, the chief diver, by winding itself around his neck and trying to strangle him. Dave Fearless, his son, was able to cut him loose. All this happened at only half a mile down. At a mile down Dave captured "two spiral whipsnaps, to use the vulgar name, and half a dozen fish which are new to science." When the divers descended to the full two mile depth they found a forest of submarine trees but were able to move the diving bell from one treetop to another by means of the crab-like claws attached to the bottom.

"At last the diving bell gained the edge of the forest and came to a rest upon one of the banks of moss of many colors. ...Should they leave the diving bell upon an exploring tour?"

They do but shortly came across "a monster as startling as it was horrible. ...It had a long, round body, fat and blubbery, with two legs in the center, two arms near the neck, and at the end the tail of a fish. The head was shaped like a huge pear, with eyes blinking savagely from either side of a nose which was as long and pointed as a cow's horn. The mouth of the demon was wide open, showing a double row of sharp, bluish teeth and a tongue covered with yellow slime. All told, the creature was at least ten feet long, and when it stood up it towered well over the heads of the two divers."

They shot the first demon only to find the area was infested by the creatures. The divers escaped to the diving bell in the nick of time and returned to the surface. The demons are presumed to belong to the lost order of "Chilusia damondaribytis" and supposed to have lived at one time upon the lost continent of Atlantis. In a later descent the divers found a "curiously shaped mound of shells, covered with moss. "'Hullo, what's this?' said Dave. 'Hang me if it doesn't look like the home of some submarine animal. Perhaps it's a meeting house for those demons'." They examined the mound, which "proved to be hollow, with the walls covered with brilliant seashells of all colors." In the center was a smaller mound which they found to contain the missing treasure. "The gold was mixed with bits of other bright metal and glass, for whoever had stored it there had known no difference in value and had simply made a collection of stuff bright to the eye."

The divers removed the treasure to the diving bell and after a final brush with the demons were hoisted aboard ship. They brought a reluctant demon with them in one of the crab-like claws of the bell. "'And the wonderful monster,' put in Doctor Barrell. 'What an odd creature! It will make a grand exhibition at the Smithsonian Institution.'"

One would think that this would happily conclude the adventures of the Fearlesses but it was not to be. It took until 1908 and two more books, The Cruise of the Treasure Ship and Adrift on the Pacific, before Amos and Dave Fearless were able to get the treasure to the United States and make a proper financial disposition of it. The latter two books have no aspects of science fiction. They were written in the early days of the Stratemeyer Syndicate and, while issued under the name "Roy Rockwood," do not appear to have Stratemeyer's writing characteristics.

The Wizard of the Sea is a strange book. It is embarrassingly reminiscent of Twenty Thousand Leagues under the Sea. In spite of some slight internal evidence, the fact that it appeared in Young Sports of America while Stratemeyer was editor, and the fact that it was printed in hardcover under the "Roy Rockwood" name, it is hard to authenticate as his writing. Even the original serial author, "Theodore Edison," is not consistent with Stratemeyer tradition. As his daughter has pointed out in connection with "D.T. Henty," another pen name sometimes associated with Stratemeyer, Stratemeyer wasn't the type of person to capitalize on another's name, and there was no need to since his professional reputation was already established. A possible answer is that as editor of Young Sports of America he was doing so much writing for it that he had to use a variety of pen names and "Edison" has a nice ring to it. This does not explain the similarity to Verne. Stratemeyer's ability to create plots, characters and situations, so evident in most of his writings, may have been affected by the pressures of his stationery store in Newark, which he was still operating at the time, together with his editing and writing. At any rate, if Twenty Thousand Leagues under the Sea is science fiction, so is The Wizard of the Sea!

For most of the first six chapters the story is concerned with the exploits of Mont Folsom at Nautical Hall, a boarding school on the seacoast. Suddenly the action changes. Mont, his chum Carl Barnaby and his "devoted follower" John Stumpton, or "Stump," are sailing in the ocean when they are run down and then rescued by the ship Golden Cross. Shortly after this the lookout on the Golden Cross sights a strange sail. "It was soon discovered that the sail was nothing more or less than a man clinging to a chicken coop, who had taken off his shirt and hoisted it on high to attract attention."

The man is Homer Woddle, Secretary to the Society for the Exploration of the Unknown Parts of the World. His ship had been sunk by "a wonderful sea monster" which was "black and long, like a gigantic eel, and threw out a phosphorescent light." When the monster shortly appeared on the scene Homer Woddle and the three boys attacked it. The monster upset their small boat and rammed the Golden Cross. The attackers found themselves on top of the submarine, for such in fact the monster was, and were eventually all dragged down into the "floating iron shell."

The captain's name was Vindex and he is "the Wizard of the Sea." The submarine Searcher had been built on a desert island in the Pacific by the twelve negroes who form the crew. Captain Vindex, like Captain Nemo, had renounced the world. Like Captain Nemo he has equipped his salon with valuable paintings, a frescoed ceiling and a "Turkey carpet." He has an organ as well although his taste in music seems a bit different. "Captain Vindex ... played Sousa's 'Liberty Bell March' with great skill." On other occasions he also played "an exquisite air of Beethoven," and "a Scotch air which had an indescribable charm about it."

The submarine is powered by electricity. "'My motive power is electricity, and I can attain a speed of thirty miles an hour.' ...'The men of the world have not yet discovered half the value of electricity.' ...'Engineering science is yet in its infancy. The world has great discoveries to make. You are at present only on the threshold of the great unknown'." Captain Vindex takes them hunting in a submarine forest. They are equipped with special self-contained diving gear and have air guns and electric bullets. They have electric lamps as well "which made their path clear and distinct...."

They make a landing on a South Sea Island and are attacked by Papouans. Captain Vindex, like Captain Nemo, electrified the submarine and the natives had a "stunning" time, as Mont put it. They visited the pearl fisheries of Ceylon and inspected a pearl worth $100,000. The smaller pearls which they picked up later made the party "all rich

men" after their escape. For some odd reason there was no
canal yet built through the Isthmus of Suez (in 1895) so the
submarine used an underground tunnel between the Red Sea
and the Mediterranean Sea, as had the Nautilus.

Captain Vindex waxed prophetic during the trip.
"'Shortly, my dear sir,' said the Captain, 'your children
--that is to say, the next generation--will travel through the
air in flying machines; your railway engines will own electricity as their motive power. There is no end to scientific
discovery; the world is in its infancy. We are just emerging
from barbarism'."

When the Searcher neared the island of Cyprus the
captives escaped from the submarine and gained the shore.
In an attempt to recapture them Captain Vindex rammed the
Searcher into the rocks, the submarine was blown to atoms
and all on board were killed. Captain Vindex never did find
his million dollar pearl.

The third of Stratemeyer's early science fiction is in a
different vein altogether. The Young Naval Captain; or,
The War of All Nations (written in 1900) takes place in 1936.
"Captain Ralph Bonehill" in the introduction to the book
says, "I wished to draw the attention of my young readers
to the fact that naval science, as well as science in all other
branches, is making wonderful strides, and that for the
future hardly anything seems impossible. In years gone by
electric lights, the telephone and telegraph, not to mention
the wireless telegraphy, navigable balloons, and even our
railroad trains would have been laughed at as impossibilities.
Yet to-day we have all these things, and many others equally wonderful, and each day we look forward to something
even more startling."

In 1936 the United States "now embraces all of North
America, from the Isthmus of Panama to Hudson Bay, and
takes in all of the West Indies, Hawaii, the Philippines, and
half a dozen other islands of the sea, as well as a corner of
China and another corner of Japan." The country has over
100 million inhabitants and nearly all are well to do. New
York City has been "built up solid as far as Yonkers."
There are four bridges between New York and Brooklyn and
two bridges from Manhattan to New Jersey. The biggest
building in the city is the Empire, which is 56 stories high
although plans are in progress to build a building 100 stories
high and three blocks long. Balloons with electric lights are
"anchored a mile in the air."

There has been a "Yellow War of 1925" in which "England, France, Germany, Russia and Japan wanted to carve
up poor China" and Uncle Sam wouldn't allow it. We had
helped the Boers to freedom in South Africa and "turned the
Turkish kingdom inside out in 1928" over an old quarrel
about money. Although the United States had "tried to

settle the many existing troubles without an appeal to arms"
they had failed. It seemed necessary to declare war against
the world. The decision was not a particularly wise one.
The armed forces numbered over a million men (no air force,
however) and the soldiers were armed with the Miles-Gilford
electric repeating rifles. The sharpshooters used telescopes
with their rifles and "could pick off an enemy at a mile
distance with ease." The combined navies of the world came
to our eastern sea coast and fought a great battle off Sandy
Hook. The United States Navy was decisively beaten, mainly
because of a German submarine, which wrecked three American warships.

In this hour of need Oscar came to the rescue. Oscar
Pelham, hero of the book "had a strong taste for electricity
and mechanics generally." After spending three years at
Edison's Electrical University at Llewellyn Park he entered
the services of the Standard Ship Yard. At 19 he perfected
the plans for a radically new submarine. The vessel was to
be powered by "two small but exceedingly powerful screws,
operated by an electric engine." She was to carry "both
natural and manufactured air" and expected to reach a speed
of 23 knots, absolutely without noise. Since he was financially independent he built a model of the craft at his own
expense and sailed it successfully on Long Island Sound.

After the disastrous battle Oscar took his model to
Washington and demonstrated it before the Secretary of the
Navy and Jefferson McKinley Adams, President of the United
States. The Navy Department immediately appropriated half
a million dollars to built the Holland XI but gave Oscar only
a month to do it in. This was plenty, however, and in 29
days he launched the ship and put it into service. Oscar
was placed in command with a Navy rank of captain and his
chum, Andy Greggs was made first lieutenant.

The Americans had lost four more warships by this time
and were preparing for a battle off Cuba. Oscar's first war
action was with the Tien-Tsin, a "monster Chinese armored
cruiser." His usual technique was to submerge, fasten a
torpedo or mine with a timing mechanism to the bottom of his
victim, and leave hurriedly. He blew the Chinese cruiser
into millions of fragments in this engagement. He next
tackled a French cruiser off the coast of Cuba but three
Yankee warships sank her first, unfortunately right on top
of the Holland. When an amunition magazine exploded on the
Republique, it freed the Holland although Oscar, who was
outside checking the damage, had to walk underwater to
Cuba where he was captured by the Japanese. After Oscar
was rescued by his crew the Holland attacked the Japanese
troops who were planning to invade Florida. They killed
enough to at least slow up the invasion.

Their next action was on the Canadian coast where an

enemy fleet of 34 warships and 66 transports was waiting to
attack. Oscar sank the British cruiser Terrible, the German
gunboat Wilhelm II and the French ship-of-the-line Philippe.
The fleet moved back out to sea. For some reason the
German submarine never again appears in this war. About
this time the enemy abducted Martha Adams, the President's
daughter, and she was reported to be a prisoner on a foreign warship. Oscar was much interested in Martha and
worried about her the rest of the book.

The next big battle started without Oscar since one of
the Holland's screws had been damaged. The battle again
went against the United States and by the end of the day
the outlook was grim. Oscar arrived on the scene just in
time to turn defeat into victory. He sank a British cruiser
and a French ship which carried "a newly-invented battery
of dynamite guns." He shot a single torpedo which tore
great holes in two German vessels and then fired two new
"hightite" bombs at the enemy which did "fearful execution."
He followed up by sinking a Turkish man-o'-war and an
Italian corvette and bombed an enemy transport. The battle
ended in a triumph for the Americans and Oscar Pelham was
the man of the hour.

After refitting the Holland at the Charlestown Navy
Yard, Oscar took her through the new Central American
Canal to tackle a fleet of 50 Chinese, Japanese and Russian
warships that was expected to attack San Francisco. He
foiled a plot to blow up the canal locks and reached San
Francisco to find the enemy had attacked the Hawaiian
Islands. It took the Holland ten days to reach Honolulu
and when they finally arrived they found that the city had
surrendered.

Oscar solved this problem by torpedoing the enemy
fleet, and things were looking up when the Holland was cast
ashore by a tidal wave and attacked by three warships.
Another tidal wave rolled her back to sea and wrecked the
enemy ships. Following this Oscar left Hawaii, searching for
the rest of the foreign fleet. His searching was interrupted
by a sportive whale who stuck his head through the trap
door opening of the submarine and had to be blown out with
a small shell.

After blowing up another Japanese warship Oscar continued his search for the enemy and found two Chinese
cruisers, two Japanese cruisers and two English men-o'-war.
He sneaked on board a British ship to get details of the
enemy's plans, was discovered, but talked his way out by
pretending to be a British spy. He returned to the Holland
with "Hang Chang," captain of one of the Chinese warships,
as a captive. Hang had the details of the abduction of Martha Adams and, encouraged by Oscar's threats of torture,
told all. Martha is on the Green Dragon, a Chinese ship.

Hang later went insane, attacked Oscar and had to be killed.
The Holland interrupted the shelling of San Francisco
but one of the anchors of the Tokio "slipped overboard and
the anchor chain became entangled in the screw of the
submarine craft." The Tokio towed the unwilling Holland to
Fisherman's Bay before Oscar was able to remove the cable,
sink the Tokio and save an American transport.

Adventures followed thick and fast as the submarine
was imprisoned in a cave under the ocean and Oscar and
Andy were attacked by a 30-foot sea serpent. After their
escape they encountered an electrical storm, which burned
out the ship's switchboard and almost sank them. It took
two days to repair all the damage. They met the enemy
fleet at Cape Nome, only to find the warships had protected
themselves by placing wires on the underside of the keels,
"stretching out in all directions, like the spokes of some
gigantic bicycle wheel." "These wires were connected with
an alarm bell...." Oscar solved this by floating a torpedo
under the Ivan II and sinking her. The rest of the fleet
lifted the bombardment of Cape Nome and fled to sea.

Oscar now had time to look for Martha Adams so the
Holland returned to the Caribbean where the Green Dragon
had been sighted. Through negligence the Holland was
captured by Spanish and Italian naval men but recaptured
by Oscar and Andy in a short time with the help of the
electric rifles. One of their captives is the traitor "Gabretti,"
for whom a fifty thousand dollar reward has been offered
but Oscar is generous. "'A fair share of it shall go to my
men,' answered Oscar."

Meanwhile a United States army had invaded England,
another army was on the way to Japan and a third was
bound for China. The enemy had won but four of 16 naval
battles and three of 22 land battles. The foreign nations
were growing tired of the war.

After surviving an underwater earthquake the Holland
rescued a Frenchman who directed them to the Green Dragon.
Just as they arrived Martha leaped overboard to avoid the
attentions of a Chinese admiral. Oscar shot the admiral and
rescued Martha in spite of being wounded himself. He then
blew up the Green Dragon and sailed the Holland back to
Chesapeake Bay--there to find that the war was over. When
the Holland showed up "it found a regular flotilla of warships
there, ready to do her honor." The President and his wife
came in person to meet Oscar and Martha. "It was a fitting
end to a most glorious campaign on land and sea."

The government profited from experience and built 12
new submarine boats of the Holland pattern with Rear Admiral Oscar Pelham as commander of all the United States
submarine craft afloat. "He was known far and wide as a
brilliant inventor and daring navy official. And his pretty

wife, Martha, was equally known for her great beauty and
her sweetness of heart."

Stratemeyer's personal interest in the technical continued to be reflected in many of the Syndicate's series. After
he formed his Literary Syndicate in about 1904 he wrote
fewer books himself, but instead plotted, outlined and edited
the books published by the Syndicate. Such series as the
Motor Boys, Dave Dashaway and the Speedwell Boys all
reflected Stratemeyer's interest--and that of American youth
--in the technical developments of the day. The emphasis
was on more-or-less true life adventures with a modern or
slightly advanced technology thrown in for good measure.
Even Tom Swift started in this vein but Tom rapidly became
a high calibre inventor with a long list of futuristic inventions to his credit.

A particularly interesting Stratemeyer series with a
strong "space travel" theme is the Great Marvel Series by
"Roy Rockwood." It qualifies as juvenile science fiction by
almost any definition. This series started in 1906 shortly
after the time Stratemeyer organized the Syndicate. Although he developed the plots, characters and general
outline of most of the books, the writing was done by contract authors. Roger Garis (in My Father Was Uncle Wiggily, McGraw-Hill, 1966, p. 77) claims his father, Howard
Garis, wrote the series. Sam Moskowitz states that the series
was "quite obviously derived from Luis Senarens' Frank
Reade, Jr., series" (p. 98 of Explorers of the Infinite).

The cast of the series featured Professor Henderson the
inventor, two orphans, Mark Sampson and Jack Darrow, who
live with Professor Henderson, and Washington White, the
Negro assistant. Mark and Jack were 15 and 16 years old
when the series started but they grew older slowly through
the years. One might have thought their adventures would
have had a rapid aging effect but apparently not. Washington White was "a big colored man, seemingly as strong as an
ox," and also engineer on the North Pole expedition. As
Professor Henderson said, "Washington and I understand
every piece of machinery. If we need any help we will call
on you." Washington was called "a genius in his way,
though somewhat inclined to use big words, of the meaning
of which he knew little and cared less." Andy Sudds, an
old hunter, and Bill Jones and Tom Smith, two young farmers, made up the rest of the crew in the early books.

The first book, Through the Air to the North Pole, was
a relatively conservative trip in an airship. "Up near the
roof of the place, which was quite high, there swayed an
immense bag of oiled silk. It was shaped like a cigar, big
in the middle and tapering at both ends. The bag was
enclosed in a net of ropes which extended down to the lower
part of the airship. This lower part, as the boys could

see, was just like a steam launch in shape, only much lighter in weight. It had a sharp bow, and a blunt stern. From the stern there extended a large propeller, the blades being made from sheets of aluminum."

This was the Monarch in which its inventor Professor Henderson and his friends successfully traveled to the North Pole and back. The somewhat primitive Monarch was followed in Under the Ocean to the South Pole by the Porpoise, a unique submarine propelled by a "water cable." "Through the entire length of the ship ran a round hole or shaft, one foot in diameter. Within this was an endless screw worked by powerful engines." The engine was a turbine, and steam was generated from heat furnished by the burning of a powerful gas, manufactured from sea water and chemicals. The combination worked beautifully and the group traveled successfully to the South Pole. They were unable to stop because the ocean was practically boiling hot right at the Pole.

In addition, they were caught in the grass of the Sargasso Sea, had to fight off monstrous suckers which grasped the boat in their powerful arms, were imprisoned within an iceberg, visited a graveyard of sunken ships and saw many strange monsters. They also found a great whirlpool that seemed to lead far into the earth and offered opportunities for further adventures.

Two years later the professor built a craft which could both sail on top of the water and navigate the air. He named it the Flying Mermaid. In this craft which "seemed like two immense cigars, one above the other," the explorers made a voyage to the interior of the earth, entering by means of the great whirlpool. Their adventures were described in Five Thousand Miles Underground. The ship was moved by the "power of compressed air. From either end of the lower hull there projected a short pipe working in a ball and socket joint, so it could be turned in any direction." The ship even contained "a small automatic piano worked by the electric current, on which popular airs could be played." The gas used had five times the lifting power of hydrogen and the gravity neutralizer also helped.

In a strange country, five hundred miles underground, they found giant man-eating pitcher plants. Jack Darrow inadvertently rolled down a hill and bounced into the opening of a monster pitcher plant, which attempted to devour him. Fortunately the others cut through the side of the flower cup and rescued Jack in the nick of time. This incident is so similar to Howard Garis's spoof, "Professor Jonkin's Cannibal Plant," which appeared in the August 1905 Argosy, that it seems most probable that Garis was the writer of at least this book.

The travelers met fish that walk and a snake-tree which

"is a plant, half animal, half-vegetable. It has long branches, not unlike a snake in shape. They can move about and grab things." The snake-tree captured Jack but again his friends rescued him. They met a creature with "the body of a bear, but the feet and legs ... of an alligator, while the tail trailed out behind like a snake, and the head had a long snout, not unlike the trunk of an elephant." They also came across a tribe of giants 10 to 15 feet tall who captured the Flying Mermaid. The explorers were rescued by King Hankos, who also gave them directions to the temple of treasure where they stocked up on gold and diamonds. They returned to the surface of the Earth in an emergency cylinder lifeboat although they had to leave the Flying Mermaid and the gold behind.

This book was possibly intended to end the series, since it states, "As the professor was getting quite old, and incapable of making any more wonderful inventions, he closed up his workshop and settled down to a quiet life." Jack and Mark, the youthful heroes, planned, however, to get a good education and after that to invent something better and take another trip. The door was left open for further adventures.

The next book in the series, Through Space to Mars, appeared in 1910, the same year as Tom Swift. It was followed by Lost in the Moon in 1911 and On a Torn-Away World in 1913. There was a 12-year gap before The City Beyond the Clouds appeared in 1925 and another four years before By Air Express to Venus was published in 1929. The last of the series, By Space Ship to Saturn, did not appear until 1935, five years after Stratemeyer's death. This was the same year that Tom Swift and His Planet Stone, last of the hardcover Tom Swifts, was published.

In Through Space to Mars Jack and Mark are students at the Universal Electrical and Chemical College and doing well, although Jack often "produced small explosions in the laboratory of the college." They are called home by Professor Henderson to meet another inventor who has a "wonderful, secret power--Etherium," with which he expects to travel to Mars. The projectile which is to take them to Mars is soon built and equipped with Etherium power as well as electric cannons. The Annihilator travels at the rate of 100 miles a second and reaches Mars in 12 days, including delays caused by a crazy stowaway machinist and a little difficulty caused by running into Donati's comet.

Mars is inhabited by a strange race of beings. "They make a special study of the sciences, and geometry and mathematics probably are their favorites." The travelers are able to communicate with the Martians through mathematics. Fifty years later Tom Swift, Jr., used the same language in his dealings with creatures from another world. Mars is a

wonderful place, full of strange and exciting novelties including "thought force" and a "mysterious red substance"
that is a source of heat, light and power. It is called
Cardite, and the members of the expedition spend most of
their time trying to steal a supply of it.

Mars is superior to Earth in many ways. "One was the
simplicity of lift." "In science they were far ahead of scientists of the earth.... That is all they do--study. That's
what makes their ears, eyes, nose and mouth so big. They
use them to listen to scientific sounds, to look at scientific
objects, smell scientific odors, and talk of scientific things."
The Martians catch the group stealing Cardite and object
violently but are neutralized by the electric cannons of the
Annihilator. It seems wisest for the Annihilator to leave
Mars at this point and return to Earth. Cardite proved to
be enormously valuable and a new motor was built to run on
it. The boys returned to college.

With the Cardite motor in the Annihilator it was a
simple matter to journey to the moon in their next adventure.
The new motor set a record of 153 miles a second, a goodly
speed for 1911. A Martian newspaper had given an account
of diamonds on the Moon and it seemed logical for our scientists to get a piece of the action. It was necessary to
wear fur-lined garments and carry "torches of life," small
iron boxes of chemicals which provided an atmosphere.
Other than that the group had made no special preparations.
"It was like being in the wildest part of the Canadian Rocky
Mountains of our earth...."

Through sheer stupidity, Jack, Mark and Andy Sudds
became lost on the moon and stumbled across a petrified
city. There were houses, animals and humans, all turned to
stone by some calamity. After being lost for a week they
discovered a field of diamonds. The Annihilator providentially appeared also, the party took all the diamonds they
wished and left for home. They took with them a petrified
man and "a history of it, in two large volumes, can be seen
in the museum where the body is exhibited."

The transportation becomes much more prosaic in On a
Torn-Away World. Mark and Jack have invented an improved
aeroplane, the Snowbird, which is capable of 50 miles an
hour or more. They fly to Alaska and are involved in a
tremendous earthquake and volcanic disturbance. Part of
Alaska is blown into space and becomes a satellite for a few
weeks. This disturbs our heroes as the force of gravity is
considerably less, their plane has been wrecked and they
are concerned about returning to earth. The satellite returns to earth of its own accord and lands in the North
Pacific. No one is hurt and the group returns to civilizaton
on board a whaler, which had also survived the trip.

When the series was resumed in 1925 with The City Be-

yond the Clouds, Jack and Mark had just built an advanced
telescope from designs by Professor Henderson. In the
intervening years they had gone to war, "both winning
medals for their heroism in action." "They had been sent to
the Universal Electrical and Chemical College, there their
rapid progress amazed their teachers." Washington White
had now degenerated to an ignorant servant although a
"prime favorite" of the boys. Even the boys had changed.
Mark now was "slightly smaller, slender and inclined to be
serious," whereas previously there had been "a certain
stoutness of which Mark never could seem to get rid." The
war may have thinned him down.

The first time they use the telescope they see a falling
aviator, 50 miles in the air. They rescue him and find he is
a famous scientist, Gustavus Hertz, who disappeared some
time ago. He has escaped from a strange, small world
located in the sky not far beyond Earth. It is inhabited by
four-foot, hideous, red dwarfs. Hertz had taken his son
and daughter exploring in an advanced plane of his design
and reached this new world. In escaping he inadvertently
left his children behind. Naturally something had to be
done about this. The boys recruit a number of old service
buddies and Hertz builds a new machine, vastly superior to
the airships of the day. By the use of a secret compound
and special wing design it was possible to attain speeds of
several thousand miles an hour. At the same time the use of
the helicopter principle allowed the plane to rise and descend
vertically.

The group needed oxygen masks but the plane had no
special problems in the lack of atmostphere and in about two
days they reached the City Beyond the Clouds. Outside of
an attack by giant grasshoppers, poison water and flowers,
they had no real problems until they met a kayo. "It had
the body of a grizzly bear and the head of a bison, but was
three times as large as any grizzly ... or any buffalo...."
It was definitely unfriendly and was killed with difficulty.

Arriving at the prison of the red dwarves they captured one and gained news about Berta and Max, Professor
Hertz's children. Events moved swiftly and the party rescued Berta from the chief's palace and took off. They were
shortly captured by the dwarves, who were nobody's fools,
and imprisoned. Max was thrown into the same prison which
made it easier when they escaped. After they killed the
king of the dwarves and as many others as possible they
struggled to the airship and "soared aloft." As they headed
for the Earth there was a tremendous explosion, which
marked the end of the planet. The ship reached earth with
no difficulties and all was well. Washington gave them a
supper that was "a triumph of the gustatory art and one
long to be remembered."

In By Air Express to Venus two mysterious comets visit the Earth and cause radios to explode. A woman in blue, gifted with mental telepathy and obviously "a being from another world," appears to ask for help. The mysterious comets are Venusian space ships. The first came to Earth on a scientific voyage and was wrecked and the second was a rescue ship that was also wrecked. One of the Venusians is injured and all are about to run out of food. They appeal to our earth scientists and inventors to build one usable space ship from the ruins of the two. Professor Henderson and associates do so and all leave hurriedly for Venus.

The space ship is run by an engine of gold and "operates on the rocket principle." They traveled at a rate exceeding 345,000 miles per hour. Outside of "ether blasts," a storm of "yellow snow," a wandering comet and a giant meteor they had few problems reaching Venus. They even tuned in to the "music of the spheres" on their radio.

When they reached Venus the negative gravity machines were thrown into gear and they landed safely. Venus was inhabited by two distinct races of people that never mingled. The expedition landed on Kar where the life-giving blue water was found. The technology was most advanced and included "thought wagons" which traveled on both land and water and "magnetic wands" which served as effective weapons. Some of the natives were "zotas" with the ability to "negative [sic] the force of gravitation." "They could rise in the air and travel by thought power."

Their first problem occurs when the Venusians they have rescued decide to keep them captives on Venus. "'It is in the interest and must be done!' said Soli." The earthlings were exhibited at various institutions of learning and kept as prisoners with the ultimate expectation of being sacrificed in an active volcano. The Professor took copious notes and they were all interested in the culture since Venusian science was more advanced than Earth science. The prospects, however, disturbed them.

Gozona, the woman in blue who started the whole thing, came to their rescue. She led then through an underground passage towards the rocket ship. They had to kill transparent snakes, horned spiders and cross a stream filled with high voltage electric eels. This they did successfully, reached the rocket ship and escaped in spite of a minor explosion which knocked them senseless. They had a near-miss with a comet, were hit by a small meteor and ran through an edge of a storm of the fatal yellow snow. After four days they reached the vicinity of Earth, set the negative gravity machines going, and landed safely less than a quarter of a mile from their home. It was good navigating.

In the last of this series of space exploration science fiction, Jack Darrow and Mark Sampson have graduated from college and are now professors at the Universal Electrical and Chemical College, specializing in astronomy. Professor Henderson and Washington White have apparently retired from the exploring business. Even Jack and Mark have little to do with these adventures. It is true they invented a selective magnetic machine which was taken on the trip to Saturn. It could be used to repel as well as attract and saved the expedition by repelling a storm of meteors.

Lucky Wright and Phil Baker, students at the college, find that Phil's uncle has built a rocket ship for a trip to Saturn. They prevail on him to go along. The college president's young son Bobby and his pet goat also go along as stowaways. A rival expedition leaves at the same time, since rocket ships have become more common. Both ships reach Saturn, both crews are captured by the natives and both groups escape and reach Earth safely. While they are on Saturn they are involved in numerous difficulties. Although they have disintegrator guns and "a generous amount of arms and ammunition" it doesn't always help. In the Cave of Perfumed Steam they found themselves shriveling up both outwardly and inwardly but escaped on the back of a cooperative Brontosaurus who carried them out of the cave. They met flying fish that uttered weird, song-like noises. The death-ray guns proved incapable of coping with the aggressive flying fish until a sea lizard, Tylosaurus dyspelor, joined in and routed the attackers.

In their travels around Saturn they picked up radio messages in Latin using geometry as a code. Here, also, they found the natives advanced in science with combination dirigible-airplanes, human magnetizers and weird machines with burnished disks. In physical appearance Saturnians were similar to humans but grew up to eight feet tall and had purple cellophane skins which they shed from time to time. They were also belligerent and imprisoned the Earth explorers who barged into the middle of a local war.

Since the language was Latin and our heroes had a classical as well as scientific education, they could communicate with little difficulty. They find television by mist has been perfected on Saturn, to say nothing of vapor or thought clouds which were used for transportation. It is interesting that thought force appears on Mars, Venus, and also on Saturn showing, possibly, interplanetary communication. The explorers are supposed to be released from prison to fight "several armies from people on the ten satellites." However, the action gets complicated. King Bazom, their captor, is conquered by King Cramii and the prisoners change captors and prisons. King Cramii makes peace with the invaders and announces the prisoners will be killed by magnetic projectiles in two days. The prisoners are concerned by this announcement so they take some spare lengths of pipe from their space ship, hook them to a geyser beneath the king's palace and, "'We'll blow up King Cramii with his palace!' said Phil joyfully."

The geyser did just that and both groups escaped to their space ships. All were saved except the goat. "Bobby and his friends had tried in vain to get back his goat, but the animal seemed to have disappeared." Before returning to Earth, Lucky and Phil's ship visits an uninhabited part of Saturn and they obtained "many more flasks of rare vapors and gases," and "several new kinds of snakes, including some large 'vapor vipers,'" as well as healing sap from a giant mushroom. They have to leave the dinosaurs behind because of space problems. In a week they were home with no further adventures except "one narrow escape from their being involved with the nebulous tail of a comet." The trip was a great success. Bobby got a new goat which he named Saturn and that was the end of the Great Marvel Series.

These books formed the major and possibly the only Syndicate "space travel" series until Tom Swift, Jr., came on the scene many years later. The casual disregard for the problems that beset modern astronauts is a credit to the inventors of the space ships and the intrepid explorers. Fortunately, their science was equal to any problem that could arise, though often just barely in time. The Great Marvel Series still reads well, many years after the books were written.

The Stratemeyer influence in juvenile science and ad- venture stories can really be traced from "Jack, the Inven- tor" in 1891 to the present day. Although Victor Appleton II is no longer recording the inventions of Tom Swift, Jr., his books are still on sale and still giving many boys their first introduction to the world of science. True, there was a gap of a few years between Toms Senior and Junior, but boys were still reading the original Tom Swift during these years. (They still do.) This makes close to 90 years of science fiction influence on the young people of America. Science and invention, futurism and space travel are all included. With the fantastic sales of some of these series, particularly Tom Swift, no one can question the influence of these books on several generations. In popular juvenile science fiction it seems quite clear that the blood lines run from Ellis to Senarens to Stratemeyer with only a minor assist from Verne.

Chapter XI

STRATEMEYER AND BLACKS

This chapter was the most difficult in the book to research and write. It involved finding, reading and studying practically every boys' book written by Edward Stratemeyer, close to 150. Another objective involved creating some kind of a frame of reference, letting the facts present the case, and maintaining as much objectivity as possible. A careful look at the evidence led to some rather unexpected findings, including a black Minuteman at Bunker Hill and books with black heroes written in the 1890's. Edward Stratemeyer, in his own writings, emerges as a much more liberal, tolerant and perceptive person, particularly for the period, than many have believed.

How did Stratmeyer regard the Blacks? The common reaction is to cite "Eradicate Sampson" of the Tom Swift Series, "Sam" and "Dinah" of the Bobbsey Twins or "Washington White" of the Great Marvel Series.* These series, however, were all products of the Stratemeyer Syndicate and practically all of the books were written by contract writers. True, they were Statemeyer's works in that he outlined them, contracted for the writing and edited them, but they were only a part, and a small part, of the tremendous production of the Stratemeyer Syndicate. Of more immediate interest is Edward Stratemeyer's own attitude towards blacks and to learn that we must examine his own writings.

To do this, we should establish guidelines. We should take his writings in their overall context and not depend on isolated examples. We should note the period in which the writing was done and the audience for whom the writing was intended. We must be aware of the social attitudes of the day and the common ways of portraying blacks in literature.

Edward Stratemeyer personally wrote approximately 150

*Paul C. Deane, "The Persistence of Uncle Tom: An Examination of the image of the Negro in Children's Fiction Series," Journal of Negro Education, vol. 37 (Spring 1968), p. 140; and Peter A. Soderbergh, "Bibliographical Essay: The Negro in Juvenile Series Books, 1899-1930," Journal of Negro History, vol. 58, no. 2 (April 1973), pp. 179-182.

boys' books between 1891 and 1926. This is exclusive of
titles he wrote for various Syndicate series. About forty of
these books appeared first as serials in various boys' magazines or story papers and were later reprinted in hard
cover. The stories were written to entertain and instruct.
The moral tone was high. Drinking, gambling, cheating and
reading dime novels were abominations and rewarded accord-
ingly. Courage and physical fitness were characteristics of
the heroes. The boys observed the Sabbath faithfully,
whenever possible, and went both to Sunday school and
church. Fortunately for the readers, the boys were also
involved in numerous interesting and generally believable
adventures.

Three of the books are science fiction and two are
presidential biographies, but most are stories of normal
American boys both of the then-present day and of historical
times. They were written to please the youthful audience of
the time and were highly successful. They also pleased the
critics, and, if the number of existing ex-library copies is
any indication, even some librarians. They did not ex-
pound any social gospel other than the American virtues of
moral integrity and aggressiveness.

Just what was the white American attitude towards the
black at this time? Sol Cohen has found that, "At the
beginning of the twentieth century the position the Negro
occupied in the eyes of most Americans was that of an irre-
sponsible child, incapable of self-determination and requiring
supervision by his Caucasian superiors." He notes that both
Jacob Riis and Ray Stannard Baker in well-documented
studies of attitudes of the period found this to be true.
"Thus we find that during the period 1890-1908, there was a
widespread view in the United States that the Negro race
was inferior; that the Negro was incapable of self-regulation,
self-discipline, or self-care" (Minority Stereotypes in Children's Literature: The Bobbsey Twins, 1904-1968," Educational Forum, vol. 34, no. 1 [November 1969], p. 120-121).

These perceptions could result in a standardized stereotype in at least some literature of the period; many writers
believe this to be so. Bette Preer comments, "In the earlier
books there was a definite attempt to show the Negro boy
and girl content with his [or her] lot in life, accepting
defeat, unambitious, menial, inferior in all respects" ("Guidance in Democratic Living through Juvenile Fiction," Wilson
Library Bulletin, vol. 22 [May 1948], p. 680-681). Paul
Deane notes that "Negroes have remained servants and
slaves, always in inferior positions" and "are also presented
as lazy, ignorant, good natured, cowardly; they are con-
sistently patronized" ("The Persistence...," op. cit., p.
142, 143). Cohen says, "He was a child who needed the
guidance of more mature and competent [Caucasian] persons

around him. These attitudes permeate the children's literature of this period" ("Minority Stereotypes...," op. cit., p.
121).
     The use of dialect is a separate issue. Deane believes
that dialect was "almost invariably degrading--it was a
source of humor and an indication of inferiority..." (op. cit.
p. 141). Soderbergh remarks, "The author's subconscious
contempt for the Negro manifested not only in the mutilated
dialect they chose for him ... but also in their adjectival
descriptions" ("Bibliographical Essay...," op. cit., p. 184).
His reference is to such terms as "nigger," "darky," "simple-
minded colored hands," and "hard-wukin' coon."
     We should remember that at that time dialect was ex-
pected in the portrayal of all ethnic and regional characters
and is practically worthless as a measure of attitude. There
is no general agreement as to syntax, spelling or vocabulary
of spoken American dialect and each writer was free to use
whatever struck his fancy. When O.G. Smith wrote to
Gilbert Patten in 1895 outlining his plans for the Frank
Merriwell series, he said, "It would be of advantage to the
series to have introduced the Dutchman, the Negro, the
Irishman, and any other dialect you are familiar with" (according to Harriet Hinsdale, ed., Frank Merriwell's Father,
University of Oklahoma Press, 1964, p. 175). The Vermonter had a dialect and the Virginian had a dialect, not as
ridicule, but as identification, and for "realism."
     Controversy over the use of dialect continued among
writers and librarians at least into the 1940's. The librarian
of the Chattanooga, Tennessee, Public Library made the
statement, "Dialect is the folk flavor in the speech of people
of all races; remove all this, and replace it with the 'king's
English,' and you have done away with much of the racy
tang of the expression among books and people" ("Negro
Dialect in Children's Books," Publisher's Weekly, October 18,
1941, p. 1556). Similarly, the word "nigger" was commonly
used for a member of any dark-skinned race and most users
were not conscious of its degrading and divisive overtones.
In similar fashion, the hateful appellations "wop," "dago,"
and "kike" were the familiar terms commonly if unconsciously
used for various ethnic groups. Racism as a concept occurred to few users of these terms 75 years ago.
     It is quite possible that we have stereotypes of the
stereotypes. The Comstock-era influence that has permeated
subsequent attitudes towards dime novels, story papers and
serious books has, through the "halo effect," affected some
writer's approach to the image of the black in series books.
Subliterary or "unsuitable" books would be expected to have
subliterary and unsuitable characterizations. The reader
might be interested in Anthony Comstock's Traps for the
Young (the 1967 Harvard Belknap Press edition).

A point to consider is why blacks were included in boys' books at all? Blacks were a minute portion of the reading population. The usual assumption seems to be that they are added either strictly for humor or by comparison to show the superiority of the white. This assumption will also be examined in connection with Stratemeyer's writings.

For comparison of ethnic stereotypes consider two well-known and respected writers of different periods. Frank R. Stockton's popular Rudder Grange was copyrighted in 1879, 1899 and 1907 and went through many editions. In it, the leading character wanted to rent a baby. Naturally he visited an Irish settlement to rent one.

"About three miles from our house was a settlement known as New Dublin. It was a cluster of poor and doleful houses, inhabited entirely by Irish people, whose dirt and poverty seemed to make them very contented and happy."

He went to a Mrs. Duffy. "It seemed to her like a person coming into the country to purchase weeds. Weeds and children were so abundant in New Dublin."

Several pages of Irish dialect later he rents little Pat and takes him home where he runs into some female resistance. "You really don't think," she said..., "that I will consent to your keeping such a creature as this in the house? Why, he's a regular little Paddy! If you kept him he'd grow up into a hod-carrier" (Rudder Grange, Scribner, 1907, p. 230-239). So much for the Irish.

Penrod was a popular and "high-class" book about boys by Booth Tarkington. The stories date from the 1913-1914 period. It is still in print as a paperback "classic." Herman and Verman are two black boys who have moved into a cottage across the alley from Penrod. They explain why.

"Mammy an' Queenie move in town an go git de house all fix up befo' pappy git out."

"Out of where?"

"Jail. Pappy cut a man, an' de police done kep' him in jail evuh sense Chris'mus-time; but dey goin tuhn him loose ag'in nex' week."

"What'd he cut the other man with?"

"Wif a pitchfawk."

One of the boys is tongue tied. The other has a finger missing. His brother was playing with an ax, "an I lay my finguh oh de do'-sill an' I say, 'Verman, chop 'er off!' So Verman he chop 'er right spang off up to de roots! Yessuh."

Penrod has several distasteful similes: "dogs are even more superstitious than boys and coloured people"; "the barber applied cooling lotions which made Penrod smell like a coloured housemaid's ideal"; and "the 'Slingo Sligo Slide' burst from the orchestra like the lunatic shriek of a gin-maddened nigger..." (Penrod, Scribner, 1915). There are apparently stereotypes and stereotypes.

With this background let us return to Stratemeyer. This review considered 137 of the boys' books which he wrote himself. Blacks appear in 92 of them--almost exactly two-thirds (admittedly, many of the appearances are minor). This still seems to be an unusually high rate of black visibility in boys' books written about white boys for a white readership. It is obviously not practical to use all references.

The selections included are believed to be representative of the wide variety of attitudes expressed. The subjects, times and places of Stratemeyer's books are almost unlimited. They cover many historical periods, geographical locations, all types of adventure, camping, sports, war, prep school stories and two presidential biographies. The attitudes presented towards the black race might be expected to vary somewhat with the period, locale and type of book. For this reason the references have been roughly grouped so that they have a reasonable continuity. The dates given are the earliest publication dates of the stories.

A measure of Stratemeyer's personal attitude, divorced from the setting of his stories, can be found in his presidential biographies. In his American Boys' Life of William McKinley (published in 1901), McKinley gave a speech "at his old homestead town, Niles." Hundreds of men he knew were there. "Then he discovered an old negro who used to tell the boys marvellous ghost stories, so that some of the lads would be afraid to be out after dark. The negro was now bent with age and almost blind, but he leaned there on his knotty stick, more than anxious to listen to what McKinley might have to say."

"There is also another story, told by an old coloured woman, which I think is worth relating, for it shows that this true-hearted American gentleman did not forget the poor and lowly, even though elevated to the highest office of the Nation." She stood in line on reception day waiting to "grasp the chief magistrate by the hand."

"'I dun stood dar jest like a fool,' she said, when relating her experience. 'He seemed to be sech a big man, I couldn't say nuffin nohow. He looked at me cu'rus like, an' all to once he says, "Ain't dis Mammy Tucker?" Den I most gasp fo' bref, an' I says, "Yes, dis is Mammy Tucker, Mister President," an' he give my hand a hot squeeze, an' he says, "Glad to see you, Mrs. Tucker. I hope you are well'.'"

They talk some more "'...an' den I had to pass on, wid everybody a-looking an' a-starin' and a-starin' at me, 'cause de blessed President had stopped to talk to a poor ole colored pusson like me.'"

Later McKinley gave her son, Washington, "a position as a cleaner in one of the public buildings, with a salary

upon which mother and son lived very nicely." This story
seems to reflect both the attitudes of the kindly white President and Stratemeyer towards the poor and lowly and also
the attitude of the poor and lowly towards themselves. The
job of cleaner is a realistic reflection of the times.

Stratemeyer discusses Roosevelt's work on the Civil
Service Commission from 1889-1895 in his American Boys' Life
of Theodore Roosevelt (published in 1904). "One of the best
and wisest acts of the Commission was to place the colored
employees of the government on an equal footing with the
white employees. In the past the colored employees had
occupied their places merely through the whim or good-will
of those over them. Now this was changed, and any colored
man who could pass the examination, and who was willing to
attend strictly to his labor, was as safe in his situation as
anybody."

An indication of attitudes in general is shown in this
passage: "President Roosevelt sympathized deeply with the
condition of the negroes in the South, and for the purpose
of learning the true state of affairs sent for Mr. Booker T.
Washington, one of the foremost colored men of this country
and the founder of the Tuskegee Industrial School for Colored People. They had a long conference at the White
House, which Mr. Washington enjoyed very much. For this
action many criticised the President severely, but to this he
paid no attention, satisfied that he had done his duty as his
conscience dictated."

Turning to the historical books, the Colonial Series tells
of events during the French and Indian Wars of the 1750's
and 60's, primarily on what was then the western frontier.
There are various references to blacks. On the Trail of
Pontiac, published in 1903, contains dialogue purporting to
give attitudes of the 1700's on slavery. Barringford is an
old frontiersman. Dave Morris and his cousin Henry are the
youthful heroes.

"'The blacks are naturally slaves--ain't good fer nuthin'
else,' put in Barringford, who had some old-fashioned ideas
on the subject.

"'I don't believe that, Sam,' came from Dave. 'Some
black people are wiser than you think. If they had the
chance to rise, they'd do it.'

"'I heard tell that some men believe in freeing the
blacks,' came from Henry.

"'Some of 'em don't want to be free,' said the old
frontiersman. 'Jest look at the slaves belongin' to old Lord
Fairfax, and to the Dinwiddies, and to the Washingtons.
Why, they all think it's an honor to belong to them families.
They wouldn't go if ye druv 'em away.'

"'Yes, I know, for I have talked to some of 'em myself,'
said Dave. 'The Washington blacks are particularly faithful.

If they were set free I don't suppose they'd know what to
do with themselves.'

"'They'd starve,' said Barringford.

"'But to come back to where we started from,' went on
Dave, 'There is a difference between being a white man's
slave and being an Indian captive. The whites don't kill
their slaves or torture them.'

"'They torture some of them,' replied Henry. 'I've
seen a negro whipped till it made my blood boil. Of course
the majority of 'em are treated fairly good.'"

The philosophical discussion continues but is interrupted by some wandering buffalo that have to be hunted
down.

Certain of the "Lt. Lounsberry" books, attributed to
Stratemeyer, have a Virginia setting of the same period. In
The Trader's Captive (published in 1904), George Lee is
surprised by two French sympathizers and the slave Hannibal. George attacked the slave.

"George, although well trained at rough and tumble,
was having a hard time of it. The slave, as had been
stated, was of huge build, and work on the plantations had
endued him with muscles of iron. The youth was outclassed."

After George saves Hannibal's life the slave becomes a
loyal friend. When George is trapped in the Virginia mansion of Hannibal's master, Hannibal rescues him and leads
him to safety at considerable danger to himself. "Ah couldn't
leave yo' to be killed by Marse Pory nohow, Marse Lee; but
if he evah finds out what Ah's done, he'll flay Hannibal's
black hide clean off'n him."

George is properly grateful and takes Hannibal with
him. "'Both Gov. Dinwiddie and Col. Washington will remember you for what you've done this day, Hannibal,' said
George." The blacks are slaves and portrayed as servants.
They are not, however, cowards or fools.

A few years later we find a northern black in the battle
of Bunker Hill. As described in The Minute Boys of Bunker
Hill (published in 1899), the battle has been raging fiercely
and the Americans are almost out of ammunition. The British
have finally taken the redoubt.

"'The day is ours!' The cry came from Major Pitcairn,
he who had ordered that first volley at Lexington....

"'De day ain't yours, anyway,' came softly from a negro
named Salem, and, lifting his flintlock quickly, he let fly his
last charge,--and Pitcairn never lived to view the victory he
had helped to make possible."

It may be considered a little surprising to find a turn-
of-the-century portrayal of a courageous black soldier--and
effective fighter as well--in this early northern battle of the
Revolutionary War. A more typical occupation is shown later
in the book. Roger Morse is in prison in Boston. "At the

same time the guard was reduced from twelve to six soldiers, with one negro cook to prepare the scanty food provided."

Stratemeyer reports a true incident of the Lewis and Clark expedition in Pioneer Boys of the Great Northwest (published in 1904). The time was 1804. The expedition had just met the Sioux. "At this time there occurred at the fort something which cannot be passed without mention. An aged Indian chief of the Minnetarees paid the expedition a visit, and after being received with distinction said he had been told that there was with the party a person who was entirely black. 'It is quite true,' said Captain Lewis.

"The chief said he would like to see the person, and York, the negro body servant, was brought forward. The aged chief was very much astonished, and tried to rub the black off with his finger, thinking it was paint. But when he saw the wooly head of the negro he was convinced that the man was really different from any he had ever seen or heard of, and he went away much mystified."

The boys of Pioneer Boys of the Gold Fields (published in 1906) are treed by some bloodhounds but rescued by a negro slave. "'What fo' you-uns come ashoah?' asked the voice, and now a burly negro put in an appearance under the tree. He had a smoky barn lantern in one hand and a stout club in the other."

When the negro was convinced they meant no harm he called off the bloodhounds, rescued the boy's scow, took them to the house where "Aunt Kate," the black cook, fed them, and let them spend the night.

Defending His Flag was written as a serial for "American Boy," expanded and published (in 1907) in hardcover as a quality "single" under Stratemeyer's own name. It is much longer than his other works and was never included in any series. The characterizations of the blacks are not flattering and some of the stereotyping is pronounced. Whether he is attempting to show Civil War attitudes realistically or whether the book reflects his own attitudes or the prevailing attitudes of 1907, is not clear.

Since this is the story of the Civil War it would be expected to find blacks in it and they are in evidence throughout the book. Louis Rockford is in the Union army and Andy Arlington in the Confederate army so their attitudes might vary. Most of the action takes place in the South.

Louis is about to be "cooled off" in a watering trough by Southerners. Andy's father, Mr. Arlington, is inquiring about him. "'Dey is dun gwine ter duck him,' explained a darky, who sat on the edge of the store stoop, too lazy to get up and witness proceedings." It is not a very flattering picture.

Once when Louis was tied up in an old mill "he heard a

broad, negro voice singing loudly..." so he called for help.
"'Wot's dat?'
"'Help me! I am tied up in the mill!'
"'Golly, who is yo'?' There was a crashing through the
woods and presently a tall darky, weighing all of two hun-
dred pounds, blocked up the entrance to the mill. 'Golly,
yere's a bit of work!'
"'Release me, will you?' asked Louis, eagerly.
"'Who tied yo' up like dat, massa??'
"'Some rascals who robbed me of my watch and money.
Cut that rope. I am almost perished with cold.'
"The negro cut the rope and released Louis and Louis
thanked him.
"'Dat's all right, massa--glad to do yo' a good turn,
sah. Yere, let me help yo' fasten dat old saddle, sah--seein'
it's de best yo' got left, sah,' and the pondrous black friend
went to work with a will. ... The negro watched him out of
sight and then went on his way, singing as before, as
though to forget the discomforts of the storm in melody."
     Andy, the Southerner, has a different experience. He
was spending the night at Parker's Mills. "Parker's Mills
was full of slaves, and it had been whispered about that
there was fear of an uprising among the colored folks. For
this reason every slave was watched closely, and if any were
found to be at all rebellious, they were chained up and
subjected to severe lashings."
     About 11 he heard a violent struggle and went down
stairs "to find the master of the house, a Mr. Rockleigh,
struggling valiantly in the grasp of two burly negroes who
were his slaves. The negroes had contemplated flight, but
before going had sneaked into the house in an attempt to
steal some money which had been left in an old-fashioned
secretary in the room."
     "'Let go, Pomp,' gasped Mr. Rockleigh. 'Let go, or
sure as I live I'll flay you alive for this.'
     "'Dun yo let go, Pomp,' put in one of the burly negroes.
'We is in dis to de end, remember!'
     "'I ain't a-lettin' go, Cuffy,' replied Pomp. 'Now,
Massa Rockleigh, yo' quit yo' noise, or I'll knock yo' ober de
head wid dis yere club. We ... is bound to hab our own
way.'
     "'You--you scoundrels!' cried the master, but even as
he spoke the club descended and the man of the house fell
back partly unconscious from a blow upon the head."
     Andy appears on the scene with a pistol. "'Don't--don't
shoot me!' yelled Cuffy, in abject terror. "Please, massa
sodger, don't shoot!" and he dropped upon his knees. He
could stand almost anything but a display of firearms.
     "'Cuffy, yo' is a fool!' howled Pomp. 'Come on, if yo'
is gwine wid me. Remember, if we is cotched now we'll be

more dan half-killed wid de lash. Take dat.'" He hurled a
heavy club at Andy who promptly shot him in the shoulder
but both slaves ran away.

One presumes that this interchange was intended to be
a reasonable picture both of blacks and Southern whites of
the period. It is not flattering of either. Cuffy is not
particularly brave, at least in front of a gun, but neither is
he a caricature. Pompey escapes but Cuffy is captured,
"chained up in one of the barns and flogged until he dropped
like one dead, from exhaustion and loss of blood."

This surprises Andy. "At home Andy had never experienced any difficulty with his father's slaves, for the colored
people were well cared for and were too happy to create any
disturbances." He thought "there was not a man or woman
on the Arlington plantation who would not have been willing
to lay down his or her life for any member of the family."

Andy belongs to the Confederate "Montgomery Grays."
"The cook was a fat darky known as Mungo, a jolly fellow
who sang from morning to night, and who could play a banjo
to perfection."

Andy is attempting to escape from the enemy when he
finds himself "face to face with a short, broad-faced, and
not unpleasant-looking negro." He forces the negro to guide
him to a cabin where an old woman gives him food.

"'Tom is a Virginia nigger, isn't he?' asked Andy and
confirmed that he was a runaway slave. Tom then takes off
with Andy's horse. "'That negro has outwitted me!'" Andy
runs after Tom and horse and they have words.

"...'You're a runaway nigger, and if you don't stop I'll
put a bullet through you.'

"...'If yo' shoot de Yankees will be down on yo' afo'
yo' kin turn yo'self,' answered the negro...."

Andy gets his horse back by a ruse but Tom is no
quitter. "'I'll git dem Union sodgers after yo' in no time!'
he sang out as he disappeared. Reaching the cabin again,
he found the old woman at the doorway, still smoking her
pipe. 'Got back your hoss, eh?' she said. 'That nigger is
a sly one.'"

We may note that the term "nigger" is used more in this
book than in most of Stratemeyer's stories. Andy is a
Southerner and the action is in Virginia. A reasonable
inference might be that it is used for realism.

Blacks are not portrayed in the Indian wars with Custer
but make up for it in the Spanish American War. Stratemeyer
wrote a number of books about this conflict with action both
in Cuba and the Philippines.

Walter has been serving on the Brooklyn in Fighting
in Cuban Waters (published in 1899). He is sick and has
become lost in the wilds of Cuba.

"He roused up to find a tall, fine-looking negro shaking

him."   Carlos Dunetta, the negro, is a spy for the Cuban
army.   He takes Walter on his back to his sister Josefina's
hut who takes care of him.   Josefina was "a short, fat negro
wench."   "Usually negro huts in Cuba are dirty and full of
vermin, but this was an exception.   In her younger days,
Josefina had worked for a titled lady of Santiago, and there
had learned cleanliness quite unusual to those of her
standing."   This, apparently, is intended to be a sympa-
thetic and factual portrayal.
        Spaniards follow Carlos to the hut.   Carlos and Walter
are hidden but when the Spaniards threaten Josefina, Carlos
goes to her defense and is shot, but not killed.   Walter is
found and the group is taken to the Spanish camp.   That
night, "Walter felt a hand steal over his shoulder."
        "'What do you think--we run for it, maybe?' whispered
Carlos.   'I'd like to run but we may get shot,' whispered
Walter in return.
        "At this Carlos shrugged his shoulders.   With two
Mauser bullets in him the tall negro rebel was still 'game.'
It was such men as he who had kept this unequal warfare in
Cuba going for three long years despite Spain's utmost
endeavors to end the conflict."   Carlos takes the initiative,
shoots the Spanish guard and captain dead, and they escape.
Eventually Carlos's brother guides Walter back to the shore.
Carlos makes Walter look like a piker!
        Captain Ponsberry in Under Dewey at Manila (published
in 1898) is annoyed with the Kanaka stevedores at Hawaii.
"'Consarn 'em!   Give me a white man for stevedore work,
every time.   The wust of 'em are worth three niggers!'"
The comment is in keeping with Captain Ponsberry's character as a bluff old salt.
        The jingoistic attitudes expressed by his crew are
typical of the time.   Hobson, an English sailor, and Striker,
a New England Yankee, are talking about modern battleships.
"'I've been told the Chinese and Japanese used some of 'em
during their late war, but them heathens don't count--not
alongside o' Anglo-Saxon blood; eh, Hobson?'"
        "'I grant you that, every time, Striker,--Anglo-Saxon
blood every trip,--against the world,' cried the Englishman,
heartily.   'Now you take it among ourselves,' he went on,
after a pause.   'The Americans and English and Germans,
and even the French, can get along together; but put a
Spaniard or a Portugese or an Italian, or one of that kind of
fellows aboard and there's trouble right away--I've seen it a
hundred times.'"
        Grandon says, "'Wish the captain had taken an English-
man or an American instead.   I can't bear those Norwegians
nor Poles nor Russians.'"   They are not a particularly
liberal crew.
        Stratemeyer's   Pan-American   series   "embraces sight-

seeing and adventures" in Central and South America. In Lost on the Orinoco (published in 1902), the boys visit Curacao.

"'I see a lot of negroes,' observed Mark....

"'The population is mostly of colored blood,' answered the professor. 'The colored people are all free, yet the few Dutchmen that are here are virtually their masters. The negroes work in the phosphate mines, and their task is harder than that of a Pennsylvania coal miner ten times over.'"

In Venezuela, "A little negro boy went around with them. He had learned to say 'Yes, mistair,' and 'No, mistair,' and he repeated these over and over again, each time bowing profoundly and rolling his eyes in a truly comical fashion. The boy's name was Bulo, and our friends took to him from the start." When the boy laughed he showed "two rows of pure white ivories."

In Young Explorers of the Isthmus (published in 1903), the boys visit Nicaragua. "'This soil would produce good crops of many things,' said the professor, as they rode along. 'But the average [Nicaraguan] Indian and negro is of a lazy nature and will not do more than is absolutely necessary. As for the better class of Nicaraguans, they will not settle in this section'...."

In Young Explorers of the Amazon (published in 1904), the boys were watching coffee being loaded on ships in Santos, Brazil. "The loading was done mostly by negroes, strong fellows, who thought nothing of carrying two bags of coffee weighing over two hundred and fifty pounds on their heads and shoulders...." Later they visit Bahia. "'Somebody was telling me about the blacks of Bahia,' said Frank. 'Are they a superior people?'"

"The population of Bahia is about half black and mulatto, and the black people are to a large extent superior to many others of the same race. Many of them are well formed and really handsome, and you will find a large number who are well educated. Their being educated is due to the fact that Bahia is second to no other city in Brazil in ecclesiastical institutions and church schools.

"They found the docks piled high with merchandise of all descriptions and negro stevedores and porters were in evidence everywhere. 'Business is certainly humming here,' observed Frank. 'And the blacks are as big and burly as one could imagine.'"

The black doesn't do too well in several books of this series. The references to such occupations as stevedoring, mining and shoe-shining are presumably factual. The comical little negro boy with his two rows of pure white ivories was a pretty standard stereotype--along with the average Indian's and negro's being lazy and the notion that steve-

dores sang and were happy. The references to the blacks
of Bahia show an awareness of differences but contain the
implication that if these blacks are superior many others of
the race are pretty inferior.

Let us examine one of Stratemeyer's science fiction
books for references to blacks. In The Wizard of the Sea,
written in 1895, three boys are having some problems with
the whites. Their sloop had been run down by the ship
Golden Cross, whose captain's name was Savage. So was the
captain. Mont (principal hero) was being flogged when the
process was interrupted to rescue another castaway from a
floating chicken coop. He turned out to be Dr. Homer
Woddle, the Secretary of the Society for the Exploration of
the Unknown Parts of the World. His ship had been sunk
by a giant submarine monster. Oddly enough, the submarine monster soon appeared in the neighborhood and Dr.
Woddle and the three boys set out in a small boat to "lay the
mighty brute low." The brute objected, rammed the ship,
killed all on board and swamped the small boat. "Mont found
himself struggling in the sea, and wondered what had become of his companions. 'Hang those monsters of the deep,'
he said to himself; 'I don't like them'."

He is hardly to be blamed. Needless to say the four
are rescued by the monster, which turns out to be a submarine manned by a mysterious Captain Vindex and a crew
of 12 blacks. The submarine was built "on a desert island
in the Pacific. I had the various parts brought in a vessel
that belonged to me from various parts of the world, and the
twelve negroes who are now with me were my only workmen."

Our heroes meet Captain Vindex and one of the crew:
"Of the two who had entered one was a negro, with intelligent but flat face, and short, woolly hair. The other was a
tall, handsome white man, with keen, searching eyes that
looked into the very soul."

John Stumpton, or Stump, the hired hand and devoted
follower of Mont, keeps exclaiming, "I know I'm only an odd
boy," and proves it regularly. He is determined to break
out of the submarine. "'If four Americans aren't a match for
a lot of niggers, and one Unknown who can't speak any
language, and doesn't belong to any country at all, it's time
we shut up shop!' went on Stump. At that moment the door
opened, and the negro who had before appeared entered.
Stump instantly threw himself upon him, and, seizing his
throat with his two hands, held him so tightly as almost to
strangle him. But being a powerful man, he soon disengaged
himself, and a fearful struggle ensued between them. 'Help,
help!' cried the negro, in excellent English."

Stump's actions are hardly fitting from one whose life
has just been saved--but fitting of Stump. The crew's
English deteriorates rapidly in later pages.

Later, the group is attacked by savages known as Papouans. "They were tall, handsome men, with an erect bearing, their features well chiseled. In their ears they wore rings of bone." The Captain is about to resume the voyage. "'And the niggers?' said Mont. 'The Papouans?' replied the captain, shrugging his shoulders..." (and apparently correcting Mont for his choice of words).

This problem was simply solved by electrifying the ship and repelling the Papouans through shocks. The rest of the adventures proceed in a manner strongly reminiscent of Jules Verne and need not concern us. The points that can be noted here are that the entire crew is black yet capable of building a fantastic submarine and operating it under the direction of an eccentric white captain. They use deep sea diving outfits for underwater exploration and perform their duties as well as anyone could be expected to. They are neither cowards, villains nor fools, although their speech leaves something to be desired.

The three prep school series--Rover Boys, Putnam Hall and Dave Porter-- have many generally minor references to blacks.

The comic relief and scapegoat of the boys' tricks at Putnam Hall is Peleg Snuggers, general utility man. He is a pretty simple person and not particularly capable--he is also white. Blacks are found as cooks and waiters. In Putnam Hall Rebellion (1909) the boys are being starved by Josiah Crabtree, a villainous teacher, but have outwitted the management and stolen considerable food. Crabtree is investigating.

"'We are following your ordars, sah,' declared the head waiter. 'Right or wrong, we are following 'em.' 'Don't you think I am in the right?' demanded Josiah Crabtree, sourly. At this the colored man shrugged his shoulders. 'That is fo' Cap'n Putnam to say, sah.' 'Ha! then you side with the boys, eh?' 'I ain't sidin' at all, sah. I obeys orders, that's all, sah.'"

When a watch is stolen in Putnam Hall Mystery (1911), suspicion falls on the servants, who are both black and white. Crabtree comments, "'Perhaps some of the new colored help took the watch'...." Crabtree doesn't like blacks but then he doesn't like anybody. It develops that the watch was stolen by a wicked white Putnam Hall student.

This series finds blacks in such occupations as pullman porter, waiter, "man of all work," manager of a hotel garage and livery driver. The roles are minor. The attitude seems to be that these were simply typical occupations for the blacks at that time.

The Rover Boys series is similar as far as the role of the black is concerned. Peleg Snuggers is still general

utility man and butt of the boys' tricks at Putnam Hall.
Blacks are still waiters. The student body and faculty are
all white. A notable variation, however, is the introduction
of Alexander Pop. He probably comes the closest to the
standard negro stereotype of the "faithful, devoted and
superstitious servant" in Stratemeyer's writings. However,
looking beyond the stereotypes, Aleck is capable, honest and
self-respecting, in spite of his referring to himself as a
"nigger" and "coon."

He is first a waiter at Putnam Hall. In The Rover
Boys at School (1899) Aleck "was a short, fat fellow, the
very embodiment of good nature." He is described differently in The Rover Boys in Camp (1904): "A box wagon
came dashing up to the depot platform, with a tall, good-
looking colored man on the seat."

In The Rover Boys in the Jungle (1899) Aleck is accused of robbing the boys of Putnam Hall. The loot has
been planted in his trunk. "'I dun' reckon sumbuddy put
up a job on dis poah coon, sah,' he continued ruefully. 'I
believe the job was put up by yourself,' answered Captain
Putnam sternly. 'If you are guilty you had better confess.' A
stormy war of words followed. Alexander Pop stoutly declared himself innocent, but in the face of the proofs discovered the master of the Hall would not listen to him. Many
were astonished to learn that he was thought guilty, but a
few declared that a 'coon wasn't to be trusted anyway.'
"'Niggers are all thieves,' said Jim Caven. 'I never yet
saw an honest one.' 'I don't believe you!' burst out Tom.
'Pop's a first-rate fellow, and the captain has got to have
more proof against him before I'll believe him guilty.' ...
'Yes, I think he's as honest as you are!' burst out Tom....."

Jim Caven attacks Tom and they begin to fight. "'I'm
going to give you the worst thrashing you ever had,' said
Caven, but in rather a nervous tone. 'All right, Caven, go
ahead and do it,' cried Tom. 'I will stand up for Aleck
Pop, and--there you are!'" The fight is inconclusive, Aleck
is hauled off to jail but escapes and "ships on one of the
outward-bound ocean vessels."

At about the same time the Rovers made a trip to Africa
to look for their father. They rescued Aleck in mid-ocean
and he accompanied them to the Congo as valet for the
crowd. Aleck doesn't do so badly in Africa. He thwarts a
plot against Randolph Rover and the boys. He "had his ear
clipped by a bullet from Captain Villaire's pistol" but did his
part in the fighting. Josiah Crabtree knocked Dick Rover
into a gully and almost killed him but Dick escaped. When he
met Crabtree again he told him, "'I am going to thrash you
to the very best of my ability, and after that, if I meet you
again I'll--I'll--' 'Dun shoot him on sight,' suggested Aleck."

When the party is surrounded and attacked by black

savages, "'I think a concerted volley from our pistols and guns will check their movements,' came from Rand. 'Dat's de talk!' cried Aleck. 'Give it to 'em hot!'" They did and routed King Susko and the savages.

It is eventually discovered that the white cadet Jim Caven had stolen the boys' jewelry and "The captain [Putnam] apologized handsomely to Aleck for the way he had treated the colored man."

"Alexander Pop remained in the employ of the two elder Rovers," however, for the remainder of the 27 books in the series. Mr. Rover thought enough of his ability in The Rover Boys out West (1900) that he sent him to Cedarville for protection.

When the boys returned home in The Rover Boys in the Mountains (1902), "There was a warm greeting from Randolph Rover also, and then the boys turned indoors, to greet faithful Alexander Pop and the others who worked about the place."

"'Yo' is a sight fo' soah eyes, 'deed yo' is, boys,' said the colored man. 'I can't tell you how much I's missed yo'!' And his face shone like a piece of polished ebony."

The black is shown in many situations in Stratemeyer's individual stories. Representative examples follow: A key to a closet was missing in The Missing Tin Box (1893). Hardwick, one of the villains, comments, "Perhaps Jackson carted it off. He's an odd sort of a coon." Jackson is apparently the janitor or caretaker of the gambling establishment. There is also a negro doorman.

The Young Auctioneers (1894) has several references to blacks which need to be considered in the total context of the book. The young auctioneers have a bad scrape with three tramps who try to hold them up. The three "would-be plunderers" are white. A jewelry store is robbed by Old Joe Yedley; he is captured and sent to jail for one year; he is white. A thief steals their horse, wagon and good; he is captured and confined; he is white.

Then, in Easton, Pennsylvania, among the crowd in their auction house "were four tall and rather ugly-looking colored men. They shoved their way forward rudely, causing some timid customers to leave in a hurry, and began to laugh and joke among themselves in a loud and coarse manner. 'I am afraid we are going to have trouble with those chaps,' whispered Matt to his partner. 'They have been drinking, and they are out for a lark.'"

Two of the black men then broke one of the showcases, and denied it. "'I won't pay for nuffin!' growled the ringleader of the quartet. 'I dun reckon somebody else in the crowd broke the glass." 'Cos da did,' replied another of the colored men. 'Maybe yo' think yo' kin lay it on us just because we is colored, hey?'

"'Not at all; a colored man can be as much of a gentleman as any one--if he wishes to be,' put in Andy. 'Do
youse mean to insinuate dat we ain't gen'men?' questioned
one of the crowd roughly. 'You are not gentlemen when you
break glass and refuse to pay for it,' returned Andy. 'That
glass is worth at least a dollar, and unless it is paid for,
somebody will be handed over to the police.'
    "'Huh! do yo' fink yo' kin scare us, boss?' 'Yo' say
another word an' we'll do up de hull place! ... We is as
good as any white trash, remember dat!'"
    One thing lead to another and the ringleader "made a
movement as if to strike the young auctioneer in the face."
At this point the police arrived, the blacks paid for the
showcase and left. But this wasn't the end of the problem.
On their way to Bethlehem they ran upon "three of the
colored men who had created the disturbance in the store."
Matt is attacked but escapes.
    "'Those negroes!' gasped Matt.... 'Come on, don't
wait, for they are three to two, and are just drunk enough
to be as ugly as sin!'" They stopped at the next farmhouse
to ask directions. "'By the way,' he went on, 'do you know
anything of the negroes that live in the cottage back a
ways?' The woman's face lost its smile and she sighed.
'Yes, I know them only too well,' she replied. 'They have
stolen so many of our chickens and so much garden truck
that my husband is going to make a complaint against them.
I wish they would leave the neighborhood.'"
    There are several interesting points in these scenes.
There are more white villains than black. The blacks are
not shown as comics or fools or stupid. They are under the
influence of drink which is made to seem at least partly
responsible for their actions. They are a pretty worthless
bunch who steal chickens and fresh vegetables but certainly
not as bad as the white villains who end up in jail. They
are also aggressive and dangerous and as worthy protagonists for our heroes as the white villains. The most interesting dialogue, particularly for 1894, is the references to
"gentlemen" and the implication that it is behavior and not
"color" that makes the difference.
    In Larry the Wanderer (1894) we find that "As he
approached the house he saw an old colored man sitting on
the porch bench, talking to Howard Bruin." (In other
words, a black sitting on the front porch with the white
owner.) "'Larry, here's a messenger to see you,' said the
artist. 'This is Abe Jackson. He works for Mrs. Noxwell."
    "'Am yo' de young gen'man wot saved Miss Maud?'
asked the negro, rising. 'Well, I did something of that
sort,' replied Larry modestly. 'Den, Mrs. Noxwell tole me to
tell yo' dat she'd be mighty pleased if yo' would cum up to
de house and call on her.'"

Abe wasn't afraid to speak his mind about his employer.
"'She am a werry close pussun,' said Abe Jackson. 'I
reckon she's about de closes' pussun you' kin meet in a
day's trabels.'" He had additional blunt comments. Outside
of the ever-present dialect there is nothing to distinguish
him from a white in a similar situation. He doesn't even call
Larry "sah."

Pickles Johnsing plays a prominent part in The Tour of
the Zero Club (1894). He was "a stout, round-faced colored
boy, with big red lips, and teeth which reminded one very
forcibly of double-blank dominoes set in twin rows. He was a
very willing and decent sort of young darky, and had many
friends in the little river town in which my story for the
present is located." His description is not flattering although his behavior is.

Our heroes invite him to ride with them in a toboggan
race. The villains are annoyed. "'Humph! If he ain't
going to take that coon on the trip!' sneered Pete Sully.
'You ain't racing niggers, are you, Pete?' questioned one of
his followers. 'I don't know as I am,' returned Pete Sully,
slowly.

"He walked over to where Harry sat on his toboggan.
'I expected to race white fellows,' he remarked, sourly.
'Pickles is all right,' said Jack Bascoe. 'He's the dark horse
to win. If you are going to race, get ready, for Harry isn't
going to wait all night for you.'"

So the boys race and Pickles does his part. "'Sit jess
a little moah to de front,' was Pickles' suggestion, and it
was immediately acted upon." Somewhat later the boys get
into a snowball fight. "Jack and Andy Bascoe had just
arrived on the scene, followed up by Pickles Johnsing, the
colored youth. These three were not slow to take in the
situation, and they sailed in vigorously. 'Dis am most lubly
sport!' cried Pickles. 'How yo' like dat, Sully? Ki!hi!
Ain't dat jess elegant, Dixon? An heah's one fo' you, Len
Spencer, fo' callin' me a coon!' And Pickles rushed to the
front, followed by Andy and Jack, and compelling Sully and
his crowd to retreat in spite of themselves."

This is pretty heady stuff for 1894--a black boy who
resents being called a coon and leads white boys in an attack
on other whites. He does even better later on. The villains
had stolen the boys' ice boat, Pickles had put them on the
track of it and gone along to help get it back. They had
recovered the ice boat and were preparing to sail home
"when Sully rushed up and tried to hit Jack in the head
with his fist."

"Pickles sprang forward and pushed the bully's arm
aside. Then he let out with his own fist, and down went
Sully flat on his back, while the Icicle sailed off, leaving

Dixon and Spencer staring at the fate of their leader in
dumb amazement."

The boys want to reward him and he pleads to be taken
on their trip. "'Say, why can't yo' fellahs take me along!'
he burst out suddenly. 'Ebery fust-class camp hab got to
hab a cook an' general util'ty man around.... I ain't much
wid a gun, but I kin trap t'ings, and yo' all knows wot I
kin do fishin' and spearin'. It an't fo' de likes of yo' to
wash de dishes and sech, an--an', to tell de truf, I wants
to go powerful bad! ... An' I kin take my banjo and mouf
harmonica along,' went on the colored youth. 'Da will come
in mighty handy-like to help kill de long evenings.'"

The boys like Pickles, "who had always stood by them
and done them more than one favor," and include him on the
excursion. As they were sailing down the river they heard
"a dismal howl that caused nearly everyone to jump in alarm.
'My gracious! what was that?' exclaimed Andy. 'Dat must
be a ghost, suah!' cried Pickles, as he sprang away from
the voice." It turned out to be the bark of a fox. As
noted later in the book, "Pickles was a firm believer in
spirits."

The following day the trip began in earnest. "'Dis am
de most glorious trip wot ever was, by golly!' cried Pickles,
as he shoved on ahead of the rest, dragging the sled behind
him. 'Dis coon is werry glad he is alibe jess about now,
boys!'" He can call himself a coon but no one else can.

"And in the exuberance of his spirits, Pickles broke
out into an old darky refrain about the history and death of
a wonderful 'Blue-tail Fly,' the chorus to which was so
catchy that they were soon every one of them singing it.
'I'm glad he came along,' whispered Jack to Harry. 'He'll
make days we can't go out seem shorter.' 'So am I, Jack,
Pickles is just the fellow for this crowd.'"

The boys go hunting and are attacked by wolves.
"Finally [the wolf] sprang at Jack, but just then came an
unexpected shot from one side. It was so close it caused
the wolf to drop almost at the boy's feet. He gave a yelp,
turned over once or twice, and was dead. They looked
around and saw Pickles standing there, a smoking shotgun
in his hands, and grinning from ear to ear. 'Dat's de time
dat wolf got dun up fo' keeps,' remarked the colored youth.
'Good for you, Pickles!' cried Jack, gratefully. 'You saved
my life!'"

In a later episode the boys are taken for chicken
thieves. Andy asked indignantly, "'Do we look like chicken
thieves?' 'Wall, I reckon a coon makes a good hen lifter!'
laughed the smallest of the farmers, with a nod towards
Pickles, which made the colored youth mad clear to his
heels.

"'Look heah!' he cried out, shaking his gun threateningly, 'yo' can't consult me dat way, yo' low down white trash! A chicken lifter, indeed! Moah likely yo' is one yourself!' 'What's thet? Don't yeou talk tew me!' roared the farmer, bristling up like a turkey cock. Maybe yeou don't know who yeou be atalkin' to?' 'I don't know, nor care!' retorted Pickles. 'I ain't no chicken lifter, an' if yo' go fo' to say so, yo'll git yo'self into a big muss wid me!'"

These are pretty strong words for a black youth of that time, but Pickle refuses to be "typical." There are certainly stereotypes of the period in the book, the description of Pickles, Pickles' fear of ghosts, the idea of blacks and chicken stealing and the love of singing, among others, but generally speaking Pickles appears in a very favorable light. He goes hunting with Boxy and the two of them shoot a deer. He shows the boys how to spear fish and how to make and use traps. He is unlettered and uncouth, perhaps, but he is a real person.

An unusual hero also appeared in The Young Oarsmen of Lakeview (1895). Blumpo Brown is part Indian and part black. "And now what of Blumpo Brown, you ask? There is little to tell at this point of our story concerning that semi-colored individual. He was alone in the world, and had lived in Lakeview some ten years. ... He was a very peculiar youth, often given to making the most ridiculous remarks...."

Blumpo wants to go on a camping trip with the boys. "'I'm not rich, nor eddicated, as you call it, and all that, but I can hunt and fish, and so on, as good as the next feller, can't I?' 'You certainly can,' put in Jerry, who had for a long time had a strange liking for the homeless youth. 'And I am as willing as the next one to do my full share of camp work--washing dishes and the like,' went on Blumpo. 'You ain't cut out for that,' he added...."

The upshot of the matter is that Blumpo goes on the trip. The "homeless youth" is a strange mixture of cowardice, bluster and bravery. He relapses into dialect on occasion, particularly when frightened. The boys go to Hermit Island. While camping there they discover the hermit. "All of the boys stared at him in blank amazement. He was a reddish-black individual, with snow white hair and long flowing beard. ... Blumpo grew so frightened that he immediately fell on his knees. 'Dee voodoo doctor, suah!' he muttered. Like many other ignorant people, he was very superstitious and believed in charms and voodooism."

The boys talk with the hermit, who speaks excellent English. It shortly develops that he is Blumpo's father. He has become a hermit because he thinks Blumpo is dead. The boys "found that the old man had quite a comfortable place among the rocks. It was elaborately furnished, showing that the hermit was well-to-do. Blumpo could scarcely believe his ears. His face began to expand, and a smile broke out on it, the like of which had never before been seen. He was a homeless waif no longer. He had found a father."

The hermit decided "he would build a cabin down by the lakeside and there he and Blumpo could live like ordinary people. 'I have several thousand dollars saved up,' he said, 'so we will not want for anything. I will buy a boat, and Blumpo can make a living by letting her out to pleasure parties.' 'Dat will suit me exactly,' cried Blumpo.

"'But you must also go to school in the winter,' went on Daniel Brown. 'And you must drop that dialect, and not say dat for that.'" Not only does Blumpo's black-Indian father speak perfect English, but he expects Blumpo to learn to do the same, the implication being that education, not race, is responsible for the dialect.

When the boys left for Lakeview the hermit went along, "and created some surprise when he appeared on the streets of Lakeview with Blumpo, his son. ... All the boys were glad that the homeless youth had found a father, who would endeavor to make something out of the good-natured and honest lad."

Blumpo did well with his boat. "'Blumpo is making money,' said Harry, 'and I am glad of it.' 'So am I,' replied our hero. 'He is an odd sort of chap, but his heart is of gold.'"

Mark Dale of Mark Dale's Stage Venture fame had a bit of a run-in with a black in an 1895 serial. He had previously been involved with a rascally lawyer (white), two wicked actors (white) and assorted miscellaneous villains (all white). He was robbed by an Italian and imprisoned by a Jewish pawnbroker. He had his problems. However, when he is searching for Marie Oldham, the heroine who has been abducted by the white rascals, he finds her in the custody of Sal Peters.

"'She de old colored gal was run out of de town half-a-dozen times.' 'She is a bad woman, then?' 'Der wurst yer ever seen, boss. She just as lief as not hit yer wid a stove plate or brick or anything she kin lay hands on. She drove her husband away more than a year ago, and not one of de neighbors kin git along wid her'."

It was a rough fight. Mark had great difficulty overcoming Sal Peters who almost brained him with her cane but finally escaped with Marie. At that point the villainous actor (white) showed up again and sat on Mark while Sal Peters recaptured Marie. Providentially Mr. Oldham appeared and, "A swift blow hurled the colored woman in the gutter, and Marie was free." Then he rescued Mark and they had the villain arrested and sent back to prison again.

Sal Peters was no worse than "Mother Caracas" an "old

Italian woman" to whom the malefactors had previously entrusted Marie. "Her face was wrinkled, her teeth gone, and her whole manner betokened avarice and cruelty. ... No pen could describe the sufferings the little actress had endured since she had been abducted."

What is the significance of this? Racially, the Italian was as bad as the black. There is no thought of the black woman's being incompetent or amusing. She happens to be a villain but an experienced and competent villain to whom the white abductors could safely entrust Marie. Again, she is a person, she is a worthy opponent, and she happens to be black.

References to blacks appear occasionally in unexpected places. In To Alaska for Gold (1899) both the heroes and rascals are white. Fred Dobson, the Squire's runaway son from Maine, follows our heroes to Alaska, arriving in pitiful shape. "'I came up by the way of Chilkoot Pass,' he said, when he felt able to speak. 'I joined a party I met in Juneau, a crowd of men from Chicago, and they promised to see me through if I would do my share of the work. But the work was too hard for me, and they treated me like a dog, and at Baker's Creek they kicked me out of camp and compelled me to shift for myself.' ... '...Cooking was the one thing I learned coming up here,' Fred explained. 'There was a negro in the party who had been a chef in a Chicago hotel; and he was the one soul in the crowd that treated me half decently.'"

Here is a black who had apparently held a responsible job, who was an equal member with the whites of his gold rush party, who was kind to the castaway when the whites were abusive and who took time to teach him to cook.

These quotations, selected from the boys' books written by Edward Stratemeyer, show a variety of attitudes. Some of the questions referred to in the beginning together with possible answers follow:

Is there a standard or common stereotype of the black in Stratemeyer's books? There is not. There are brave blacks and cowardly blacks. There is a hero at Bunker Hill and there are gallant black patriots in Cuba. There is also a black horse thief in Oklahoma and a black sneak thief in New York. Blacks are given major roles in two of the books.

Is the black portrayed as a comic character? Practically never, certainly no more so than his white counterparts. He may be shown occasionally as a devoted servant contented with his "place" but he is not pictured as a comic clown.

Is the black shown as lazy? The quotations show only two actual examples of this. The trait is certainly not emphasized.

Does Stratemeyer use dialect as an indication of low mentality? No, he does not. Blumpo's father specifically refers to education as a means of eliminating dialect and improving speech. Jews, Italians, Germans and Irish all use dialect.

Is the black portrayed as happy and carefree? Yes, to some extent. There are various references to singing, the playing of musical instruments and a relaxed attitude towards life.

Is the black portrayed as doing menial work? Generally, yes, by modern standards, although many exceptions have been quoted. By the standards of the day, however, as noted in the excerpt from the Life of McKinley, the portrayals were intended to represent real life job opportunities for the blacks. We must remember that so-called menial work was a way of life in this country for people of all races at that time.

Certainly there are stereotyped incidents but Stratemeyer shows a great deal of awareness of the black as a person. His attitude seems basically friendly and positive. He is never vicious, for example, as Tarkington is. He undoubtedly reflects to some extent the benevolent paternalism of the kindly and enlightened white of that time, but this is a far cry from the stereotypes that critics Cohen and Deane discuss (see the beginning of the chapter). There are a number of black villains and there are a number of white villains. When cast as villains the blacks perform as well as their white counterparts. Stratemeyer seems to take the black seriously and certainly to be conscious of him. In sum, it would seem that Stratemeyer in his own writings of boys' books appears as unusually objective and liberal for the times in his literary treatment of the blacks.

Part Five. Stratemeyer Bibliography.

INTRODUCTION AND
PUBLISHING HISTORY

It is to be hoped that Harriet Adams, in her definitive history of the Stratemeyer Syndicate, will list all the series published both by her father and, later, herself. No accurate and complete listing exists, outside of the Syndicate offices. The common series are legion--Bunny Brown, Honeybunch, Bobbsey Twins, Six Little Bunkers, Tom Swift, Hardy Boys, Ruth Fielding, Nancy Drew, and the Dana Girls are some of the more obvious--but what about the uncommon series? The Young Reporter and Dick Hamilton series under Howard Garis's name were both Syndicate series. The "Payson" Boy Scout Series have been reported as Syndicate but they definitely were not. Stratemeyer published very little with a Scout theme, for good reason (see Chapter III).

It is possible, however, to trace the majority of Edward Stratemeyer's personal series and also the individual boys' books written by him under various pen names. Many of these first appeared in story papers or magazines and were reprinted in hard cover.

The Bibliography that follows this Introduction is pioneering in the sense that it attempts to show both the origins and publishing history of nearly all early boys' books actually written by Stratemeyer. The majority predate the Syndicate (1904.) The supplemental listing of hardcover books first published as serials should be a help to the growing number of Stratemeyer collectors.

In recent years many articles have appeared on Nancy Drew, Tom Swift, the Hardy Boys and the Bobbsey Twins. These articles generally discuss the modern series and sometimes the methods and operations of the Stratemeyer Literary Syndicate. They seldom give much attention to the writings of Edward Stratemeyer himself, especially his early writings. From 1889 to the formation of the Literary Syndicate in about 1904, however, Stratemeyer wrote boys' serials for at least ten magazines or story papers, edited two of them and published one. In addition, over 100 titles of his hardcover boys' books were published under various pen names in the period from 1894 through 1905. Of the 20 or more boys' series which Stratemeyer personally wrote, practically all were written or at least started before the days of the Syndicate. He is generally reported to have written "over 150 books" in his lifetime, but this figure seems low. The actual numbers are difficult to determine because of his use of pen names as well as his reported technique of personally writing one or more of the later series before turning the series over to contract writers. This following Bibliography includes over 150 books alone, attributed to Stratemeyer. The very volume of his writing is significant in its effect on the youth of this country. This chapter will attempt to trace his writing activities by means of the boys' serials and later the hardcover books that he personally wrote.

Even knowledgeable collectors and writers about boys' books often know of neither the early series and single titles by Stratemeyer nor the connection between the hardcover titles and the serials that were first published in story papers. As an example, a recent article on the attitudes of series books towards blacks referred to The Young Auctioneers as copyrighted in 1903. This was superficially correct, but it was also copyrighted in 1897 and was first published as a serial in Good News in 1894-1895. A difference of nine years in such a situation can be most significant.

It is worth noting that many of Stratemeyer's books were published in high quality hardcovers and sold for 75¢ to $1.25 each during the 1890's. They received critical acclaim from such newspapers as the Christian Advocate, The Churchman, and the Boston Herald. Ironically perhaps, some of the best of these books were reprints of story paper serials, showing, as writer-publisher Edward Ellis once pointed out, that some people are more concerned about the quality of the package than the contents. During the same period many of his serials were reprinted in paper covers and some were printed both in paperback and in hardcover.

As time passes, it becomes more and more difficult to determine with certainty which of the serials, shorts, "libraries" or other writings of the 1890's and 1900's were written by Stratemeyer. Earlier researchers, though men of tremendous scholarship and integrity, have sometimes given little proof for their claims. The original Street & Smith records are not readily available if, indeed, they still exist. One thing that is known without question is that Stratemeyer produced a tremendous body of fiction in a period of about 15 years, some of which remains to be positively identified.

A brief chronology may be helpful in connection with these listings. In the late 1880's Edward Stratemeyer was working in his step-brother's tobacco store. He had a strong desire to write, which did not please his father, who wanted him to go into the commercial field. Edward secretly

wrote his first short story on brown wrapping paper and
sent it to Golden Days. "His success in the field of children's literature was immediate" (according to a letter from
Andrew E. Svenson, October 25, 1963). This story was the
serial, "Victor Horton's Idea," published November 2, 1889.
The sale of this story for $75 encouraged him to write a
number of other serials in the early 1890's for various magazines or story papers--Munsey's Argosy, Ellis's The Holiday,
Street & Smith's Good News and Elverson's Golden Days.
In addition to his writing and editing activities, he owned
and managed a stationery store in Newark, New Jersey,
from 1890 to 1896.

In 1893 he was hired by Street & Smith as editor of
Good News, a weekly boys' story paper. It was Stratemeyer
who hired Gilbert Patten of "Frank Merriwell" fame under
such good terms for Street & Smith that Patten never for-
gave him. Patten noted with satisfaction in his autobiography
that "Edward Stratemeyer had made me dislike him, and I
was well pleased when, not long thereafter, his position of
editor of Good News was given to Arthur Dudley Hall" (Harriet Hinsdale, ed., Frank Merriwell's Father, University of
Oklahoma Press, 1964, p. 164).

If this was a setback, it was a minor one, for in 1895
he was writing much of Young Sports of America, for Frank
J. Earll. He became an editor when the title was changed to
Young People of America (J.P. Guinon, "The Young Sports
Series," Dime Novel Round-Up. vol. 26, no. 8 [August 15,
1958], p. 113). In 1896 Stratemeyer became publisher of
Bright Days, originally a juvenile monthly and later a weekly.
As J.P. Guinon notes, Bright Days and Young People of
America had the same publishing address and Bright Days
republished material from Young People of America. He
suspects that Richard K. Fox, financial backer of Young
Sports and Young People of America, was also backing
Bright Days ("Young Sports Series," op. cit., p. 114).

The National Cyclopaedia of American Biography reports
that Stratemeyer sold this magazine in 1899 "in order to
devote his entire time to the writing of full-length books and
serials for boys" (vol. 32, p. 167-168). Since the last
known issue of Bright Days is February 27, 1897, this seems
to be in error. The same source also states that Stratemeyer
left Street & Smith in 1896, but returned in 1902 as a part-
time editor.

On the other hand, Quentin Reynolds, referring to the
1898-1899 period of Street & Smith, says, "Edward Stratemeyer ... was now doing everything but set type. He was
writing dime novels under the names of Jim Bowie, Nat Woods
and Jim Daly, and writing serials aimed at women for the
'Weekly' under the name of Julie Edwards. He was also

acting as a sort of editor-in-chief without title for the firm"
(The Fiction Factory, Random House, 1955, p. 116-117).
Stratemeyer's first book was Richard Dare's Venture;
or, Striking Out for Himself, published by Merriam in 1894.
Johanssen and others call Richard Dare's Venture the first
of the Bound to Win Series and one source claims that by
1897 this series contained nine books, three each under the
names Stratemeyer, Bonehill and Winfield. This is incorrect.
As noted later, the Bound to Succeed Series was first published by Merriam between 1894 and 1897 and later by Lee &
Shepard.   The Bound to Win Series was published by W.L.
Allison during the 1897-1900 period and contained 12 books
by Stratemeyer, Bonehill and Winfield. An ad in Fighting for
His Own, published by W.L. Allison Co. and copyrighted
1897, lists Working Upward Series, Bright and Bold Series,
Young Sportsman's Series and Young Hunter Series, for a
total of 13 books, just by this one publisher. These titles,
with the addition of Young Hunters of Porto Rico, were
identical with the Bound to Win titles.
A Merriam ad of about 1896 lists three titles in the
Bound to Succeed Series with one of them "in press" and
notes the series is to be completed in six volumes.   The
same ad lists the Ship and Shore Series of three volumes,
one of which was also "in press." It now appears that
Merriam actually published four titles, two in each series.
With the ealier Merriams, Stratemeyer had apparently about
six series and 16 books in hardcover at the time of the
Spanish-American War.
In 1898 he published Under Dewey at Manila, first of
six books in the Old Glory Series. This series quickly went
through several editions and greatly increased his popularity.
In succeeding years he wrote a number of stories with a
military setting, such as the Flag of Freedom Series, Mexican
War Series, Between Boer and Briton and the Minute Boys
Series.   His next major success was the Rover Boys Series,
which ran from 1899 to 1926.
Stratemeyer had a remarkable ability to sense the interests of youth and to note trends and changes in interests.
This was probably developed by his extensive editing and
publishing activities in the juvenile field. He was certainly
aware of the success of "Frank Merriwell" and his prep
school and college days, whose start preceded that of the
"Rover Boys" by three years. Stratemeyer himself had
written "The Schooldays of Fred Harley; or, Rivals for All
Honors" for Good News in 1894 and had published the first
part of the serial "Chap Fullalife, Frank and Free; or, the
Boys of the Boarding School" in his own Bright Days before
it ceased operations in 1897. Where others followed trends,
he anticipated them.

Stratemeyer wrote sports stories, adventure stories, science fiction (including a rather unusual book, The Young Naval Captain, a war of the world which takes place in 1936), historical stories and presidential biographies. This was in addition to his women's writings under pen names like Edna Winfield and Julia Edwards. He also completed An Undivided Union by "Oliver Optic" and completed and edited the "Rise in Life" Horatio Alger series, which were published after Alger's death. With his ambition, initiative and imagination, it is small wonder that about 1904 he initiated a Literary Syndicate, on the order of the Balzac and Dumas operations, where he developed the general format, plots and characters for series and hired other professional writers for the actual writing. He continued personally to write certain series but spent the majority of his time in the other operations of the Syndicate.

The pen names of Edward Stratemeyer is a separate study in itself. Limiting the list to those used just for his hardcover boys' books from 1894 to about 1906 restricts us to fewer than half a dozen that can be considered proven. His most famous pen names were "Arthur M. Winfield" and "Captain Ralph Bonehill" and it is generally accepted that everything published under those names was actually written by Stratemeyer. It is probable that some of the "Lt. Lionel Lounsberry" books, as discussed later, were by Stratemeyer. Since "Roy Rockwood" and "Allen Chapman" were well-known Syndicate house names it is assumed that story paper serials or single titles under these names were written by Stratemeyer. This is not necessarily proven, since a reading of the books reveals a marked difference in both style and general quality. For example, "The Wizard of the Deep; or, Over and Under the Ocean in Search of the $1,000,000 Pearl" by "Theodore Edison" appeared in 1895 in Young Sports of America. It was printed in hardcover in 1900 by Mershon as The Wizard of the Sea; or, A Trip Under the Ocean, by "Roy Rockwood." If it were not for Stratemeyer's known connection with Young Sports of America and the "Rockwood" name, it would be difficult to identify this book as his writing.

"Clarence Young," a well-known Syndicate house name, was also used in the 1890's, presumably by Stratemeyer, but no known hardcover titles were issued under this name before the Syndicate's Motor Boys series which started in 1906. Roy B. Van Devier states that the first three volumes of this series were by Stratemeyer ("Edward Stratemeyer," Dime Novel Round-Up, vol. 26, no. 3 [March 15, 1958], p. 20). Others believe Howard Garis did the actual writing. The first "Bobbsey Twins" by "Laura Lee Hope" published in 1904 by Mershon is thought to be definitely by Stratemeyer himself. The Optics and Algers with which Stratemeyer was connected are included in the Bibliography, but Optic and Alger are not considered pen names in the usual sense.

One would think a list of the hardcover boys series by Edward Stratemeyer would pose few problems. Harry K. Hudson has a very complete listing of the various series in his excellent A Bibliography of Hard-Cover Series-Type Boys Books (1123 Waterview Dr., Inverness FL 32650). Unfortunately the matter is not that simple. Various writers list series that are unknown or questionable. Examples are the Zero Club Series, 1902, and Camp Life and Sport Series (1904-1905) (National Cyclopaedia of American Biography, vol. 32, p. 167-168). The Tour of the Zero Club by Street & Smith has "Zero Club Series" on the cover but only the one volume was issued as far as is known. No other reference to either of these series has been found.

Another example is the Young Pioneer Series by "Harrison Adams." Contemporary Authors attributes the entire series to Stratemeyer although St. George Rathborne is generally conceded to be the author and his obituary lists the Young Pioneer Series as his work (Johannsen, House of Beadle and Adams, 1950, vol. 2, p. 231). Complicating this issue is the known fact that Rathborne wrote for Stratemeyer. Nancy Axelrad has verified that the Young Pioneer Series is a Stratemeyer Syndicate one.

Some writers mention the Great America Industries Series. It is true that Two Young Lumbermen has "Great American Industries Series" on its cover in the first edition but it, also, was the only volume issued in the series. Two Young Lumbermen was then issued as a "single" and finally as part of the Popular Series. Similarly, the War and Adventure Stories listed only two titles, On to Pekin and Between Boer and Briton. With the writing of sequels to On to Pekin, this book became No. 1 of the Soldiers of Fortune Series and Between Boer and Briton became a separate title until it, in turn, was added to the Popular Series. The Popular Series grew to include a large number of formerly separate titles as well as titles from earlier series printed years before.

Another example is the Flag and Frontier Series, which was simply a reissue of the Flag of Freedom Series and the Frontier Series, printed together as one series. The Mexican War Series was issued first under the pen name of "Captain Ralph Bonehill" and later as by Stratemeyer. The first two volumes of the Lakeport Series were published as single titles by "Bonehill," the titles were later changed and they became the first two books of the series as by Edward Stratemeyer.

The Deep Sea Series by "Roy Rockwood" is a different problem. "Roy Rockwood" was used both by Stratemeyer and as a Syndicate house name. The first volume of this series was written as a serial, quite definitely by Stratemeyer, but the second and third volumes are questionable. Such statements as the following from "For It Was Indeed He" are often made: "He was the father of this fifty-cent literature. He wrote the first of it (The Motor Boys, or Chums Through Thick and Thin), the most of it (under literally hundreds of pseudonyms), its best seller (Tom Swift), its worst failure (The White Ribbon Boys), its latest success (Nancy Drew)" (Fortune, April 1934, p. 87).

While Stratemeyer undoubtedly prepared the plots and outlined the books a careful reading of these and many other Syndicate series shows no clear-cut evidence of his writing style. For this reason, regardless of numerous statements to the contrary, this listing is conservative in attributing Syndicate titles to Stratemeyer except for those by "Bonehill" and "Winfield."

The 11 "Alger" titles are included in the Bibliography for good reason. Regardless of how much was originally Alger material, the final edited version of these books resembles Stratemeyer more than Alger. Stratemeyer publicly spoke of the Algers he completed, although he insisted, with support from Street & Smith, that he only finished and edited them. Harriet Adams has recently discovered letters from Alger and his sister asking Stratemeyer to continue with his unfinished work.

Stratemeyer had legal possession of these Alger books. He published them under the Rise in Life Series through the Mershon complex until 1908. Professor David Mitchell has brought to light interesting notices in Publishers Weekly, March 7, 1908, "that the litigation which has been carried on since October, 1907, between Chatterton-Peck Company and Stitt Publishing Co., The Mershon Co., W.L. Mershon and Edward Stratemeyer ... has been settled so far as Edward Stratemeyer was concerned, he having arranged for the purchase of all stock and publication rights to the following books: ... Rise in Life Series...." The same issue carried the announcement by Grosset & Dunlap that "We have just completed an arrangement with Mr. Edward Stratemeyer, owner of the plates and copyrights ... whereby we have taken over the publication of the following well-known books: ... The Rise in Life Series by Horatio Alger, Jr...." Joe the Hotel Boy (Cupples & Leon, 1906) and Ben Logan's Triumph (Cupples & Leon, 1908) were not included, although they were later added to the series.

It is not the intent of this listing to include paperback series or "libraries" except as they relate to the boys' serials and hardcover titles. One exception is an interesting appearance of a "Roy Rockwood" story, "Flyer Fred, the Cyclist Ferret; or Running Down the Rough and Ready Rascals." It appeared in Beadle & Adams' Banner Weekly, vol. 14, no. 722, September 12 to October 17, 1896, and in the Half-Dime Library, no. 1047, August 17, 1897.

A link in the chain of Stratemeyer's writing activities is the Street & Smith paperback Alger Series. The first 96 titles are by Horatio Alger but include Stratemeyer "Algers" as well. The remaining titles of the first 123 are all by Stratemeyer. As pointed out by J.R. Chenu, these were apparently printed from the hardcover plates and new titles were sometimes used. "For example, Boys of the Wilderness; or, Down in Old Kentucky (no. 113) shows inside page tops reading 'With Boone on The Frontier'; The Young Pearl Hunters; or, In Hawaiian Waters (no. 118) shows 'Off for Hawaii,' and On Fortune's Trail (no. 121) shows 'With Custer In the Black Hills'." On Fortune's Trail has been reported in hardcover but this has not been verified. The Stratemeyer titles are these:

98. The Last Cruise of the Spitfire
99. Reuben Stone's Discovery
100. True to Himself
101. Richard Dare's Venture
102. Oliver Bright's Search
103. To Alaska for Gold
104. The Young Auctioneer
105. Bound to Be an Electrician
106. Shorthand Tom
107. Fighting for His Own
108. Joe the Surveyor
109. Larry the Wanderer
110. The Young Ranchmen
111. The Young Lumbermen
112. The Young Explorers
113. Boys of the Wilderness
114. Boys of the Great Northwest
115. Boys of the Goldfields
116. For His Country
117. Comrades in Peril
118. The Young Pearl Hunters
119. The Young Bandmaster
120. Boys of the Fort
121. On Fortune's Trail
122. Lost in the Land of Ice
123. Bob the Photographer

PHOTOGRAPHS OF
SELECTED BOOK COVERS

As it would be too expensive to provide an illustration of the cover of each of Stratemeyer's books, the following 22 are merely representative.

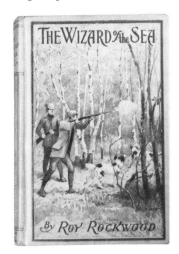

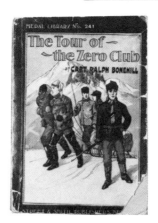

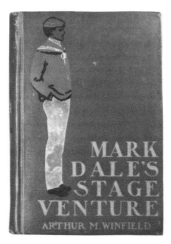

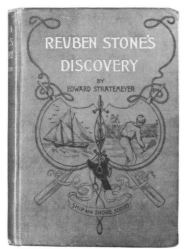

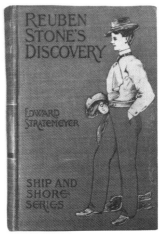

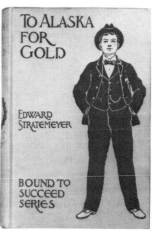

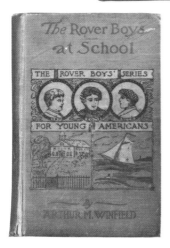

TOM AND TOM, JR.:
A COMPLETE LIST

Collectors have attempted to find all 38 hardcover Tom Swifts in the uniform tan binding. They do not exist. Grosset & Dunlap published the uniform bindings only through number 35, Tom Swift and his Giant Magnet. The last three were printed only in orange, as far as can be determined.

The Whitman reprints are another source of confusion. Andrew E. Svenson once wrote the author that Whitman reprinted the following: " Tom Swift and His Wireless Message (1911) and from 1926 to 1934 eight books, Airline Express, Circling the Globe, And His Talking Pictures, And His House on Wheels, His Big Dirigible, His Sky Train, His Television Detector and His Ocean Airport."

The reprint formats are many and varied. They are both standard size and oversize. They are both cloth and paper bound. Examples are Green paper with red letters, Red cloth with black letters, Brown simulated leather paper with black letters, Blue paper with red letters, Orange cloth with black letters, Brown paper with red letters, Green cloth with black letters and others, all by Whitman.

Even the Grosset & Dunlap uniform tan bindings varied significantly throughout the years and knowledgeable collectors recognize this. The best clue to the actual date of printing is the last title listed in the advertisements in the particular book in question.

Each of the titles in both lists that follow begin with the words "Tom Swift" (most but not all then have "and His). Note that the word "Jr." does not appear in the titles of the second series.

Tom Swift

1. and His Motor Cycle; or, Fun and Adventure on the Road. 1910
2. and His Motor Boat; or, The Rivals of Lake Carlopa. 1910
3. and His Airship; or, The Stirring Cruise of the Red Cloud. 1910
4. and His Submarine Boat; or, Under the Ocean for Sunken Treasure. 1910

5. and His Electric Runabout; or, The Speediest Car on the Road. 1910
6. and His Wireless Message; or, The Castaways of Earthquake Island. 1911
7. Among the Diamond Makers; or, The Secret of Phantom Mountain. 1911
8. in the Caves of Ice; or, The Wreck of the Airship. 1911
9. and His Sky Racer; or, The Quickest Flight on Record. 1911
10. and His Electric Rifle; or, Daring Adventures in Elephant Land. 1911
11. in the City of Gold; or, Marvelous Adventures Underground. 1912
12. and His Air Glider; or, Seeking the Platinum Treasure. 1912
13. in Captivity; or, A Daring Escape by Airship. 1912
14. and His Wizard Camera; or, The Perils of Moving Picture Taking. 1912
15 and His Great Searchlight; or, On the Border for Uncle Sam. 1912
16. and His Giant Cannon; or, The Longest Shots on Record. 1913
17. and His Photo Telephone; or, The Picture That Saved a Fortune. 1914
18. and His Aerial Warship; or, The Naval Terror of the Seas. 1915
19. and His Big Tunnel; or, The Hidden City of the Andes. 1916
20. in the Land of Wonders; or, The Search for the Idol of Gold. 1917
21. and His War Tank; or, Doing His Best for Uncle Sam. 1918
22. and His Air Scout; or, Uncle Sam's Mastery of the Sky. 1919
23. and His Undersea Search; or, The Treasure on the Floor of the Atlantic. 1920
24. Among the Fire Fighters; or, Battling with Flames from the Air. 1921
25. and His Electric Locomotive; or, Two Miles a Minute on the Rails. 1922
26. and His Flying Boat; or, The Castaways of the Giant Iceberg. 1923
27. and His Great Oil Gushers; or, The Treasure of Goby Farm. 1924
28. and His Chest of Secrets; or, Tracing the Stolen Inventions. 1925
29. and His Airline Express; or, From Ocean to Ocean by Daylight. 1926

30. Circling the Globe; or, The Daring Cruise of the Air Monarch. 1927
31. and His Talking Pictures; or, The Greatest Invention on Record. 1928
32. and His House on Wheels; or, a Trip to the Mountain of Mystery. 1929
33. and His Big Dirigible; or, Adventures Over the Forest of Fire. 1930
34. and His Sky Train; or, Overland Through the Clouds. 1931
35. and His Giant Magnet; or, Bringing Up the Lost Sub-marine. 1932
36. and His Television Detector; or, Trailing the Secret Plotters. 1933
37. and His Ocean Airport; or, Foiling the Haargolanders. 1934
38. and His Planet Stone; or, Discovering the Secret of Another World. 1935
39. and His Giant Telescope [no subtitle]. 1939
40. and His Magnetic Silencer [no subtitle]. 1941

Tom Swift, Jr.

1. and His Flying Lab. 1954
2. and His Jetmarine. 1954
3. and His Rocket Ship. 1954
4. and His Giant Robot. 1954
5. and His Atomic Earth Blaster. 1954
6. and His Outpost in Space. 1955
7. and His Diving Seacopter. 1956
8. in the Caves of Nuclear Fire. 1956
9. on the Phantom Satellite. 1956
10. and His Ultrasonic Cycloplane. 1957
11. and His Deep-Sea Hydroplane. 1958
12. in the Race to the Moon. 1958
13. and His Space Solartron. 1958
14. and His Electronic Retroscope. 1959
15. and His Spectromarine Selector. 1960
16. and the Cosmic Astronauts. 1960
17. and the Visitor from Planet X. 1961
18. and the Electronic Hydrolung. 1961
19. and His Triphibian Atomicar. 1962
20. and His Megascope Space Prober. 1962
21. and the Asteroid Pirates. 1963
22. and His Repelatron Skyway. 1963
23. and His Aquatomic Tracker. 1964
24. and His 3-D Telejector. 1964
25. and His Polar-Ray Dynasphere. 1965
26. and His Sonic Boom Trap. 1965

27. and His Subocean Geotron. 1966
28. and the Mystery Comet. 1966
29. and the Captive Planetoid. 1967
30. and His G-Force Inverter. 1968
31. and His Dyna-4 Capsule. 1969
32. and His Cosmotron Express. 1970
33. and the Galaxy Ghosts. 1971

-D-

SERIALS AND BOOKS
BY STRATEMEYER

The listings below are restricted to the following: (1) Story paper and magazine serials for boys by Edward Strate-meyer and their printing history, where known, in paper-back and hardcover. (2) The hardcover boys' series and separate titles written or presumed written by Edward Strate-meyer himself, and the Stratemeyer titles from the paperback Alger Series. (3) Books or series with which he was con-nected, i.e., Alger and "Optic."

THE SERIALS
(in chronological order)

GOLDEN DAYS, 1890-1895. James Elverson, publisher [see note 1, page 168]

As Edward Stratemeyer:
    1. "Victor Horton's Idea," vol. 10, nos. 49-1, November 2 to November 30, 1889. Reprinted in vol. 27, nos. 5-9, December 9, 1905 to January 6, 1906. No author given.
    2. "Captain Bob's Secret; or, The Treasures of Bass Island," vol. 11, nos. 16-26, March 15 to May 24, 1890. Reprinted in vol. 26, nos. 46-3, September 23 to November 25, 1905, as by the author of "Clearing His Name."

As "Ralph Hamilton" [see note 2]:
    3. "Alvin Chase's Search; or, The Mystery of Cedar Cove," vol. 11, nos. 46-4, October 11 to December 20, 1890. Reprinted in vol. 25, nos. 45-1. September 11 to November 12, 1904, as by the author of "Clearing His Name."
    4. "Clearing His Name," vol. 12, nos. 39-45, August 22 to October 3, 1891. Reprinted in vol. 24, nos. 15-21, Feb-ruary 21 to April 4, 1903, as by Edward Stratemeyer.
    5. "The Hermit's Protege; or, The Mystery of Wind Ridge," vol. 13, nos. 4-14, December 19, 1891, to February 27, 1892. Reprinted in vol. 25, nos. 1-11, November 14, 1903 to January 23, 1904, as by Dr. Willard MacKenzie. Possible but not considered proven.
    6. "Judge Dockett's Grandson" vol. 13, nos. 33-43, July

147

9 to September 17, 1892. Reprinted in vol. 27, nos. 51-9, October 27, 1906 to January 5, 1907, as by the author of "Captain Bob's Secret."
  7. "Paul Raymond's Rovings; or, In Quest of Name and Fortune," vol. 16, nos. 36-46, July 27 to October 5, 1895. (In Number 37 the author is given as Edward Stratemeyer.)

ARGOSY, 1891-1893. Frank A. Munsey, publisher [see note 3]

As Edward Stratemeyer:
  8. "Richard Dare's Venture; or, Striking Out for Himself," vol. 11, nos. 423-433, January 10 to March 21, 1891. Copyright 1894 by Merriam. Copyright 1899 by Lee & Shepard (rev. ed.). Vol. 1 of Bound to Succeed Series; vol. 4 of Popular Series; and vol. 101 of Alger Series.
  9. "True to Himself; or, Roger Strong's Struggle for Place," vol. 13, nos. 463-475, October 17, 1891, to January 9, 1892. Copyright 1900 by Lee & Shepard. Listed as "in press" by Merriam ca.1896 but apparently not published. Vol. 3 of Ship and Shore Series; vol. 3 of Popular Series; and vol. 100 of Alger Series.
  10. "Luke Foster's Grit, or, The Last Cruise of the Spitfire," vol. 13, nos. 477-487, January 23 to April 2, 1892. Copyright 1894 by Merriam as The Last Cruise of the Spitfire; or, Luke Foster's Strange Voyage. Copyright 1900 by Lee & Shepard (rev. ed.). Vol. 2 of Ship and Shore Series; vol. 3 of Popular Series, and vol. 98 of Alger Series.
  11. "Reuben Stone's Dicovery; or, The Young Miller of Torrent Bend," vol. 14, nos. 503-515, July 23 to October 15, 1892. Copyright 1895 by Merriam; copyright 1900 by Lee & Shepard (rev. ed.) as vol. 2 of Ship and Shore Series. Vol. 2 of Popular Series; vol. 99 of Alger Series.

As "Arthur M. Winfield":
  12. "Fighting for His Own; or, The Fortunes of a Young Artist," vol. 14, nos. 494-503, May 21 to July 23, 1892. Copyright 1897 by W.L. Allison as by Edward Stratemeyer. Vol. 4 of Working Upward Series; Vol. 11 of Popular Series.
  13. "One Boy in a Thousand; or, The Mystery of the Aurora Mine," vol. 15, nos. 519-531, November 12, 1892, to February 4, 1893. Copyright 1895 by the Merriam Co. as Oliver Bright's Search; or, The Mystery of a Mine as by Edward Stratemeyer. Copyright 1899 by Lee & Shepard (rev. ed.). Vol. 2 of Bound to Succeed Series; Vol. 5 of Popular Series.

THE HOLIDAY, 1891. Woodfall Pub. Co. (Edward Ellis) [see note 4]

As Edward Stratemeyer:
14. "Jack, the Inventor; or, The Trials and Triumphs of a Young Machinist," vol. 3, nos. 18-25, April 25 to June 3, 1891. Unfinished. Denis Rogers believes there is a possibility that No. 26 did, in fact, appear. This would have completed the serial. Reprinted in Good News and Bright Days. Copyright 1901 by Saalfield as A Young Inventor's Pluck; or, The Mystery of the Willington Legacy (slightly rev.) as by Arthur M. Winfield.

GOOD NEWS, 1891-1896. Street & Smith, publishers [see notes 4 and 5]

As Edward Stratemeyer:
15. "Jack the Inventor; or The Trials and Triumphs of a Young Machinist," vol. 4, nos, 90-100, January 23 to April 2, 1892. Reprinted from The Holiday, vol. 3, nos. 18-25, April 25 to June 3, 1891. Copyright 1901 by Saalfield as A Young Inventor's Pluck; or, The Mystery of the Willington Legacy as by Arthur M. Winfield. Hardcover ed. slightly rev. from serial in The Holiday.
16. "The Tin Box Mystery; or, The Stolen Railroad Bonds," vol. 6, nos. 154-164, April 15 to June 24, 1893. Copyright 1897 by W.L. Allison as The Missing Tin Box; or, Hal Carson's Remarkable City Adventures, as by Arthur M. Winfield. No. 4 in the Bright and Bold Series. The Donohue reprint (ca.1905) reverts to the original subtitle.
17. "Camera Bob; or, The Thrilling Adventures of a Travelling Photographer," vol. 7, nos. 179-194, October 7, 1893, to January 20, 1894. Vol. 123 of Alger Series. Copyright by Wessels, 1902, as Bob the Photographer.
18. "Shorthand Tom; or, The Exploits of a Young Reporter," vol. 8, nos. 196-207, February 3 to April 21, 1894. The initial appearance of "Tom Swift." Reprinted as vol. 106 of Alger Series. Copyright 1897 by W.L. Allison as Shorthand Tom the Reporter; or, The Exploits of a Smart Boy. Vol. 3 of the Working Upward Series; Copyright 1903 by Lee and Shepard. Vol. 10 of the Popular Series. ("Ned Newton; or, The Fortunes of a New York Bootblack," by Arthur Lee Putnam (Horatio Alger) appeared in Golden Argosy, vol. 5, nos. 227-252, April 9 to October 1, 1887. Both Ned and Tom underwent a considerable transformation before they appeared again in Tom Swift and His Motorcycle.)
19. "Joe, the Surveyor; or, The Value of a Lost Claim," vol. 9, nos. 209-221, May 5 to July 28, 1894. Vol. 108 of

Alger Series. Copyright 1903 by Lee and Shepard. Vol. 6 of Popular Series.
   20. "Larry, the Wanderer; or, The Ups and Downs of a Knockabout," vol. 9, nos. 223-235, August 11 to November 3, 1894. Vol. 109 of Alger Series. Copyright 1904 by Lee and Shepard as Larry the Wanderer; or, The Rise of a Nobody. Vol. 12 of Popular Series.
   21. "The Young Auctioneer; or, The Polishing of a Rolling Stone," vol. 10, nos. 241-253, December 15, 1894, to March 9, 1895. Vol. 104 of Alger Series. Copyright 1897 by Allison as The Young Auctioneers; or, The Polishing of a Rolling Stone. Vol. 1 of the Working Upward Series. Copyright 1903 by Lee and Shepard. Vol. 8 of Popular Series.

As "Arthur M. Winfield":
   22. "Missing Money; or, The Young Bank Messenger's Discovery," vol. 8, nos. 183-195, November 4, 1893, to January 27, 1894. Vol. 269 of Medal Library. Copyright 1902 by Street & Smith as Young Bank Clerk.
   23. "Stolen Gold; or, The Brightest Messenger in Boston," vol. 8, nos. 198-211, February 17 to May 19, 1894.
   24. "The Schooldays of Fred Harley; or, Rivals for All Honors," vol. 9, nos. 229-241, September 22 to December 15, 1894. Copyright 1897 by W.L. Allison Co. Vol. 2 in Bright and Bold Series.

As "Emerson Bell":
   25. "The Electric Air and Water Wizard," vol. 8, nos. 185-196, November 18, 1893, to February 3, 1894.
   26. "Overhead Steve; or, The Wizard of the Wires," vol. 12, nos. 289-301, November 16, 1895, to February 8, 1896.

As "Harvey Hicks" [see note 6]:
   27. "The Tour of the Zero Club; or, Perils by Ice and Snow," vol. 10, nos. 243-255, December 29, 1894, to March 23, 1895. Vol. 241 of Medal Library; Vol. 67 of Round the World Library. Copyright by Street & Smith 1902 as by Captain Ralph Bonehill and published as Zero Club Series. Published by David McKay in The Boys Own Library series.
   28. "By Pluck Alone; or, Ralph Nelson's Upward Struggle," vol. 11, nos. 277-289, August 24 to November 16, 1895. Copyright by Street & Smith 1902 as by Arthur M. Winfield, as The Young Bridge Tender; or, Ralph Nelson's Upward Struggle. Published as Silver Lake Series.
   29. "Ned Purcell, the Boy Engineer; or, The Hero of the 'Valley Central'," vol. 13, nos. 319-331, June 13 to September 5, 1896. The style is completely unlike Stratemeyer. The author is not identified in the S & S listing of Good News serials. Authorship by Stratemeyer very doubtful.

As "Manager Henry Abbott":
    30. "A Footlight Favorite; or, Born to Be an Actor," vol.
10, nos. 257-269, April 6 to June 29, 1895. Vol. 279 of
Medal Library. Copyright 1902 by Street & Smith and published as Mark Dale's Stage Venture as by Arthur M. Winfield.
    31. "Neka, King of Fire; or, A Mystery of the Variety
Stage," vol. 12, nos. 295-307, December 28, 1895, to March
21, 1896. Vol. 250 of Medal Library. Copyright 1902 by
Street & Smith and published as Neka, the Boy Conjuror by
Captain Ralph Bonehill.

As "Walden F. Sharp":
    32. "For His Honor's Sake; or, The Richest Boy Detective
in New York," vol. 11, nos. 271-283, July 13 to October 5,
1895.

As "Peter":
    33. "Dot Poy Hans," vol. 12, nos. 289-299, November 23,
1895, to January 25, 1896.
    34. "That Coon Rastus," vol. 11-12, nos. 271-277, August
24 to November 9, 1895.

YOUNG SPORTS OF AMERICA (nos. 1-22 [see note 7]) and
    YOUNG PEOPLE OF AMERICA (nos. 23-43), 1895-1896.
    Frank J. Earll, publisher.

As "P.T. Barnum, Jr.":
    35. "Limber Leo, Clown and Gymnast; or, With the Great-
est Show on Earth," nos. 1-5, May 25 to June 29, 1895.
Copyright 1897 by W.L. Allison as Leo the Circus Boy; or,
Life Under the Great White Canvas as by Captain Ralph
Bonehill. Vol. 3 of Young Sportsman Series.

As "Roy Rockwood":
    36. "Joe Johnson, the Bicycle Wonder; or, Riding for the
Championship of the World," nos. 2-7, June 1 to July 13,
1895. Copyright 1897 by W.L. Allison as The Rival Bicyclists;
or, Fun and Adventure on the Wheel as by Captain Ralph
Bonehill. Vol. 1 of Young Sportsman's Series.
    37. "Nat Donald, King of the Air; or, The Marvelous Ad-
ventures of a Young Balloonist," nos. 8-13, July 20 to
August 24, 1895.

As "Captain Ralph Bonehill":
    38. "Single Shell Jerry; or, The Rival Oarsmen of Lake-
view," nos. 4-9, June 15 to July 27, 1895. Copyright 1897
by W.L. Allison as Young Oarsmen of Lakeview; or, The
Mystery of Hermit Island.   Vol. 2 of Young Sportsman's
Series.

39. "Gun and Sled; or, The Young Hunters of Snowtop Island," nos. 26-32, November 23, 1895, to January 4, 1896. Copyright 1897 by W.L. Allison. Vol. 1 of Young Hunter's Series. Also published in Young Sportsman's Series by Donohue.

As "Theodore Edison":
40. "The Wizard of the Deep; or, Over and Under the Ocean in Search of the $1,000,000 Pearl," nos. 11-16, August 10 to September 14, 1895. Copyright 1900 by Mershon as The Wizard of the Sea; or, A Trip Under the Ocean, as by Roy Rockwood.

As "Captain Young of Yale" (first 2 installments) and "Clarence Young" (last 5):
41. "Quarterback Dan, the Football Champion; or, Kicking for Fame and Fortune," nos. 22-28, October 26 to December 7, 1895. Copyright 1897 by W.L. Allison as By Pluck, Not Luck; or Dan Granbury's Struggle to Rise as by Arthur M. Winfield.

As "Albert Lee Ford":
42. "Poor but Plucky; or, The Mystery of a Flood," nos. 23-30, November 3 to December 21, 1895. Copyright 1897 by W.L. Allison as by Arthur M. Winfield. Vol. 1 of Bright and Bold Series.
43. "A New Year's Hold-Up; or, A Brave Boy's Reward," no. 32, January 4, 1896. (Serial length story complete.)

As "Arthur M. Winfield":
44. "Lester Fleming's Struggles; or, The Fortunes of an Artist," nos. 24-34, November 9, 1895, to January 18, 1896. Reprinted from Argosy, vol. 14, nos. 494-503, May 21 to July 23, 1892. Copyright 1897 by W.L. Allison as Fighting for His Own; or, The Fortunes of a Young Artist by Edward Stratemeyer. Vol. 4 of Working Upward Series; vol. 11 of Popular Series.

As Edward Stratemeyer:
45. "Three Ranch Boys; or, The Great Winthrop Claim," nos. 27-37, November 30, 1895, to February 8, 1896. Copyright 1901 by Saalfield as Three Young Ranchmen; or, Daring Adventures in the Great West as by Captain Ralph Bonehill.

As "Philip A. Alyer":
46. "A Nobody Schoolboy; or, Backbone Against the World," nos. 28-39, December 7, 1895, to February 22, 1896. Copyright 1900 by Mershon as A Schoolboy's Pluck; or, The Career of a Nobody, as by Roy Rockwood.

BRIGHT DAYS, 1896-1897.   Bright Days Pub. Co. (Edward
Stratemeyer) [see note 8]

As "Roy Rockwood":
  47. "The Rival Bicyclists; or, Fun and Adventure on the
Wheel," nos. 1-3, April to June 1896.   Reprinted from Young
Sports of America, nos. 2-7, June 1 to July 13, 1895.
Copyright 1897 by W.L. Allison as by Captain Ralph Bonehill.
Vol. 1 of Young Sportsman's Series.
  48. "The Schoolboy Cadets; or, Fun and Mystery at Washington Hall," nos. 6-10, September 5 to October 3, 1896.
  49. "The Schoolboy's Mutiny; or, Lively Times at River-
dale," nos. 16-20, November 14 to December 12, 1896.
  50. "Tom Fairwood's Schooldays; or, The Boys of River-
dale," nos. 11-15, October 10 to November 7, 1896.

As "Arthur M. Winfield":
  51. "Bound to Be an Electrician; or, A Clear Head and a
Stout Heart," nos. 1-5, April to August 1896.   Vol. 105 of
the Alger Series.   Copyright 1897 by W.L. Allison as Bound
to Be an Electrician; or, Franklin Bell's Success   as   by
Edward Stratemeyer.   Vol. 2 of Working Upward Series.
Copyright 1903 by Lee and Shepard.   Vol. 9 of Popular
Series.

As Edward Stratemeyer:
  52. "The Island of Caves; or, The Remarkable Adventures
of the Bixby Twins," nos. 1-6, April to June 1896.
  53. "Just from the Farm; or, Don Borden's Metropolitan
Adventures," nos. 6-13, September 5 to October 3, 1896.
  54. "The Young Civil Engineer; or, The Perils of the
Backwoods," nos. 13-21, October 24 to December 19, 1896.
  55. "A Young Inventor's Pluck; or, The Wellington Legacy," nos. 30-31, February 20 to 27, 1897 (unfinished).
Reprinted from The Holiday, vol. 3, nos. 18-25, and Good
News, vol. 4, nos. 90-100.   Copyright 1901 by Saalfield as
A Young Inventor's Pluck; or, The Mystery of the Willington Legacy as by Arthur M. Winfield.   Hardcover ed.
slightly rev.

As "Albert Lee Ford":
  56. "The Young Florists of Spring Hill; or, The New Heliotrope," nos. 2-4, May to July 1896.   Copyright 1900 by
Mershon as Boys of Spring Hill; or, Bound to Rise as by
Allen Chapman.

As "Theodore Barnum":
  57. "Carl, the Juggler and Magician; or, A Hundred Stage
Tricks Revealed," nos. 8-14, September 19 to October 31,
1896.
  58. "Leo, the Circus Boy; or, Life Under the Great White

Canvas," nos. 3-6, June to September 5, 1896. Reprinted from Young Sports of America, nos. 1-5, May 25 to June 29, 1895. Copyright 1897 by W.L. Allison as by Captain Ralph Bonehill. Vol. 3 of Young Sportsman's Series.

As "Louis Charles":
    59. "The Land of Fire; or, A Long Journey for Fortune," nos. 9-16, September 26 to November 14, 1896. Copyright 1900 by Mershon Co. (This pen name was authenticated in a letter from the Stratemeyer Syndicate to Captain Mayo.) Harriet Adams told this writer that the book was finished by Louis Charles Stratemeyer, Edward Stratemeyer's brother; whether Fortune Hunters of the Philippines was written by both Stratemeyers is not clear.

As "Allen Chapman":
    60. "For Name and Fame; or, Walter Loring's Strange Quest," nos. 10-15, October 3 to November 14, 1896. Copyright 1900 by Mershon; printed as Walter Loring's Career as the second part of Boys of Spring Hill; or, Bound to Rise.

As "Captain Ralph Bonehill":
    61. "Balloon Boys; or, Adventures among the Clouds," nos. 12-17, October 17 to November 21, 1896.
    62. "Camp and Diamond; or, The Outing of the Young Victors," nos. 4-8, July to September 19, 1896.

As "D.T. Henty" [see note 9]:
    63. "Malcolm, the Waterboy; or, A Mystery of Old London," nos. 15-22, November 7 to December 26, 1896. Copyright 1901 by Mershon Co.

As "Clarence Young":
    64. "Football Dan; or, Pluck, Not Luck," nos. 17-25, November 21, 1896, to January 16, 1897. Reprinted from Young Sports of America, nos. 22-28, October 26 to December 7, 1895. Copyright 1897 by W.L. Allison as By Pluck, Not Luck; or, Dan Granbury's Struggle to Rise, as by Arthur M. Winfield. Vol. 3 in Bright and Bold Series.

As "Philip A. Alyer":
    65. "Among South Sea Savages; or, The Last Cruise of the Comet," nos. 18-24, November 28, 1896, to January 9, 1897.

As "Maurice Monroe" [see note 10]:
    66. "Always on Time; or, The Young Engineer of the Overland Express," nos. 29-31, February 13 to February 27, 1897. A suggestion has been made that this could be one of the Railroad Series, written by "Allen Chapman" and published by the Stratemeyer Syndicate. The first of this series was copyrighted in 1906 by Mershon and Ralph on the

Overland Express was not copyrighted until 1910 by Grosset & Dunlap. It is the opinion of this writer, an opinion with which J. Edward Leithead agreed, that the style of the Railroad Series resembles W. Bert Foster much more than Stratemeyer. A textual comparison has not yet been made.

GOLDEN HOURS, 1898-1903. N.L. Munro, publisher [see note 11]

As "Captain Ralph Bonehill":
    67. "Pawnee Bill, the Hero Scout of Oklahoma; or, Wild Adventures in the Wild West. A True Life Tale of the Hero of the Plains," nos. 537-546, May 14 to July 16, 1898.
    68. "May Lillie, Princess of the Prairie; or, Pawnee Bill's Wild Ride for Life," nos. 547-555, July 23 to September 17, 1898.
    69. "The Young Bandmaster; or, Solving a Mystery of the Past," nos. 576-585, February 11 to April 15, 1899. Copyright 1900 by Mershon as The Young Bandmaster; or, Concert Stage and Battlefield. Vol. 4 of Flag of Freedom Series.

As "Hal Harkaway":
    70. "Holland, the Destroyer; or, America Against the World," nos. 669-676, November 24, 1900, to January 12, 1901. Copyright 1902 by Thompson and Thomas as The Young Naval Captain; or, The War of All Nations as by Captain Ralph Bonehill. The same book was reprinted by Donahue as Oscar the Naval Cadet.
    71. "Bob Ready, Reporter; or, The Mystery of the Poisoned Dagger," nos. 686-693, March 23 to May 11, 1901. Not proven.

As "Roy Rockwood":
    72. "Lost in the Land of Ice; or, Bob Baxter at the South Pole," nos. 670-678, December 1, 1900, to January 26, 1901. Copyright 1902 by A. Wessels as Lost in the Land of Ice; or, Daring Adventures Around the South Pole as by Captain Ralph Bonehill.
    73. "Rival Ocean Divers; or, A Boy's Daring Search for Sunken Treasure," nos. 675-682, January 5 to February 23, 1901. Copyright 1905 by Stitt as Rival Ocean Divers; or, The Search for a Sunken Treasure. Vol. 1 of Deep Sea Series. Published as Dave Fearless After a Sunken Treasure; or, The Rival Ocean Divers as Vol. 1 of Dave Fearless Series.
    74. "Brave Larry Barlow; or, The Fire Fighters of New York," nos. 693-702, May 11 to July 13, 1901. Copyright 1902 by Saalfield as Larry Barlow's Ambition; or, The Adventures of a Young Fireman as by Arthur M. Winfield.

As Horatio Alger, Jr.":
    75. "Young Captain Jack; or, The Son of a Soldier,"
nos. 701-710, July 6 to September 7, 1901. Vol. 89 of Alger
Series. Shown as "Completed by Arthur M. Winfield."
Copyright 1901 by Mershon.

BOYS OF AMERICA, 1901-1903. Street & Smith, publishers
    [see note 12]

As "Manager Henry Abbott":
    76. "Footlight Phil; or, From Call Boy to Star," nos.
10-15, December 7, 1901, to January 11, 1902. Vol. 205 of
Brave and Bold Series. Not proven.
    77. "Nimble Nip; or, The Call Boy of the Olympic Theatre,"
nos. 79-81, April 4 to April 18, 1903. Vol. 5 of Nugget
Library; vol. 182 of Diamond Dick Library. Not proven.

As "Ned St. Meyer":
    78. "Match as a Fakir; or, The Pumpkinville County
Fair," nos. 71-74, February 7 to February 28, 1903. Vol.
56 of Nugget Library. Not proven.

THE POPULAR MAGAZINE, 1903-1904. Street & Smith,
    publishers

As Edward Stratemeyer:
    79. "Snow Lodge," vol. 1, nos. 2-3, December 1903 to
January 1904. Rev. and copyrighted 1904 by A.S. Barnes
as The Island Camp; or, The Young Hunters of Lakeport as
by Captain Ralph Bonehill. Copyright by Lothrop, Lee and
Shepard as The Gun Boys of Lakeport; or, The Island
Camp. Vol. 1 of Lakeport Series by Stratemeyer.
    80. "Building the Line," vol. 2, nos. 3-4, July to
August, 1904.

THE AMERICAN BOY, 1906-1907.

As Edward Stratemeyer:
    81. "In Defense of His Flag," [May 1906] to June 1907.
Copyright 1907 by Lothrop, Lee & Shepard as Defending His
Flag.

NEW BUFFALO BILL WEEKLY, 1913-1915. Street & Smith,
    publishers [see note 13]

As "Lt. Lionel Lounsberry":

82.   "By Order of the Colonel; or, The Captain of the Young Guardsmen," nos. 49-55, August 16 to September 27, 1913. Vol. 15 of Boys of Liberty Library.

83.   "Fighting for Freedom," nos. 101-109, August 16 to September 27, 1913.   Vol. 2 of Boys of Liberty Library.

84.   "A Call to Duty; or, The Young Guardsman on Detached Service," nos. 110-114, October 11 to November 14, 1914. Vol. 19 of Boys of Liberty Library.

85.   "The Trader's Captive; or, The Young Guardsman and the French Spies," nos. 155-161, August 28 to October 9, 1915. Vol. 26 of Boys of Liberty Library.

86.   "In Glory's Van; or, The Young Guardsman at Louisburg," nos. 162-171, October 16 to December 18, 1915. Vol. 28 of Boys of Liberty Library.

THE BOY'S BOOKS
In alphabetical order of pen names
showing full title, (first book publisher),
copyright date, and [original publication]

HORATIO ALGER, JR. [see note 14]

1.   Ben Logan's Triumph; or, The Boys of Boxwood Academy (Cupples and Leon), 1908.
2.   Falling in with Fortune; or, The Experiences of a Young Secretary (Mershon Co.), 1900.
3.   From Farm to Fortune; or, Nat Nason's Strange Experience (Stitt & Co.), 1905.
4.   Jerry, the Backwoods Boy; or, The Parkhurst Treasure (Mershon Co.), 1904.
5.   Joe the Hotel Boy; or, Winning Out by Pluck (Cupples & Leon), 1906.
6.   Lost at Sea; or, Robert Roscoe's Strange Cruise (Mershon Co.), 1904.
7.   Nelson the Newsboy; or, Afloat in New York (Mershon Co.), 1901.
8.   Out for Business; or, Robert Frost's Strange Career (Mershon Co.), 1900.
9.   Randy of the River; or, The Adventures of a Young Deckhand (Chatterton-Peck), 1906.
10.   The Young Book Agent; or, Frank Hardy's Road to Success (Stitt & Co.), 1905.
11.   Young Captain Jack; or The Son of a Soldier (Mershon Co.), 1901 [Golden Hours, 1901].

CAPTAIN RALPH BONEHILL

Individual Titles

1. The Boy Land Boomer; or, Dick Arbuckle's Adventures in Oklahoma (Saalfield, 1902).
2. Tour of the Zero Club; or, Adventures amid Ice and Snow (Street & Smith, 1902) [Good News, 1894-1895, as by "Harvey Hicks"].
3. Three Young Ranchmen; or, Daring Adventures in the Great West (Saalfield, 1901) [Young People of America, 1895-1896, as "Three Ranch Boys; or, The Great Winthrop Claim," as by Edward Stratemeyer].
4. Lost in the Land of Ice; or, Daring Adventures Around the South Pole (A. Wessels, 1902) [Golden Hours, 1900-1901, as "Lost in the Land of Ice; or, Bob Baxter at the South Pole," as by "Roy Rockwood"].
5. Neka, the Boy Conjurer; or, A Mystery of the Stage (Street & Smith, 1902) [Good News, 1895, as "Neka, King of Fire; or, A Mystery of the Variety Stage," as by "Manager Henry Abbott"].
6. The Young Naval Captain; or, The War of All Nations (Thompson and Thomas, 1902); also as Oscar the Naval Cadet [Golden Hours, 1900-1901, as "Holland, the Destroyer; or, America Against the World," as by "Hal Harkaway"].
7. The Island Camp; or, The Young Hunters of Lakeport (Barnes, 1904) [The Popular Magazine, 1903-1904, as "Snow Lodge" by Edward Stratemeyer, vol. 1 of his Lakeport Series].
8. The Winning Run; or, The Baseball Boys of Lakeport (Barnes, 1905) [Vol. 2 of Lakeport Series].

Bonehill "Boy Hunter Series"

1. Four Boy Hunters; or, The Outing of the Gun Club (Cupples & Leon, 1906).
2. Guns and Snowshoes; or, The Winter Outing of the Young Hunters (Cupples & Leon, 1907).
3. Young Hunters of the Lake; or, Out with Rod and Gun (Cupples & Leon, 1908).
4. Out with Gun and Camera; or, The Boy Hunters in the Mountains (Cupples & Leon, 1910).

Bonehill "Flag of Freedom Series"

1. When Santiago Fell; or, The War Adventures of Two Chums (Mershon Co., 1899).
2. A Sailor Boy with Dewey; or, Afloat in the Philippines (Mershon Co., 1899).

3. Off for Hawaii; or, The Mystery of a Great Volcano (Mershon Co., 1899).
4. The Young Bandmaster; or, Concert, Stage and Battle-field (Mershon Co., 1900) [Golden Hours, 1899 as "The Young Bandmaster; or, Solving a Mystery of the Past"].
5. Boys of the Fort; or, A Young Captain's Pluck (Mershon Co., 1901).
6. With Custer in the Black Hills; or, A Young Scout Among the Indians (Mershon Co., 1902).

Bonehill "Frontier Series"

1. With Boone on the Frontier; or, The Pioneer Boys of Old Kentucky (Mershon Co., 1903).
2. Pioneer Boys of the Great Northwest; or, With Lewis and Clark Across the Rockies (Mershon Co., 1904).
3. Pioneer Boys of the Gold Fields; or, The Nugget Hunt-ers of '49 (Stitt & Co., 1906).

Bonehill "Mexican War Series" [see note 15]

1. For the Liberty of Texas (Estes, 1900).
2. With Taylor on the Rio Grande (Estes, 1901).
3. Under Scott in Mexico (Estes, 1902).

Bonehill "Young Hunters Series"

1. Gun and Sled; or, The Young Hunters of Snow-Top Island (W. L. Allison Co., 1897) [Young People of America, 1895].
2. Young Hunters in Porto Rico; or, The Search for a Lost Treasure (W. L. Allison Co., ca.1899. Allison ads list this book but the book itself says copyright 1900 by Donohue Brothers. Allison ads also noted another vol-ume in preparation in this series but there is no record of it).

Bonehill "Young Sportsman's Series"

1. The Rival Bicyclists; or, Fun and Adventures on the Wheel (W. L. Allison Co., 1897) [Young Sports of America, 1895, as "Joe Johnson, the Bicycle Wonder; or, Riding for the Championship of the World" as by "Roy Rockwood"].
2. Young Oarsmen of Lakeview; or, The Mystery of Hermit Island (W. L. Allison Co., 1897) [Young Sports of America, 1895, as "Single Shell Jerry; or, The Rival Oarsmen of Lakeview"].
3. Leo, the Circus Boy; or, Life Under the Great White

Canvas (W.L. Allison Co., 1897) [Young Sports of America, 1895, as "Limber Leo, Clown and Gymnast; or, With the Greatest Show on Earth" as by P.T. Barnum, Jr.].

ALLEN CHAPMAN

1. Boys of Spring Hill; or, Bound to Rise [and] Walter Loring's Career (Mershon Co., 1900) [Bright Days, 1896, as "The Young Florists of Spring Hill; or, The New Heliotrope," as by "Albert Lee Ford," and "For Name and Fame; or, Walter Loring's Strange Quest"].
2. The Young Builders of Swiftdale (apparently Chatterton-Peck; information is needed on this title--not proven).

LOUIS CHARLES [see note 16]

1. Fortune Hunters of the Philippines; or, The Treasure of the Burning Mountain (Mershon Co., 1900).
2. The Land of Fire (Mershon Co., 1900) [Bright Days, 1896].

LT. LIONEL LOUNSBERRY [see note 13 for listing]

OLIVER OPTIC

An Undivided Union, Lee & Shepard, 1899. Completed by Edward Stratemeyer; last book of the Blue and Gray--On Land Series of William T. Adams.

ROY ROCKWOOD

1. A Schoolboy's Pluck; or, The Career of a Nobody (Mershon Co., 1900) [Young People of America, 1895-1896, as "A Nobody Schoolboy; or, Backbone Against the World," as by "Philip A. Alyer"].
2. The Wizard of the Sea; or, A Trip Under the Ocean (Mershon Co., 1900) [Young Sports of America, 1895, as "The Wizard of the Deep; or, Over and Under the Ocean in Search of the $1,000,000 Pearl"].
3. Rival Ocean Divers; or, The Search for a Sunken Treasure (Stitt & Co., 1905) [Golden Hours, 1900-1901; no. 1 of Deep Sea Series and Dave Fearless Series].
4. The Cruise of the Treasure Ship; or, The Castaway of Floating Island (Stitt & Co., ca.1906); not proven [no. 2 of Deep Sea Series and Dave Fearless Series].

EDWARD STRATEMEYER

Individual Title [see note 17]

Defending His Flag; or, A Boy in Blue and a Boy in Gray
   (Lothrop, Lee & Shepard, 1907) [The American Boy,
   May 1906 to June 1907, as "In Defense of His Flag"].

Stratemeyer "American Boys Biographical Series"

1. American Boys' Life of William McKinley (Lee & Shepard,
   1901).
2. American Boys' Life of Theodore Roosevelt (Lee & Shepard, 1904; rev. 1906).

Stratemeyer "Bound to Succeed Series"

1. Richard Dare's Venture; or, Striking Out for Himself
   (Merriam Co., 1894) [Argosy, 1891]. Copyright 1899
   by Lee & Shepard.
2. Oliver Bright's Search; or, The Mystery of a Mine (Merriam Co., 1895) [Argosy, 1892-1893, as "One Boy in a
   Thousand; or, The Mystery of the Aurora Mine," as by
   Arthur M. Winfield]. Copyright 1899 by Lee & Shepard.
3. To Alaska for Gold; or, The Fortune Hunters of the Yukon (Lee & Shepard, 1899) [see note 18].

Stratemeyer "Colonial Series"

1. With Washington in the West; or, A Soldier Boy's Battles
   in the Wilderness (Lee & Shepard, 1901).
2. Marching on Niagara; or The Soldier Boys of the Old
   Frontier (Lee & Shepard, 1902).
3. At the Fall of Montreal; or, A Soldier Boy's Final Victory
   (Lee & Shepard, 1903).
4. On the Trail of Pontiac; or, The Pioneer Boys of the Ohio
   (Lee & Shepard, 1904).
5. The Fort in the Wilderness; or, The Soldier Boys of the
   Indian Trails (Lothrop, Lee & Shepard, 1905).
6. Trail and Trading Post; or, The Young Hunters of the
   Ohio (Lothrop, Lee & Shepard, 1906).

Stratemeyer "Dave Porter Series" (all published by Lothrop,
   Lee & Shepard)

1. Dave Porter at Oak Hall; or, The School Days of an American Boy (1905).
2. Dave Porter in the South Seas; or, The Strange Cruise of
   the Stormy Petrel (1906).
3. Dave Porter's Return to School; or, Winning the Medal of

Honor (1907).

4. Dave Porter in the Far North; or, the Pluck of an American Schoolboy (1908).
5. Dave Porter and His Classmates; or, For the Honor of Oak Hall (1909).
6. Dave Porter at Star Ranch; or, The Cowboy's Secret (1910).
7. Dave Porter and His Rivals; or, The Chums and Foes of Oak Hall (1911).
8. Dave Porter on Cave Island; or, A Schoolboy's Mysterious Mission (1912).
9. Dave Porter and the Runaways; or, Last Days at Oak Hall (1913).
10. Dave Porter in the Gold Fields; or, The Search for the Landslide Mine (1914).
11. Dave Porter at Bear Camp; or, The Wild Man of Mirror Lake (1915).
12. Dave Porter and His Double; or, The Disappearance of the Basswood Fortune (1916).
13. Dave Porter's Great Search; or, The Perils of a Young Civil Engineer (1917).
14. Dave Porter Under Fire; or, A Young Army Engineer in France (1918).
15. Dave Porter's War Honors; or, At the Front with the Fighting Engineers (1919).

Stratemeyer "Lakeport Series"

1. The Gun Club Boys of Lakeport; or, The Island Camp (Barnes, 1904, as The Island Camp; or, The Young Hunters of Lakeport as by Captain Ralph Bonehill) [The Popular Magazine, 1903-1904, as "Snow Lodge" by Edward Stratemeyer].
2. The Baseball Boys of Lakeport; or, The Winning Run (Barnes, 1905, as The Winning Run; or The Baseball Boys of Lakeport as by Captain Ralph Bonehill).
3. The Boat Club Boys of Lakeport; or, The Water Champions (Lothrop, Lee & Shepard, 1908).
4. The Football Boys of Lakeport; or, More Goals Than One (Lothrop, Lee & Shepard, 1909).
5. The Automobile Boys of Lakeport; or, A Run for Fun and Fame (Lothrop, Lee & Shepard, 1910).
6. The Aircraft Boys of Lakeport; or, Rivals of the Clouds (Lothrop, Lee & Shepard, 1912).

Stratemeyer "Minute Boys Series" [see note 19]

1. The Minute Boys of Lexington (Estes & Lauriat, 1898).
2. The Minute Boys of Bunker Hill (Estes, 1899).

Stratemeyer "Old Glory Series" (all Lee & Shepard)

1. Under Dewey at Manila; or, The War Fortunes of a Castaway (1898).
2. A Young Volunteer in Cuba; or, Fighting for the Single
   Star (1898).
3. Fighting in Cuban Waters; or, Under Schley on the Brooklyn (1899).
4. Under Otis in the Philippines; or, A Young Officer in the
   Tropics (1899).
5. The Campaign of the Jungle; or, Under Lawton Through
   Luzon (1900).
6. Under MacArthur in Luzon; or, Last Battles in the Philippines (1901).

Stratemeyer "Pan American Series"

1. Lost on the Orinoco; or, American Boys in Venezuela (Lee
   & Shepard, 1902).
2. The Young Volcano Explorers; or, American Boys in the
   West Indies (Lee & Shepard, 1902).
3. Young Explorers of the Isthmus; or, American Boys in
   Central America (Lee & Shepard, 1903).
4. Young Explorers of the Amazon; or, American Boys in
   Brazil (Lee & Shepard, 1904).
5. Treasure Seekers of the Andes; or, American Boys in
   Peru (Lothrop, Lee & Shepard, 1907).
6. Chased Across the Pampas; or, American Boys in Argen-
   tina and Homeward Bound (Lothrop, Lee & Shepard,
   1911).

Stratemeyer "Popular Series"

1. The Last Cruise of the Spitfire; or, Luke Foster's
   Strange Voyage. See Ship and Shore Series.
2. Reuben Stone's Discovery; or, The Young Miller of
   Torrent Bend. See Ship and Shore Series.
3. True to Himself; or, Roger Strong's Struggle for Place.
   See Ship and Shore Series.
4. Richard Dare's Venture; or, Striking Out for Himself.
   See Bound to Succeed Series.
5. Oliver Bright's Search; or, The Mystery of a Mine. See
   Bound to Succeed Series.
6. Joe the Surveyor; or, The Value of a Lost Claim (Lee
   & Shepard, 1903) [Good News, 1894].
7. To Alaska for Gold; or, The Fortune Hunters of the
   Yukon. See Bound to Succeed Series.
8. The Young Auctioneer; or, The Polishing of a Rolling
   Stone. See Working Upward Series.
9. Bound to Be an Electrician; or, Franklin Bell's Success.
   See Working Upward Series.

10. Shorthand Tom, the Reporter; or, The Exploits of a
    Bright Boy. See Working Upward Series.
11. Fighting for His Own; or, The Fortunes of a Young
    Artist. See Working Upward Series.
12. Larry, the Wanderer; or, The Rise of a Nobody (Lee
    & Shepard, 1904) [Good News, 1894, as "Larry the
    Wanderer; or, The Ups and Downs of a Knockabout"].
13. Between Boer and Briton; or, Two Boys' Adventures in
    South Africa (Lee & Shepard, 1900).
14. Two Young Lumbermen; or, From Maine to Oregon for
    Fortune (Lee & Shepard, 1903).
15. First at the North Pole; or, Two Boys in the Arctic
    Circle (Lothrop, Lee & Shepard, 1909).

Stratemeyer "Ship and Shore Series"

1. The Last Cruise of the Spitfire; or, Luke Foster's Strange
   Voyage (Merriam Co., 1894) [Argosy, 1892, as "Luke
   Foster's Grit; or, The Last Cruise of the Spitfire"].
   Copyright 1900 by Lee & Shepard.
2. Reuben Stone's Discovery; or, The Young Miller of Torrent Bend (Merriam Co., 1895) [Argosy, 1892]. Copyright 1900 by Lee & Shepard.
3. True to Himself; or, Roger Strong's Struggle for Place
   (Lee & Shepard, 1900) [Argosy, 1891-1892].

Stratemeyer "Soldiers of Fortune Series"

1. On to Pekin; or, Old Glory in China (Lee & Shepard,
   1900).
2. Under the Mikado's Flag; or, Young Soldiers of Fortune
   (Lothrop, Lee & Shepard, 1904).
3. At the Fall of Port Arthur; or, A Young American in the
   Japanese Navy (Lothrop, Lee & Shepard, 1905).
4. Under Togo for Japan; or, Three Young Americans on
   Land and Sea (Lothrop, Lee & Shepard, 1906).

Stratemeyer "Working Upward Series"

1. Young Auctioneer; or, The Polishing of a Rolling Stone
   (W.L. Allison Co., 1897) [Good News, 1894-1895].
2. Bound to Be an Electrician; or, Franklin Bell's Success
   (W.L. Allison Co., 1897) [Bright Days, 1896, as "Bound
   to be an Electrician; or, A Clear Head and a Stout
   Heart," as by "Arthur M. Winfield"].
3. Shorthand Tom, the Reporter; or, The Exploits of a Smart
   Boy (W.L. Allison Co., 1897) [Good News, 1894, as
   "Shorthand Tom; or, The Exploits of a Young Re-
   porter"].
4. Fighting for His Own; or, The Fortunes of a Young Artist
   (W.L. Allison Co., 1897) [Argosy, 1892, as by "Arthur
   M. Winfield"].

ARTHUR M. WINFIELD

Individual Titles

1. A Young Inventor's Pluck; or, The Mystery of the Willington Legacy (Saalfield, 1901) [The Holiday, 1891, as
by Edward Stratemeyer].
2. Bob, the Photographer; or, A Hero in Spite of Himself
(A. Wessels, 1902) [Good News, 1893-1894, as "Camera
Bob; or, The Thrilling Adventures of a Travelling
Photographer"].
3. Larry Barlow's Ambition; or, The Adventures of a Young
Fireman (Saalfield, 1902) [Golden Hours, 1901, as "Brave
Larry Barlow; or, The Fire Fighters of New York," as
by "Roy Rockwood"].
4. Mark Dale's Stage Venture; or, Bound to Be an Actor
(Street & Smith, 1902) [Good News, 1895, as "A Foot-
light Favorite; or, Born to Be an Actor," as by "Manager Henry Abbott"].
5. The Young Bank Clerk; or, Mark Vincent's Strange Discovery (Street & Smith, 1902) [Good News, 1893-1894,
as "Missing Money; or, The Young Bank Messenger's
Discovery"].
6. The Young Bridge Tender; or, Ralph Nelson's Upward
Struggle (Street & Smith, 1902) [Good News, 1895, as
"By Pluck Alone; or, Ralph Nelson's Upward Struggle,"
as by "Harvey Hicks"].

Winfield "Bright and Bold Series"

1. Poor but Plucky; or, The Mystery of a Flood (W.L. Allison Co., 1897) [Young People of America, 1895, as by
"Albert Lee Ford"].
2. School Days of Fred Harley; or, Rivals for All Honors
(W.L. Allison Co., 1897) [Good News, 1894]. The book
mentions a sequel, Fred Harley the Castaway; or, The
Mystery of the Floating Island, but there is no record
of it.
3. By Pluck, Not Luck; or, Dan Granbury's Struggle to Rise
(W.L. Allison Co., 1897) [Young People of America,
1895, as "Quarterback Dan, the Football Champion; or,
Kicking for Fame and Fortune," as by "Clarence
Young"].
4. The Missing Tin Box; or, Hal Carson's Remarkable City
Aventures (W.L. Allison Co., 1897) [Good News, 1893,
as "The Tin Box Mystery; or, The Stolen Railroad
Bonds"].

Winfield "Putnam Hall Series"

1. The Putnam Hall Cadets; or, Good Times in School and

Out (Mershon Co., 1901).

2. The Putnam Hall Rivals; or, Fun and Sport Afloat and Ashore (Mershon Co., 1906).
3. The Putnam Hall Champions; or, Bound to Win Out (Grosset & Dunlap, 1908).
4. The Putnam Hall Rebellion; or, The Rival Runaways (Grosset & Dunlap, 1909).
5. The Putnam Hall Encampment; or, The Secret of the Old Mill (Grosset & Dunlap, 1910).
6. The Putnam Hall Mystery; or, The School Chums' Strange Discovery (Grosset & Dunlap, 1911).

Winfield "Rover Boys Series"

1. The Rover Boys at School; or, The Cadets of Putnam Hall (Mershon Co., 1899).
2. The Rover Boys on the Ocean; or, A Chase for a Fortune (Mershon Co., 1899).
3. The Rover Boys in the Jungle; or, Stirring Adventures in Africa (Mershon Co., 1899).
4. The Rover Boys Out West; or, The Search for a Lost Mine (Mershon Co., 1900).
5. The Rover Boys on the Great Lakes; or, The Secret of the Island Cave (Mershon Co., 1901).
6. The Rover Boys in the Mountains; or, A Hunt for Fame and Fortune (Mershon Co., 1902).
7. The Rover Boys on Land and Sea; or, The Crusoes of Seven Islands (Mershon Co., 1903).
8. The Rover Boys in Camp; or, The Rivals of Pine Island (Mershon Co., 1904).
9. The Rover Boys on the River; or, The Search for the Missing Houseboat (Stitt & Co., 1905).
10. The Rover Boys on the Plains; or, The Mystery of Red Rock Ranch (Mershon Co., 1906).
11. The Rover Boys in Southern Waters; or, The Deserted Steam Yacht (Mershon Co., 1907).
12. The Rover Boys on the Farm; or, The Last Days at Putnam Hall (Grosset & Dunlap, 1908).
13. The Rover Boys on Treasure Isle; or, The Strange Cruise of the Steam Yacht (Grosset & Dunlap, 1909).
14. The Rover Boys at College; or, The Right Road and the Wrong (Grosset and Dunlap, 1910).
15. The Rover Boys Down East; or, The Struggle for the Stanhope Fortune (Grosset & Dunlap, 1911).
16. The Rover Boys in the Air; or, From College Campus to the Clouds (Grosset & Dunlap, 1912).
17. The Rover Boys in New York; or, Saving Their Father's Honor (Grosset & Dunlap, 1913).
18. The Rover Boys in Alaska; or, Lost in the Fields of Ice (Grosset & Dunlap, 1914).
19. The Rover Boys in Business; or, The Search for the

Missing Bonds (Grosset & Dunlap, 1915).
20. The Rover Boys on a Tour; or, Last Days at Brill College (Grosset & Dunlap, 1916).

Winfield "Rover Boys"--Second Series [see note 20]

21. The Rover Boys at Colby Hall; or, The Struggles of the Young Cadets (Grosset & Dunlap, 1917).
22. The Rover Boys on Snowshoe Island; or, The Old Lumberman's Treasure Box (Grosset & Dunlap 1918).
23. The Rover Boys Under Canvas; or, The Mystery of the Wrecked Submarine (Grosset & Dunlap, 1919).
24. The Rover Boys on a Hunt; or, The Mysterious House in the Woods (Grosset & Dunlap, 1920).
25. The Rover Boys in the Land of Luck; or, Stirring Adventures in the Oil Fields (Grosset & Dunlap, 1921).
26. The Rover Boys at Big Horn Ranch; or, The Cowboy's Double Round-up (Grosset & Dunlap, 1922).
27. The Rover Boys at Big Bear Lake; or, The Camps of the Rival Cadets (Grosset & Dunlap, 1923).
28. The Rover Boys Shipwrecked; or, A Thrilling Hunt for Pirates' Gold (Grosset & Dunlap, 1924).
29. The Rover Boys on Sunset Trail; or, The Old Miner's Mysterious Message (Grosset & Dunlap, 1925).
30. The Rover Boys Winning a Fortune; or, Strenuous Days Afloat and Ashore (Grosset & Dunlap, 1926).

BOUND TO WIN SERIES (Bonehill, Stratemeyer and Winfield)

The titles in the Working Upward Series (Stratemeyer), the Bright and Bold Series (Winfield), the Young Sportsman's Series (Bonehill) and Gun and Sled from the Young Hunters Series (Bonehill) were also issued by W.L. Allison Co., as the Bound to Win Series. This is not the same as the Bound to Succeed series although the two are often confused. The listing is taken from The American Catalogue 1895-1900.

1. Bound to Be an Electrician
2. School Days of Fred Harley
3. Gun and Sled
4. Shorthand Tom
5. Missing Tin Box
6. Young Oarsmen of Lakeview
7. Young Auctioneers
8. Poor but Plucky
9. Rival Bicyclists
10. Fighting for His Own
11. By Pluck, Not Luck
12. Leo the Circus Boy

NOTES

1. See Steinhauer, Donald L., "Bibliographic Listing
of 'Golden Days'," Dime Novel Round-Up, n.d.
2. Neither "Franklin Calkins" nor "Dr. Willard Mackenzie" are accepted as proven pen names of Stratemeyer.
"Ralph Hamilton" was a house name for Golden Days and
"Dr. Willard Mackenzie" was also. It seems incorrect to
attribute all "Ralph Hamilton" serials to Stratemeyer. Johannsen notes that "Off to the Southwest; or, The Adventures of the Twin Manlys," by "Franklin Calkins," appeared
in Golden Days, Vol. 5, August 16, 1884, which was as by
"Ralph Hamilton"--Albert Johannsen, The House of Beadle
and Adams (Norman: University of Oklahoma Press, 1950),
vol. 2, p. 265. Stratemeyer's first serial was for Golden
Days but not until 1889, some years later. Two serials by
"Franklin Calkins" and one by "Ralph Hamilton" appeared in
1882. Two serials by "Dr. Willard MacKenzie" appeared in
1888 and two in 1889, before Stratemeyer's first serial.
Therefore no serials published before Stratemeyer's "Victor
Horton's Idea" are included in the listing. Stanley A.
Pachon has pointed out that Franklin W. Calkins was a real
author who was on the staff of Youth's Companion for around
40 years.
3. See Pachon, Stanley A., "Bibliographic Listing of
'Golden Argosy' and 'Boys' World'," Dime Novel Round-Up,
March 1962.
4. See Mayo, Capt. Chester G., "Bibliographic Listing
of 'Good News'," Dime Novel Round-Up, September 1960, p.
28.
5. Ralph Adimari, in listing Stratemeyer's pen names
in the Dime Novel Round-Up says, "The following for Good
News which he edited from the start. 1890-'Frank,' 'Jack,'
'Uncle Ned,' 'Ned St. Meyer.' 'W.B. Lawson'"--Ralph Adimari,
"The Ralph Adimari Pseudonyms," Dime Novel Round-Up,
vol. 27, no. 9 (September 1959), p. 78. Stratemeyer apparently became editor in 1893, not 1890. The W.B. Lawson
stories "Canoe and Camp Fire" and "Shifting Winds" were
reprinted as by St. George Rathborne and Captain Mayo
does not attribute any of the Lawson stories to Stratemeyer.
"Uncle Ned" and "Ned. St. Meyer" were not used as pen
names for any serials in Good News. The serials under
"Frank" and "Jack" were all published between May 15,
1890, and January 10, 1892. Stratemeyer's first serial in
Good News under his own name was "Jack the Inventor,"
and was published from January 23 to April 2, 1892 (reprinted from Ellis's The Holiday of the preceding year).
Johannsen and others have stated that Stratemeyer became

editor in 1893 "and during the next two years wrote many
stories for it"--Johannsen, House of Beadle and Adams,
1950, vol. 2, p. 264. The recent discovery of the S & S
authors list for Good News serials does not show Stratemeyer
as using any of the above pen names.

    6. The "Harvey Hicks" stories ran from October 29,
1892, to September 5, 1896, but only "The Tour of the Zero
Club" and "By Pluck Alone" can definitely be ascribed to
Stratemeyer. The "Mat Merriman" stories by "Hicks" are
given as "English reprints, revised," by the S & S author
lists. These lists show E.H. Lewis as the author of the Tom
Truxton stories. They were printed by McKay in hardcover
as by "Lt. Lionel Lounsberry," a Street and Smith house
name. There were 12 serials published in Good News under
the pen name "Lt. Lounsberry." Captain Mayo ascribes four
of them to Prentiss Ingraham and eight to Henry Harrison
Lewis but none to Stratemeyer. McKay's Boys Own Library
listing under "Lt. Lounsberry" includes both Ingraham and
Lewis "Lounsberry" serials from Good News as well as the
two "Tom Truxtons." Leithead (Note 13), however, ascribes
other "Lounsberry" serials to Stratemeyer and Adimari lists
"Lt. Lounsberry" as a pen name for Stratemeyer. It is
thought by this writer that Stratemeyer's Good News serials
later published in hardcover were issued only under his own
pen names, "Bonehill" or "Winfield."

    7. See Guinon, J.P., "The Young Sports Series,"
Dime Novel Round-Up, vol. 26, no. 8 (August 15, 1958), p.
113, and LeBlanc, Edward T., ed., "Bibliographic Listing of
'Young Sports of America'," n.p., n.p., n.d.

    8. See Mayo, Capt. Chester G., "Bibliographic Listing
of 'Bright Days'," Edward T. LeBlanc, publisher, n.p.,
n.d.

    9. Believed by Van Devier to be a Stratemeyer pen
name but not proven--Mayo, "Bibliographic Listing of 'Bright
Days'," op. cit. p. 15. See also the G.A. Henty Bibliography by Robert L. Dartt.

    10. Believed by Van Devier to be a Stratemeyer pen
name but not proven--Mayo, "Bibliographic Listing of 'Bright
Days'," op. cit. p. 15.

    11. Steinhauer, the Rev. Donald L., "Bibliographic
Listing of 'Golden Hours'," Edward T. LeBlanc, publisher,
n.p., n.d.

    12. See LeBlanc, Edward T., ed., "Bibliographic
Listing of 'Boys of America'," n.p., n.p., n.d.

    13. See Leithead, J. Edward, "Bibliographic Listing of
'New Buffalo Bill Weekly'," Dime Novel Round-Up, suppl. no.
5, May 15, 1970. These serials were copyrighted by Street
& Smith circa 1904 and published by McKay in hardcover in
the Boys of Liberty Library. The original printing is unknown. Their authorship by Stratemeyer is considered not
proven. "Lt. Lionel Lounsberry" was a Street & Smith house

name and used by several authors. The hardcover books under that name together with the true author where known are given below, in this fashion: Title, "by Pen Name" (Publisher)--Actual Author (Authority). First, the Boys Own Library:

Cadet Kit Carey, "by Lt. Lounsberry" (Good News)--Prentiss Ingraham (Mayo)

Captain Carey, "by Lt. Lounsberry" (Good News)--Prentiss Ingraham (Mayo)

Kit Carey's Protege, "by Lt. Lounsberry" (Good News)--Prentiss Ingraham (Mayo)

Lieut. Carey's Luck, "by Lt. Lounsberry" (Good News)--Prentiss Ingraham (Mayo)

Out with Commodore Decatur, "by J. Gibson Perry, USN" (Good News)--H.H. Lewis (S & S)

Randy, the Pilot [further information is unknown]

Tom Truxton's School Days, "by Harvey Hicks" (Good News)--H.H. Lewis (S & S)

Tom Truxton's Ocean Trip, "by Harvey Hicks" (Good News)--H.H. Lewis (S & S)

Treasure of Golden Crater, "by Lt. Lounsberry" (Good News)--H.H. Lewis (Mayo)

Won at West Point, "by Lt. Lounsberry" (Good News)--H.H. Lewis (S & S)

And for the Boys of Liberty Library:

The Quaker Spy, "by Jasper W. Wildwood" (New York Weekly-Good News)--"Old Weekly Reprint" (S & S)

The Trader's Captive [by Unknown] -- Stratemeyer (Leithead)

Fighting for Freedom, "by J. Gibson Perry, USN" (Good News)--H.H. Lewis (S & S)

By Order of the Colonel [by Unknown]--Stratemeyer (Leithead)

A Call to Duty [by Unknown]--Stratemeyer (Leithead)

In Glory's Van [by Unknown]--Stratemeyer (Leithead)

The Young Patriot [further information is unknown]

14. See Gardner, Ralph D., Horatio Alger; or, The American Hero Era. Mendota, Ill.: Wayside Press, 1964.

15. Reprinted by Lothrop, Lee & Shepard as by Stratemeyer.

16. See Ethridge, James M., et al., eds., Contemporary Authors (Detroit: Gale Research), vols. 19 and 20).

17. Information obtained in a letter from Charles L. Messecar, February 27, 1975.

18. The original Merriam Bound to Succeed Series listed vol. 3 as Larry the Wanderer; or, The Polishing of a Rolling Stone and said the series will be completed in six volumes. The Stratemeyer Syndicate has verified that Merriam published only two volumes in this series. Merriam went bankrupt in 1897.

19. The remaining volumes of this series were written by "James Otis."

20. This series recounts the adventures of the next generation of Rovers.

CHRONOLOGY OF STRATEMEYER'S BOYS'
BOOKS FIRST PUBLISHED AS SERIALS

Data are given in the following order: Book Title (Serial Title, dates first published, by Serial Author), Book Publisher, date of book, by Book Author.

1. Richard Dare's Venture (Argosy, 1/91-3/91, by Stratemeyer), Merriam, 1894, by Stratemeyer.
2. A Young Inventor's Pluck (The Holiday, 4/91-6/91, by Stratemeyer), Saalfield, 1901, by Winfield.
3. True to Himself (Argosy, 10/91-1/92, by Stratemeyer), Lee & Shepard, 1900, by Stratemeyer.
4. The Last Cruise of the Spitfire (Argosy, 1/92-4/92, by Stratemeyer), Merriam, 1894, by Stratemeyer.
5. Fighting for His Own (Argosy, 5/92-7/92, by Winfield), Allison, 1897, by Stratemeyer.
6. Reuben Stone's Discovery (Argosy, 7/92-10/92, by Stratemeyer), Merriam, 1895, by Stratemeyer.
7. Oliver Bright's Search (Argosy, 11/92-2/93, by Winfield), Merriam, 1895, by Stratemeyer.
8. The Missing Tin Box (Good News, 4/93-6/93, by Stratemeyer), Allison, 1897, by Winfield.
9. Bob the Photographer (Good News, 10/93-1/94, by Stratemeyer, Wessels, 1902, by Winfield.
10. Young Bank Clerk (Good News, 11/93-1/94, by Winfield), Street & Smith, 1902, by Winfield.
11. Shorthand Tom the Reporter (Good News, 2/94-4/94, by Stratemeyer), Allison, 1897, by Stratemeyer.
12. Joe the Surveyor (Good News, 5/94-7/94, by Stratemeyer), Lee & Shepard, 1903, by Stratemeyer.
13. Larry the Wanderer (Good News, 8/94-11/94, by Stratemeyer), Lee & Shepard, 1904, by Stratemeyer.
14. Schooldays of Fred Harley (Good News, 9/94-12/94, by Winfield), Allison, 1897, by Winfield.
15. The Young Auctioneers (Good News, 12/94-3/95, by Stratemeyer), Allison, 1897, by Stratemeyer.
16. The Tour of the Zero Club (Good News, 12/94-3/95, by Harvey Hicks), Street & Smith, 1902, by Bonehill.
17. Mark Dale's Stage Venture (Good News, 4/95-6/95, by Manager Henry Abbott), Street & Smith/McKay, 1902, by Winfield.

18. The Young Bridgetender (Good News, 8/95-11/95, by Harvey Hicks), Street & Smith/McKay, 1902, by Winfield.
19. Neka, the Boy Conjuror (Good News, 12/95-3/96, by Manager Henry Abbott), Street & Smith, 1902, by Bonehill.
20. Leo, the Circus Boy (Young Sports of America, 5/95-6/95, by P.T. Barnum, Jr.), Allison, 1897, by Bonehill.
21. Young Oarsmen of Lakeview (Young Sports of America, 6/95-7/95, by Bonehill), Allison, 1897, by Bonehill.
22. The Rival Bicyclists (Young Sports of America, 6/95-7/95, by Rockwood), Allison, 1897, by Bonehill.
23. The Wizard of the Sea (Young Sports of America, 1/95-9/95, by Theodore Edison), Mershon, 1900, by Rockwood.
24. By Pluck, Not Luck (Young People of America, 10/95-12/95, by Young), Allison, 1897, by Winfield.
25. Poor but Plucky (Young People of America, 11/95-12/95, by Albert Lee Ford), Allison, 1897, by Bonehill.
26. Gun and Sled (Young People of America, 11/95-1/96, by Bonehill), Allison, 1897, by Bonehill.
27. Three Young Ranchmen (Young People of America, 11/95-2/96, by Stratemeyer), Saalfield, 1901, by Bonehill.
28. A School Boy's Pluck (Young People of America, 12/95-2/96, by Philip A. Alyer), Mershon, 1900, by Rockwood.
29. Bound to Be an Electrician (Bright Days, 4/96-8/96, by Winfield), Allison, 1897, by Stratemeyer.
30. Boys of Spring Hill [and] Walter Loring's Career (Bright Days, 5/96-7/96; 10/96-11/96, Boys... by Albert Lee Ford; Walter... by Chapman), Mershon, 1900, by Chapman.
31. Land of Fire (Bright Days, 9/96-11/96, by Louis Charles), Mershon, 1900, by Charles.
32. Malcolm the Waterboy [not proven] (Bright Days, 11/96-12/96, by D.T. Henty), Mershon, 1901, by D.T. Henty.
33. The Young Bandmaster (Golden Hours, 2/99-4/99, by Bonehill), Mershon, 1900, by Bonehill.
34. The Young Naval Captain   [Oscar the Naval Cadet] (Golden Hours, 11/00-1/01, by Hal Harkaway), Thompson & Thomas, 1902, by Bonehill.
35. Lost in the Land of Ice (Golden Hours, 12/00-1/01, by Rockwood), Wessels, 1902, by Bonehill.
36. Rival Ocean Divers (Golden Hours, 1/01-2/01, by Rockwood), Stitt, 1905, by Rockwood.
37. Larry Barlow's Ambition (Golden Hours, 5/01-7/01, by Rockwood), Saalfield, 1902, by Winfield.
38. The Island Camp (Popular Magazine, 12/03-1/04, by Stratemeyer), Barnes, 1904, by Bonehill.
39. Defending His Flag (American Boy, 5/06-6/07, by Stratemeyer), Lothrop, Lee & Shepard, 1907, by Stratemeyer.

These early book titles not yet identified with serials:
1. Young Hunters in Porto Rico, published by Allison or Donohue Bros., 1899 or 1900, as by Bonehill.

2. To Alaska for Gold, published by Lee & Shepard, 1899, as by Stratemeyer.

3. Between Boer & Briton, published by Lee & Shepard, 1900, as by Stratemeyer.

4. Boy Land Boomer, published by Saalfield, 1902, as by Bonehill.

5. Two Young Lumbermen, published by Lee & Shepard, 1903, as by Stratemeyer.

6. The Winning Run, published by Barnes, 1905, as by Bonehill.

BIBLIOGRAPHY OF
SECONDARY SOURCES

Blanck, Jacob. Harry Castlemon, Boys' Own Author. Waltham, Mass.: Mark Press, 1969.

Bleiler, E.F. (ed.). Eight Dime Novels. New York: Dover, 1974.

Butler, Francelia (ed.). Children's Literature: The Great Excluded. Storrs, Conn., 1972-77.

Comstock, Anthony. Traps for the Young (1883), edited by Robert Bremner. Cambridge, Mass.: Harvard University Press, 1967.

Dartt, Robert L. G.A. Henty: A Bibliography. Cedar Grove, N.J.: Dar-Web, 1971.

Dunlap, George T. The Fleeting Years. Privately printed, 1937.

Gardner, Martin, and Nye, Russel B. The Wizard of Oz and Who He Was. Lansing: Michigan State University Press, 1957.

Gardner, Ralph D. Horatio Alger; or, The American Hero Era. Mendota, Ill.: Wayside Press, 1964.

Garis, Roger. My Father Was Uncle Wiggly. New York: McGraw-Hill, 1966.

Harris, Louise. A Comprehensive Bibliography of C.A. Stephens. Providence, R.I.: Brown University, 1965.

Hinsdale, Harriet (ed.). Frank Merriwell's Father. Norman: University of Oklahoma Press, 1964.

Hoyle, Karen Nelson. Girls' Series Books 1900-1975. Minneapolis: University of Minnesota, 1978.

Hudson, Harry A. A Bibliography of Hard-Cover Boys' Books. Tampa, Fla.: Data Print, 1977.

Johannsen, Albert. The House of Beadle and Adams. Norman: University of Oklahoma Press, 1950.

Kilgour, Raymond L. Lee and Shepard Publishers for the People. Hamden, Conn.: Shoe String Press, 1965.

McFarlane, Leslie. Ghost of the Hardy Boys. New York: Methuem/Two Continents, 1976.

Mason, Bobbie Ann. The Girl Sleuth. Old Westbury, N.Y.: Feminist Press, 1975.

Moskowitz, Sam. Explorers of the Infinite. Cleveland: World, 1960.

Mott, Frank Luther. A History of American Magazines, 1885-1905. Cambridge, Mass.: Harvard University Press, 1957.

Noel, Mary. Villains Galore; The Heyday of the Popular Story Weekly. New York: Macmillan, 1954.

Nye, Russel Blaine. The Unembarrassed Muse: The Popular Arts in America. New York: Dial Press, 1970.

Prager, Arthur. Rascals at Large; or, The Clue in the Old Nostalgia. Garden City, N.Y.: Doubleday, 1971.

Reynolds, Quentin. The Fiction Factory. New York: Random House, 1955.

Scharnhorst, Gary. Horatio Alger, Jr. Boston: Twayne Publishers, 1980.

_____, and Bales, Jack. Horatio Alger, Jr.: An Annotated Bibliography of Comment and Criticism. Metuchen, N.J.: Scarecrow Press, 1981.

Smith, Henry Nash. Virgin Land: To the American West as Symbol and Myth. Cambridge, Mass.: Harvard University Press, 1950.

Thompson, John Cargill. The Boys' Dumas. Cheadle, Cheshire, England: Carcanet Press, 1975.

Turner, E.S. Boys Will Be Boys. London: Michael Joseph, 1948.

PERIODICALS

The Baum Bugle. Barbara S. Koelle, editor. 244 Haverford Ave., Swarthmore PA 19081.

The Boys Book Collector. T.E. Dikty, publisher, 1969-1973 (out of print but has much valuable information).

Dime Novel Round-Up. Edward T. LeBlanc, editor. 87 School Street, Fall River MA 02720. Published since 1931 (by far the best single source for accurate information on popular children's literature).

The Mystery and Adventure Series Review. Fred Woodworth, editor. 837 E 8th St., Tuscon AZ 85719.

Newsboy (Horatio Alger Society). Jack Bales, editor. 1407A Winchester St., Fredericksburg VA 22401.

The Piegan Storyteller. David C. Andrews, editor. Box 53, Andes NY 13731.

Yellowback Library. Gil O'Gara, editor. 2019 SE 8th St., Des Moines IA 50315.

SELECTED LISTINGS FROM DIME NOVEL ROUND-UP

Le Blanc, Edward T. Boys of America, n.d.

_____. Young Sports of America, n.d.

Leithead, J. Edward. New Buffalo Bill Weekly, May 15, 1970.

Mayo, Chester G. Bright Days, n.d.

_____. Good News, September, 1960.

Pachon, Stanley A. Golden Argosy and Boys World, March,
    1962.
Steinhauer, Donald L. Golden Days, n.d.
_____. Golden Hours, n.d.

INDEX

Abbott, Manager Henry 151,
  156
Adams, Harriet S. 2, 28,
  43, 52, 55, 57, 58, 131,
  137, 154
Adams, William T. 8; also
  see Oliver Optic
Adimari, Ralph 168
Alger, Horatio, Jr. 1, 8,
  9, 10, 12, 72, 74, 138;
  bibliography 157
Allen, Capt. Quincy 72
Alyer, Philip A. 152, 154
The American Boy: bibli-
  ography 156
American Boys Biograph-
  ical Series: bibliography
  161
"American Dream" 1, 4, 14
American Library Associ-
  ation 16
The American Novels 88
American society 4
Ann of Green Gables 16
Appleton, Victor 2, 8, 57
Argosy: bibliography 148
Asimov, Isaac 87, 90
atomic energy 50
Axelrad, Nancy 136

Bailey, J.O. 89
Barbour, Ralph Henry 3,
  73, 75, 76
Barnum, P.T., Jr. 151
Barnum, Theodore 153
Baum, L. Frank 1

Bell, Emerson 91, 150
Betsey books 16
Betty Gordon 27
Bird Boys 73
Bleiler, E.F. 88
"Blowing Out the Boy's
  Brains" 24
The Boat Club 9
Bobbsey Twins 1, 13, 16ff,
  44, 58, 131, 135
Bomba the Jungle Boy 2
Bonehill, Captain Ralph 8,
  72, 76, 92, 96, 151, 154,
  155; also see Stratemey-
  er--pen names 113, 135;
  Stratemeyer--bibliography
  158-160
book covers (photographs)
  139-142
Borrowers series 16
Bound to Succeed series
  134; bibliography 161
Bound to Win series 134;
  bibliography 167
Boy Allies with the Army
  63; bibliography 65
Boy Allies with the Navy
  63; bibliography 66
Boy Hunter series 158
Boy Scouts Year Book
  (1934) 26
The Boy Troopers series
  66
Boys of America: bibliog-
  raphy 156
Boys of Business 44
The Boys of Liberty Li-
  brary: bibliography 170

179